TATTERED HUNTRESS

THRILL OF THE HUNT
BOOK ONE

HELEN HARPER

Cover created by JoY Cover Design

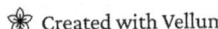 Created with Vellum

CHAPTER

ONE

I should make it clear from the start that a bogle wouldn't be my first choice of drug dealer. And Arbuthnot wouldn't be my first choice of bogle. Unfortunately, I wasn't in a position to be picky.

I'd spent the last three nights exhausting my other options, which was why I found myself standing in front of Arbuthnot in a dark, brooding nook along Fleshmarket Close. I'd known him for a dozen years, and I was certain that it had been at least another dozen years before then since he'd abandoned his natural countryside habitat in favour of the city. I'd never asked him why he'd come to Edinburgh; in my experience it is better not to know about the skeletons in other people's closets. Those doors are shut for a reason.

Arbuthnot's watery eyes were fixed on a random point somewhere over my shoulder. It made me feel I was about to be jumped from behind by one of his cronies, even though I knew nobody was there. 'I've got white dust, skunk and 'shrooms,' he mumbled.

I ignored the flash of panic that clawed at my throat and remained still. Bogles don't like sudden movements. 'I'm not

HELEN HARPER

looking for any of that,' I said. 'All I want is spider's silk.' All I ever wanted was spider's silk.

'All?' Arbuthnot's voice rose to a high-pitched squeak as if he didn't already know what I was there for. '*All?*'

'I have the money.'

He twisted his head slowly from side to side, making his long, matted hair shiver. 'Silk is in high demand. There's not a lot of it about, and the authorities are cracking down.'

The knot in my stomach eased. If he truly didn't have any, he'd be extolling the dubious virtues of his other products. Arbuthnot was simply trying to drive up his price. It was a dance with which I was more than familiar.

I took a step back. 'Oh. I'll try somewhere else, then.'

His hand shot out, grasped my shoulder and pinched it hard. 'I have *some*,' he said. 'Just not a lot.'

'Is it pure?'

His answer was too swift to be anything but a lie. 'One hundred percent.'

I maintained a blank expression but my spirits sank; I'd be lucky if it were fifty percent pure, then. But I was out of options because the withdrawal symptoms were already kicking in with a vengeance. I'd be hallucinating soon. I didn't have time to find an alternative.

'I'll give you two hundred quid for ten.' That would see me through to pay day when I could find a different dealer with higher standards.

Arbuthnot wheezed, his derisive laugh echoing down the alleyway. 'Five hundred.'

'Three,' I countered. I could manage that.

'I won't break even at three. But I like you, Daisy.' He tapped his thin lips and pretended to be deep in thought. 'Tell you what, I'll do you a special deal. Four hundred and the pills are yours.'

I ran the numbers in my head. I still had to pay my electricity bill and I owed Kat fifty pounds, but there was enough food in the cupboard to last me until the end of the month. It could be worse.

'Three-fifty.'

'Four.'

'Three-sixty.'

'Four.' He tilted his head and I recognised the dangerous gleam that suddenly lit his eyes. 'Offer less again and the price goes up.'

He was probably bluffing but unfortunately I didn't dare test that theory. Arbuthnot had the spider's silk I needed, and that meant he had all the power. My position was too weak – and I was too damned desperate.

I cursed inwardly then dug into my pocket until I found the crumpled wad of notes. I thrust them in his direction. He all-but snatched the money from me, sticking his tongue out as he counted it. He lost count halfway through and had to start again while my skin itched and my hands trembled. Eventually he grunted in satisfaction and waved me away. 'Jimmy's waiting at the bottom of the steps. He will sort you out.'

I nodded. Before I could twist away to collect what I'd paid for, Arbuthnot's eyes snapped to my face and met my gaze for the first time. 'It'll kill you in the end, you know.'

He was the last person I needed health advice from. And, yeah, it would kill me in the end. Being an addict sucked but spider's silk was the only thing I'd found that could control the wild magic inside me. Before I'd started taking it, I'd been in real danger of inadvertently killing someone because of my lack of self-control. I'd rather be an addict than a murderer – though I wouldn't tell any of that to Arbuthnot.

'Yes,' I said simply. 'I know.'

I marched briskly down the well-trodden steps. The narrow

gullies on either side, where rivulets of blood from the butchers who used to do business here once flowed, had been filled in decades ago but even so I stayed away from them. There was no sense in treading over bloody history unnecessarily. It was important to me to respect the past, even when it had no bearing on my future. Call it an odd quirk, if you like. We all have them.

Jimmy, a large, muscled human whose face was etched with a criss-cross of ugly, shiny scars, held out a small, sealed bag as I approached. I took it from him and counted: ten little white pills, each one marked with a crude S. I tried not to let my relief show, though I didn't have the patience or the willpower to wait. As soon as I turned my back on him, I fumbled inside the bag for a pill and threw it into my mouth, holding it on my tongue until I felt the familiar bitter fizz. Then I swallowed. Everything would be okay now. *I* would be okay now.

I waited for the spider's silk to take effect. It was manufactured in a grotty lab somewhere and had nothing to do with actual arachnids – not as far as I was aware. It was only called spider's silk because once you were caught in its web there was almost no chance of escape, no matter how hard you struggled to free yourself.

Withdrawal symptoms started with shaking and nausea before moving on to hallucinations, hysteria and palpitations. They usually ended up in total insanity followed by cardiac arrest. I'd come dangerously close a few times in the past and I had no desire to experience them again, regardless of the long-term risks of taking the drug.

I held my breath as the night sky slowly sharpened and my blood started to tingle. That was when the high-pitched scream ripped through the chill air.

I whipped around, my gaze snagging with Jimmy's. He

blinked at me slowly and raised his massive shoulders in a shrug. 'Didn't hear nothing,' he said.

I hissed in irritation then sprinted in the scream's direction.

I saw the woman as soon as I left Fleshmarket Close. She'd been backed into a corner, her spine pressed against a doorway as her hands, still clutching her handbag, flailed in front of her face. One of her shoes had come off, a high-heeled black-lacquered thing whose design would do no-one other than the wealthy designer any favours. It lay uselessly on the cobbles, the only obstacle between her and the snarling vampire who was on all fours in front of her.

Cumbubbling bollocks. I watched the vampire advance on her for a single frozen second, then I rolled my eyes and launched myself at him.

What most people don't realise is that vampires are stupid. The general public focus on the idea that vamps are extraordinary predators with terrifying skills instead of the fact that once they've latched onto a target they don't notice anything else – even when they're about to be attacked them-selves. Even when I'd leapt onto the vampire's back, wrapped my arm around his neck and begun to squeeze, the undead creature still only had eyes for its intended victim.

The woman, whose terror had enveloped her like a shroud, squeaked. Unfortunately, that sound only increased the vampire's bloodlust. I grunted, doing my best to hold back his foul, rotting body as his dirt-caked hands scrabbled towards her.

I tightened my grip on his neck but it obviously wasn't enough, so I gritted my teeth and smashed the elbow of my other arm into the side of his head. I heard the crunch of bone as his cheekbone shattered. Needless to say, the injury didn't slow him down – I wasn't sure that he'd even noticed.

I dropped my legs on either side of his body until I was

straddling him, then dug my heels into the ground to ensure that he couldn't advance any further.

The woman began chanting a trembling litany, her words running into each other until they were barely intelligible. 'I don't want to die, Idontwanttodie, Idonwanodie.'

I could feel the vampire's sinewy muscles straining against me. My hold on him was slipping and he jerked forward an inch. Then another.

'Idonwanodie.'

'Lady,' I muttered, 'you need to be quiet.'

'Idonwanodie.'

Confronted with her own mortality, she was beyond hearing me. I yanked harder on the vamp's neck and was rewarded with a brief moan, but my hold wasn't enough. I ran my tongue over my lips and focused. It had rained recently and there was a helpful trail of puddles to my right. I half-closed my eyes.

'Idonwan—'

The dirty water from the largest puddle flew through the air and smacked the woman in the face. She gasped, stopping her chant in favour of blinking rapidly in my direction as the water dribbled down her cheeks and merged with her tears. Good. That was what I'd been aiming for.

'You're panicking,' I said, raising my voice so she could hear me above the vampire's guttural snarl. 'I need you to grab your shoe and pass it to me.' The woman stared at me through her mascara-streaked tears. I tried again. 'Pick up your shoe and give it to me.'

I waved my free hand in the air but that was a mistake because it relaxed my grip on the vampire's neck. He lurched forward, his fangs snapping.

I half-expected the woman to lose her brief return to sanity once again, but the vamp's lunge had the opposite effect. She darted forward, scooped up her fallen shoe and threw it to me. Thankfully, I caught it.

Immediately I clutched the toe, twisted my wrist and slammed the pointed heel into the vampire's ear. Three inches of designer steel embedded itself in his head with a loud crunch followed by a soggy squelch. Damn, that was satisfying. That silly stiletto had its uses after all.

I let go of the vamp's neck and he crashed forward, his skull thudding onto the damp cobbles. As I stood up and brushed myself off, the woman rushed forward to give me a grateful hug. I frowned and quickly held up my hand, indicating that she needed to stay back. 'Don't get too close,' I warned. 'He's not dead.' Not yet.

She squeaked again and jumped into the doorway as the vamp's legs twitched. I circled around his body and considered, then dug my hand into one of my back pockets and retrieved an old receipt that was scrunched up inside it. It wasn't ideal kindling but it would do in a pinch.

Concentrating hard, I tossed the little piece of paper towards the vampire and it began to smoke and curl at the edges. I concentrated harder until it finally caught fire as it landed on the nub of the vampire's bony spine.

I nipped around, grabbed the woman by the shoulders and hauled her away.

'Wh-what?'

'We need to get to a safe distance,' I explained.

'But—'

I yanked her another few feet further away. 'Count to five,' I told her.

I could feel her trembling but she did as I asked. 'One, two, th-three,' she stuttered. 'Four, five.'

We stared at the vampire's body. The little receipt had

already burned out. 'Is something supposed to happen?' the woman asked.

That was embarrassing. I delved into my pocket again, hoping to find another useful scrap of paper.

A moment later, the vampire burst into flames. About bloody time.

The woman dived behind me, using my body to shield hers, then she seemed to realise what she was doing and I heard a muffled apology – although she stayed where she was. I waited, watching the vamp be incinerated into ash. It would have been far more impressive if he'd actually combusted when she'd finished counting. Oh well; I suppose the end result was the same.

'You shouldn't be wandering the streets at night on your own if you don't have proper protection,' I said, once it was clear that the vampire definitely wouldn't rise again.

'I had an argument with my boyfriend,' the woman said shakily. 'And I couldn't get a taxi. There aren't supposed to be many vampires around at the moment. I thought it would be safe.'

I bit back my admonition that it obviously *wasn't* safe. 'At the very least arm yourself with some vamp spray for next time.'

Her eyes widened. 'I did! It didn't work!' She held up her bag, which she was still clinging on to and pulled out a little bottle.

I frowned, took it from her and sprayed it into the air in front of me. It was supposed to be a combination of holy water and wild garlic but, as far as I could tell, this particular version was nothing more than water laced with a synthetic garlic scent. 'You were conned,' I said.

Her shoulders dropped. 'Yeah,' she mumbled. 'I realise that.' She looked beyond me. 'Is my shoe—?'

'Burnt to a crisp. You'll be hobbling home. Where do you live?'

'Chambers Street,' she whispered.

It wasn't far. 'I'll walk you there.'

Her eyes filled with tears. 'Thank you.' She stared at me. 'How did you know what to do? How did you know how to beat him?'

'Practice,' I said, although I knew what she was really asking. I am a skinny, five-foot-five, unarmed woman and I don't look as if I could beat up a small child, let alone a vampire.

I sighed and relented, tucking my hair behind my ears so she could see the truth.

'You're an elf,' she breathed. She looked me up and down again. 'But—'

'I'm a low elf,' I told her. 'I'm not high born.'

She nodded as if she understood. Perhaps she did; some humans recognised the difference. High elves have power, wealth, copious amounts of elemental magic and good looks; low elves have zero power, no wealth, a mere smattering of barely controlled magic – and they usually have acne, too. It sucks. But I'd long since learned that complaining about things I couldn't change was a highway to nowhere.

'Can I do something?' the woman asked. 'Or give you something? As a heartfelt thank you for saving my life?'

I was tempted to ask her for some spare cash, but that seemed cruel considering what she'd just been through. 'No.' I smiled. 'It was my pleasure to help.'

'If you don't want money, I can owe you a favour instead,' she said. 'Whatever you need in the future, you can come to me and—'

'No!' My refusal was louder and more forceful than I'd intended. She winced and I softened my tone. 'Never do that. Never grant anyone an unnamed future favour, especially someone with magic. You could end up giving away everything that's ever mattered to you.'

She blanched. 'Oh. Okay. Sorry.'

I wondered how on earth this woman had managed to get through life unscathed thus far. 'Come on,' I said, before she promised me her first born. 'Let's get you home.'

CHAPTER

TWO

Although I'd been somewhat clumsy with the vampire, my success at saving a stranger's life coupled with the easing of my withdrawal symptoms meant that I was in a buoyant mood when I pitched up at work the following morning. My good humour was probably why I didn't immediately become suspicious at my boss's overly-bright smile.

'Daisy!' he beamed. 'You're looking fabulous this morning. You must have had a good night's sleep.'

'I did sleep well, thank you,' I said. Telling Mr McIlvanney the truth would have terrified him out of his wits.

'I'm so pleased to hear that,' he said. 'I've been worried about you these past few days. You've been looking very tired.'

A faint warning bell started to ding deep in the recesses of my brain. Alas, I wasn't sharp enough to pay it attention. 'Well,' I said, 'I'm feeling a whole heap better now.'

He bobbed his head vigorously. 'Good, good. Still, it's important not to overdo things. We can't afford for our best delivery driver to end up on long-term sick leave.'

The warning bell grew louder. This time I gave it more notice.

'That's why,' McIlvanney continued, 'I made sure to keep your deliveries to a minimum today. I don't want to over-stretch you.'

I met his eyes and belatedly noted his flicker of anxiety. Oh no. 'Boss—' I began.

He interrupted me. 'So you only have three deliveries to make. Lucky you!'

I folded my arms across my chest. Three deliveries was unheard of; I usually did more than a hundred, even when there were a lot of rural runs. 'And where are these three deliveries?'

'Well,' he said hesitantly, 'the first one is near Peebles.'

I tapped my foot. 'Where exactly near Peebles?'

'Neidpath Castle. It's for Hugo Pemberville.' McIlvanney paused. '*The* Hugo Pemberville. The treasure-hunter bloke. He's the housewives' favourite these days.'

An image flashed into my head of the tawny-haired high elf. Hugo Pemberville was well-known up and down the country; somehow I had the feeling that McIlvanney was trying to distract me with celebrity.

'How many housewives do you actually know?' I asked.

'It's a turn of phrase. I don't mean anything by it. Don't you find him attractive? Everyone else seems to.'

Yep, he was definitely trying to distract me. 'What about the other two deliveries?' I asked, my suspicions growing by the second.

'Oh.' He waved a hand airily. 'They're close to Neidpath Castle.'

'Where *exactly*?'

'One is at Westloch.'

I dredged my memory for previous runs up there. 'The holiday homes?'

'That's the place.' McIlvanney turned away.

'Boss,' I said. He started to whistle tunelessly. I raised my voice. 'Mr McIlvanney.'

'Mmm?'

'Where's the third delivery?'

He mumbled something.

'Can you repeat that?'

Reluctantly he looked over his shoulder then turned to face me and sighed. 'Hurley Cave.'

There we go; that was why I only had three deliveries today. 'Hurley Cave,' I said flatly.

The words fell out of him in a rush. 'You're the only person I can trust to do it, Daisy!'

My expression didn't alter. 'You mean I'm the only person you can trust to come back with all my limbs intact. Probably.'

'I can't send anyone else. I've asked. They've all said no.'

I sniffed. 'I'm saying no, too.'

'*Please*, Daisy. We have to at least attempt the delivery. We can't afford to lose the contract for the entire area because of one address – and it's only one box. You can leave it at the entrance.'

'You know what happened when Billy tried to do that last year.'

'We're SDS. We deliver when it counts,' McIlvanney regurgitated the firm's motto. His voice began to wheedle. 'She likes you.'

'She doesn't like anyone.'

'That's not true. I really think she likes you a lot.'

That was bullshit and we both knew it; she barely knew who I was. However, I also knew that McIlvanney was desperate. I clicked my tongue. 'What's it worth?' I asked, pretending I didn't spot the hope flaring in his expression.

'I can't afford to give you a pay rise.'

I raised my eyebrows.

'But you're due a holiday!' he said quickly. 'How about you take it next week? I'll tack on a few extra days in case you want to get away somewhere nice. You could go and see your folks. They'd like that.'

It had been quite a long time since I'd stayed with them, and I could do with a break from work. In fact, the extra days off would give me more than enough time to find another spider's silk supplier. I thought about it then I conceded – grudgingly. 'Alright.'

The sudden smile that broke across McIlvanney's face was almost wide enough to make my day, even with a trip to Hurley Cove on the horizon. 'Thank you, Daisy!'

'You're welcome.' I smiled back, although I was certain I was going to deeply regret this. Perhaps I ought to nip home and pick up some protective gear first. A hazmat suit. And body armour. An iron shield might be helpful, although as an elf I couldn't actually abide the touch of the cold metal. Hell, a flame thrower would be good. If only I actually owned any of those items, I thought with a sigh. Oh, well.

It was an hour's drive from the warehouse to Neidpath Castle. As I certainly wasn't in any rush to make the third delivery at Hurley Cove, I took my time trundling down the road past the towns of Dalkeith and Bonnybridge then the smaller villages of Howgate, Leadburn and Eddleston.

Eventually I turned into Peebles and navigated the streets until I reached the turn off for the castle. The road narrowed and crossed over an arched stone bridge before veering left where, all of a sudden, the castle came into view.

It was located on a gentle slope, nestled between a meandering river on one side and a steeper hill on the other. Despite its sturdy, fortress-like appearance and narrow windows, it was surprisingly pretty. I parked outside the old walls, leaving my van wedged between a gleaming Mercedes and a battered Land Rover with the personalised numberplate HUG5. I smirked slightly before loping around to the van's rear doors to retrieve the parcel.

I hefted it in my arms then walked through a stone archway towards the castle's main entrance, which appeared to be a plain black door. It was, I supposed, considerably less daunting than a portcullis would have been.

I knocked loudly. Although the parcel required a signature, I didn't expect that anyone would hear my knock and open the door for me; this was a castle, not a small tenement flat. But barely twenty seconds after my knock, the door creaked open to reveal a cheerful-looking woman wearing an apron. 'Hello there!' she said.

I smiled. 'I have a delivery. I need a quick signature.'

Her eyes crinkled. 'That'll be Mr Pemberville's box. He's been waiting for it. If you follow me, I'll take you to him.'

'That won't be necessary,' I said. 'You can sign and give it to him.'

She shook her head in alarm. 'Oh no. He wants it taken directly to him so he can sign for it himself.'

Why on earth was that necessary? I gazed down at the innocuous cardboard box and suddenly felt curious about its contents. However, it wasn't my business to know what was inside – and it certainly wasn't my business to question the whim of a famous high elf. I shrugged and followed her inside. At least I'd get a bit of a nosey at the castle's interior.

The woman, who introduced herself as Marianne, chattered away non-stop as she led me through the hallway. 'It's been a grand busy morning so far,' she told me. 'People coming and going all the time! There's even a film crew setting up in the library. It's not normally like this.'

'He's on television quite a lot though, isn't he?' I asked, certain that I'd seen Hugo Pemberville on *The One Show* on numerous occasions. 'Didn't he find that old Viking treasure up in the Shetland Isles last month?'

'Oooh, yes, he did. He's got a whole team of people working with him and they're all staying here, too. They call themselves the Primes.' There was a faintly disapproving edge to Marianne's voice, suggesting she was unimpressed by the egotistical name.

I glanced at her curiously. 'Don't you work with him?'

'Oh goodness, no!' She laughed as if the idea were ridiculous. 'I work for the family who own Neidpath Castle. Mr Pemberville is only renting it for a season while his own home undergoes repairs. He's had terrible problems with waterwights. They've finally been encouraged to move elsewhere, but there is still work to be done. Until it's completed, Mr Pemberville is staying here.'

If vital repairs had to be done to my flat, I'd be lucky to stay on a friend's sofa for the duration. I certainly wouldn't be able to rent out an entire bloody castle. How the other half lived.

'When you say waterwights—' I began.

'Oh, yes. Mr Pemberville has a moat. Of course there's a permanent bridge there now instead of a drawbridge, but it's still a moat.'

Marianne flicked her eyes from side to side, afraid somebody would overhear her, then reached into her apron, pulled out her phone and brought up an image of a stunning castle. My jaw dropped. It looked like something out of a fairy tale. Neidpath Castle, in comparison, was rather a slum.

'Get a look at Pemberville Castle. It's near Loch Lomond.' She dropped her voice further. 'He calls it "the bone zone".'

My brow furrowed in confusion, then I got it. In a flash my admiration for the building's beauty changed to disgust. 'Oh.'

Marianne gave me a meaningful look. Suddenly I had an inkling as to why I was to deliver the parcel personally: Marianne had a big mouth and was not to be trusted, even with sealed boxes. I got the impression that she was waiting for me to ask her for more secrets about her celebrity guest and I pinned my mouth firmly shut. I'd already heard far more than I wanted to.

Thankfully she seemed to sense that her audience was unwilling to take part. Instead of chatting further, she picked up speed and led me to a closed oak door towards the back of the castle. She paused for a moment and tried to listen, but if I couldn't hear anything through the thick wood then she certainly couldn't.

She knocked once and opened it.

'I told you we weren't to be disturbed again,' I heard a smooth, cultured voice say with restrained politeness that didn't quite mask a trace of irritation.

'Yes, sir,' Marianne said. 'It's only that your parcel has arrived. The delivery girl is here.' She beckoned me forward. I nodded, trying not to react to being called a girl when I was most definitely a full-grown woman, and peered into the room.

There were eight people inside, seven of whom were seated. Although they were dressed casually, their clothes testified to their wealth. I was reasonably certain that at least four were elves. Only a couple of them glanced in my direction; most were hunched over a long table and concentrating on a pile of papers. The one person who was standing was Hugo Pemberville. Damn. He was even better looking in person than he was on screen.

His soft tawny hair, with its gold and chestnut brown highlights, fell artlessly across his forehead, and his smooth, tanned skin spoke of a life spent mostly outdoors. Frankly, his healthy glow was insulting. His pointed elven ears were only just visible but I could see that they were both adorned with tiny golden cuffs indicating his high-elf status. There was a smattering of tiny freckles across his nose and cheekbones. He was wearing a white shirt with rolled-up sleeves and a simple pair of chinos. The curve of his muscular biceps and the way his trousers moulded to the lower part of his body mocked my scrawniness.

When he looked at me with his velvet blue eyes, I felt an unnerving kick of attraction. It got worse when the corners of his mouth crooked up into a smile; I could swear my heart skipped a beat.

'Thank you so much for taking the time to bring it to me in person,' he said. 'I'm aware that your schedule must be hectic.'

Not today. I cleared my throat, sternly told myself not to blush, and handed over the parcel. 'No problem. I just need a signature and I'll be on my hectic way.'

'Of course.' He strode over and grabbed a pen from a young woman at the table who was holding it out to him.

I smiled slightly, wondering how long it had been since he'd last had something hand-delivered. 'I have a tablet,' I said. 'You don't need a pen.'

He grinned good-humouredly, took the parcel and reached for my tablet. As he did, he looked into my eyes – and his grin suddenly vanished. It wasn't only his mouth that altered; the look in his eyes grew frosty as he snatched the tablet and stepped back as if he were suddenly repelled by my presence.

My jaw clenched. I didn't know many other elves, even low ones, because my background precluded moving in such circles. However, I did know that most elves weren't observant enough to notice the flecked ring of silver around my pupils that indicated I was a spider's silk user. Usually only those who were addicts themselves noticed and recognised it for what it was.

The few high elves I'd met either hadn't spotted it or hadn't cared.

Clearly that wasn't the case with Hugo Pemberville; he'd seen the rings of silver and he knew what they meant. He stared at me for another moment as if I were nothing more than a dirty cockroach that deserved to be squashed, then he scribbled his signature with his fingertip onto the tablet and thrust it back at me.

'You can go now,' he said in such a cold, hard voice that several of his well-dressed underlings looked up in surprise. Next to me, Marianne flinched.

'Is everything alright, Hugo?' asked a pretty blonde who was sitting near to where I was standing.

I glanced at her concerned expression then at the papers strewn in front of her and the words scrawled on them: *Black abyss. Four hills. Sulphur?*

'Everything will be fine in about ten seconds' time,' Hugo Pemberville bit out. He glared at me pointedly. 'I said you can go now. We don't want your kind lingering here.' He paused. 'So fuck off.' A moment later, he slammed the heavy oak door in my face.

'My goodness,' Marianne murmured, sounding faintly astonished. 'Do you two already know each other?'

Hot, furious shame burned through me. 'No,' I answered shortly.

I curled my fingers tightly around the tablet. I didn't think I'd ever been made to feel quite so worthless in such a short space of time. I glowered at the closed door for another long second, then I spun on my heel and left.

CHAPTER

THREE

I should have used the time it took to travel to the holiday homes at Westloch to calm down, but the further I drove from Neidpath Castle the more my shame turned to fury. Alright, so I wasn't perfect – but nobody was. Hugo Wankstain Pemberville definitely wasn't.

The only life that was being destroyed by my addiction to spider's silk was mine, and he had no fucking clue what had driven me to it in the first place. That bastard thought he could judge me from his lofty pedestal of privilege and position – well, screw him. I slammed my fists on the steering wheel. *Screw him.*

I pulled up outside the Westloch address and took several moments to breathe in and out, inhaling air into my lungs slowly and steadily. When that didn't work, I leaned across and opened the glovebox. I'd been planning to wait until after I'd been to Hurley Cave but Arbuthnot's batch of spider's silk wasn't very strong and I needed another hit now.

I tore open the small plastic bag, took out another pill and stared at it in the palm of my hand. Then I bared my teeth and shrugged angrily. I wasn't hurting anyone. I might be weak, but

I wasn't bad to the bone. I tossed the pill into my mouth and swallowed it. This was my life to mess up.

This time the parcel didn't require a signature, so when nobody came to answer the door I left it in the porch where it would be safe from both prying eyes and the weather. I only had Hurley Cave to go, and after Hugo Pemberville that would be a breeze. I put the old van into gear, slammed my foot down on the accelerator and sped towards it. Suddenly, I was looking forward to the distraction.

Hurley Cave isn't a natural cavern; it was originally created as part of a designed landscape a few hundred years ago and is actually an artificial tunnel. To be honest, a real cave with stagnant water, stalagmites and bats would have been far more pleasant because it wouldn't have been occupied by Duchess, a large misanthropic troll with a penchant for violence.

The package she'd ordered was both cumbersome and heavy; knowing what I did of Duchess, it wouldn't have surprised me if it contained the severed fingers of vestal virgins or the discarded fur from tortured bunny rabbits. I parked as close to the cave as I could, collected it from the back of the van and shifted it in my arms until it was comfortable to carry.

Tentatively, I approached the small bridge in front of the dark doorway but stopped a metre or two short of it. I wouldn't attempt to cross it – I wasn't that stupid.

I coughed loudly to announce my presence then called out, 'Hello?'

There was no answer. I took a shuffling baby step forward and tried again. 'Hello? Duchess?'

I could hear a few wood pigeons cooing overhead and the muted babble of the water underneath the bridge but nothing else. I allowed myself to take another tiny step, then another. And another...

It was only when my toes were an inch from the bridge that

there was finally a deep rumble from somewhere underneath. The ground trembled beneath my feet and a clawed hand appeared and gripped the low bridge wall. I waited.

In a lithe movement that belied her size and shape, Duchess threw herself upwards and planted her bare feet on top of the bridge's moss-covered surface. Her lower half, which was partly covered by a grubby linen skirt that only just skimmed her thighs, was dripping wet, and rivulets of water were running down her bony green legs. Her upper half boasted a lichen-covered breastplate that didn't do much to conceal her sagging flesh. She had slicked-back hair, a heavy monobrow, and her grey eyes were narrowed as she leered at me.

I tried not to look nervous. 'Hi, Duchess.'

'You made a grave mistake coming here, girlie.' She pawed at the air in front of her . 'There might not be much meat on you but I can still crunch your bones and suck out all that juicy marrow. This is my home and you will pay the ultimate penalty for intruding.'

'You invited me here.' Sort of.

'I did no such thing,' Duchess snorted. She took a heavy step forward and, without warning, swiped her left hand towards me with the sort of speed any predator would envy. The sharp nail on her index finger scraped my cheekbone and immediately drew blood.

I held my ground, aware that stepping back or showing pain or fear would only spur her on to attack properly.

Duchess chuckled and placed her finger to her lips. After licking off the tiny beads of my blood, she smacked her lips. 'You're tastier than you look.'

I dropped into a half-curtsey of mock gratitude before nodding awkwardly at the box in my arms. 'I'm not trying to cross the bridge,' I told her. 'I don't want to sneak into your home or hurt you.'

Duchess threw back her head and laughed. The sound bounced wetly off the walls of the cave behind her. 'As if the pathetic likes of you could ever hurt *me*. I dare you to try, girlie. Go on, give it your best shot and in return I'll show you what real pain feels like.'

If anyone else had said those words, their comic-book-villain melodrama would have sounded amusing, but Duchess spoke with complete sincerity that negated any humour. She wasn't bluffing. Duchess didn't bluff.

I nodded again at the box. 'I'm here from SDS. Swift Delivery Service? I've got a parcel for you. You've met me before, more than once.' Several times, in fact.

Her brow furrowed slightly. 'Really?'

'Really.'

She squinted at me then clicked her massive fingers as realisation dawned. 'You're Kat! Kitty Kat! We were going to test whether you have nine lives or not.'

I shook my head. 'I'm Daisy. Daisy Carter.'

Duchess's frown deepened. 'The elf?'

'That's me,' I said with forced cheeriness. It wasn't her memory that was the problem but her incredibly poor eyesight; that was probably part of the reason why she was so grumpy and quick to attack.

'I hate elves,' she grumbled. 'Especially elves like you.'

I was still feeling a tad touchy after my encounter with Hugo Pemberville. 'Like me?'

'You know.' She waved an irritated hand. 'High-born idiots who have more magic than they know what to do with.'

I relaxed slightly. 'I'm not a high elf.'

Duchess squinted again. 'Are you sure?'

'Yep.'

She pursed her lips. 'Are you really from SDS?'

'I am.'

'Why didn't they send that tasty boy like last time?'

Presumably she was talking about Billy. 'Because last time you covered him head to toe in troll snot and it took him a week to wash it all off.' Troll snot is like tar, but worse. Sometimes, when the wind blew the wrong way, I could still catch the odd rank whiff of it from Billy even though it was months since she'd doused him with it.

Duchess giggled. 'Yeah, I did do that.' She grinned and pointed to the parcel. 'Hand it over.'

'You have to promise not to attack me once you've got it.'

A crafty look came into her grey eyes. 'Why would I attack you? Hand it over.'

I stayed where I was. 'Promise.'

'Just give me it! It's mine! I've paid for it and I need it! These candles are the only things that work.'

Now it was my turn to squint. 'Candles?'

'Lavender and honey scented,' Duchess told me. 'It stinks in here. It's dark and gloomy, and hardly anybody ever drops in. Count yourself lucky that you don't have to live here.'

'You could move.' If she did that, she might fall under the jurisdiction of a different delivery company. That would be great; I'd get employee of the month if I managed to persuade Duchess to relocate.

Without warning, Duchess lunged towards me and her right hand snapped out, curling around my throat. I felt her claws digging into my flesh. Uh-oh; I must have said the wrong thing. 'Move?' she screeched. 'Move where? Where else is there to go?'

I resisted the temptation to resort to magic to defend myself. It would only rile Duchess further and she was already on the verge of losing her temper completely. 'I know the perfect place,' I whispered, struggling to get the words out as my throat closed up.

She pulled her hand away and tilted her head. I doubled over and gulped fresh air into my lungs. 'Where?'

I rubbed my aching neck and straightened up. 'Pemberville Castle. It's got a moat and a bridge that would be perfect for you, and you'd have it all to yourself. It's near Loch Lomond.'

'I know where it is!' Duchess snapped. 'I also know that it's filled with waterwights.' She advanced on me again.

I hastily held up the box as a makeshift – and probably useless – shield. 'They've gone. The waterwights have left. It's a good place, Duchess. You'll see a lot more people than you do here – and I bet it doesn't smell. You won't need any more scented candles.'

Duchess continued to gaze at me suspiciously, but there was a flicker of hope in her eyes. She really did want to move.

'I'm not lying,' I told her. 'If it doesn't work out, you can always come back here, but it's got to be worth a try, right? You don't have anything to lose.' I was telling the truth: Duchess wouldn't lose anything, but Hugo Pemberville would.

No, I still didn't think I was a bad person – though I'd happily admit to being petty.

'Give me my parcel,' Duchess snarled. I clutched it to my chest. She sighed, exasperated. 'I won't hurt you. I promise.'

I examined her face carefully to see if she were lying. As satisfied as I could be that she wasn't, I passed it to her.

'You're sure the waterwights have gone?' she asked.

'I'm sure.'

She thought for a moment or two. 'I suppose I could give it a try,' she said finally.

'Definitely.' I started to back up inch by inch.

'There would be a lot more space.'

'There would indeed.'

'And it's an elf castle. There will be lots of them to annoy.'

'It'll be great fun,' I assured her.

'I could get some fairy lights,' she mumbled. 'Brighten the place up a bit if it needs it.'

'It won't be like living next to a damp cave,' I agreed. There was now considerable space between us. I raised my hand. 'I'll see you around, Duchess.'

She muttered distractedly – then her head jerked up. 'Oi!' she called. I froze. 'Next time, make sure you deliver my parcels there instead of here.'

I grinned. 'Absolutely.'

'Pemberville Castle,' Duchess whispered to herself. 'Yes. It's about time I moved up in the world.'

My grin grew. I couldn't agree more.

FOUR

A loud cheer rippled through the Hanging Bat when I walked through its doors. Unsurprisingly, it was Billy who grabbed me first, hauled me into a bear hug and made a show of sniffing me. 'No troll snot!' he declared. 'How did you do it?'

'I won her over with my delightful personality,' I told him.

Billy snorted. 'Yeah, right.'

I winked at him. 'SDS. We deliver when it counts.'

He rolled his eyes then we ambled over to our usual table. Kat had already got in the drinks and she handed me a gin and tonic before I even sat down. 'Chin-chin,' she said.

I took a sip of the cool drink and smacked my lips. 'Thanks, Kat.'

'You're very welcome, darling.'

I settled on the chair next to her and we clinked glasses. 'To better times ahead.'

She grinned. 'I'll drink to that.'

Billy plonked himself next to me and pointed at the television screen behind the bar. 'Look who's on.'

I followed his finger and stiffened when I saw Hugo

Pemberville's face. Kat leaned towards me. 'I heard that you didn't only persuade Duchess to move but that you also met *him*. What's he like in real life?' Her eyes danced. 'Did you get an autograph?'

'I did when he signed for his parcel,' I said, unwilling to re-hash what had happened.

Billy scowled. 'I don't understand what the big deal is.'

'Well,' Kat said, 'he's a high elf and that means serious power. And he's smooth, suave and sophisticated.'

I tried not to choke on my drink.

'I'm smooth, suave and sophisticated,' Billy said.

'Not like hunky Hugo, you're not.' Kat raised her chin and called to the bartender. 'Could you put the sound up?'

He found the remote control and a moment later we could hear Hugo Pemberville's dulcet, cultured tones. 'Oh, yes, Deborah,' he said to the coiffed interviewer on the sofa. 'It's incredibly exciting. We've narrowed down the possible locations where the necklace might have been hidden after it was stolen in the late nineteenth century. There are only a few places to investigate, so I'm confident that we'll find it soon.'

'Can you tell us where these locations are?' Deborah asked.

Hugo tapped his nose and winked at her. 'Close to Edinburgh. That's the most I'm saying.'

Deborah giggled, clearly charmed by him. Next to me, Billy rolled his eyes. 'Looks like Pemberville is getting lucky tonight.'

I barely heard him; instead my mind had flashed to the scribbled notes I'd seen in the drawing room at Neidpath Castle. *Black abyss. Four hills. Sulphur?* Hmm.

'Also joining us today,' Deborah said, 'is Sir Nigel Hannigan, who is helping to fund the search for the necklace. Sir Nigel, you must be extraordinarily excited that it might finally be found after so many years.'

The camera panned to an older gentleman who clearly

didn't pander to any contemporary fashion norms. He was wearing a bow tie, a checked waistcoat and sporting an extraordinary handlebar moustache that had been waxed to perfection.

'I'm terribly thrilled,' he said. 'Of course, once the necklace is found it will be restored and then displayed to the public in the British Museum. That way everyone can enjoy it for generations to come.'

Deborah smiled at him, although there was a much less flirtatious edge to her expression than she'd displayed for Hugo Pemberville. 'I'm also told,' she said, glancing towards an invisible autocue, 'that you have other exciting plans on the horizon.'

'Indeed. We've found some interesting documents in the archives that we believe may lead to the treasure of Loch Arkaig. It holds a large amount of gold that Spain gave to the Jacobites in 1745 to help with the uprising against the English. It was hidden away and then lost before it could be put to its intended use. I'm funding a competition to locate this treasure. Several teams from across the British Isles will join the search for it, including Hugo and his Primes. Whoever finds the Arkaig treasure will receive a substantial reward.'

'And I'm looking forward to receiving that reward,' Hugo said.

Deborah laughed again before the camera cut away to a different segment.

'See?' Kat said, dropping her gaze from the screen. 'He's so sexy that even Deborah Drummond wants to shag him.'

Billy harrumphed. 'I'd rather have the treasure than shag Hugo Pemberville.'

'Well, I'd rather shag Hugo Pemberville.' She nudged me. 'Right, Daisy?'

I didn't answer.

'Daisy?'

I licked my lips. 'I know where it is,' I whispered.

She frowned. 'What?'

Billy turned to me. 'The Loch Arkaig treasure? *You* know where it is?'

I shook my head. 'Not that. I think I know where that necklace is.'

Kat and Billy stared at me. Finally Kat said, 'I guess the next drinks are on you then.'

'What are we waiting for?' Billy said. 'Let's get out of here and go find it! Is it gold? Will it make us rich?'

I shrugged. I didn't know anything about the necklace, but if the notes I'd spotted were accurate then I knew its location. I'd spent enough time driving around the lowlands of Scotland delivering random items to rural places to know exactly where it was.

Kat shook her head. 'We won't get rich. There might be a small finder's fee, but objects like that belong to the country rather than the person who digs them up. Treasure-trove law.' She pointed at the television screen again, even though it was now showing a skein of ducks instead of treasure hunters. 'I've heard Hugo Pemberville talk about it before.'

Her face brightened. 'Instead of getting the necklace ourselves, we should tell him where it is. He'll be eternally grateful.' She smirked saucily and I knew she was imagining all the ways Hugo Pemberville could display his gratitude. Knowing Kat, they probably involved strawberry-flavoured lubricant and vanilla massage oil. A *lot* of massage oil.

I leaned back in my chair and took another long gulp of my gin and tonic. 'Nah. He said he's already narrowed down the location. He'll probably have it in his privileged paws before the end of the week. He doesn't need our help.'

I'd had enough dealings with the man and I certainly didn't

want to go rushing in to help his daft treasure hunt. I didn't have any inclination to find the necklace myself; I'd make more money by turning up to my job instead of chasing after vague dreams, and I had no doubt that he'd have found it by the time my holiday started next week. Besides, I didn't want to allow Hugo Pemberville to take up any more space in my head.

I'd taken my petty revenge and my dealings with him – brief as they had been – were over.

~

By the time Friday rolled around, I'd forgotten the turmoil at the start of the week and was focused on my upcoming time off. My parents were thrilled to hear that I was dropping by for a few days, which made me feel guilty for staying away for so long.

I made plans to head to my family home for three days then return to Edinburgh. I'd have more than enough free time to locate a new supplier for spider's silk. I might even spring clean my little flat. Stranger things had happened.

It was with those happy thoughts that I skipped into the warehouse to pick up my delivery orders for the day. With any luck they'd be in and around the city so I could be sure of a timely finish.

I waved at Billy, who was loading up his van by the main warehouse doors and wandered inside to find Mr McIlvanney. To my surprise, he wasn't in the small staff kitchen making his usual pot of tea but waiting for me by the door to his office.

'Ah. Daisy.' He offered an uncomfortable smile which, I noticed, didn't reach his eyes. 'Can I have a quiet word?'

A quiet word. Four syllables that can strike terror into anyone's heart. My zippy mood vanished. I nodded jerkily and followed McIlvanney into his office. When he gestured for me to close the door, my spirits sank further. 'Have a seat, Daisy,' he said.

I crossed my arms. 'I'd rather stand.'

He sighed. 'As you wish.'

I watched as he sat down behind his utilitarian desk. He shuffled some papers in front of him and twitched several times.

'Let me guess,' I said flatly. 'We're short staffed so you want me to delay my holiday next week.'

McIlvanney started; from his expression, he'd entirely forgotten about my vacation. 'No,' he said. 'It's not that.'

I eyed him. 'What is it then?'

He looked away, unwilling to meet my gaze. 'There's no easy way to say this, Daisy. I'm afraid we've had a very serious complaint about you.'

I had my faults, but I was good at my job. I met my targets and I tried to be a supportive co-worker; in fact, I genuinely enjoyed working as a delivery driver. I got to see a lot of the country, plus I'd been here almost four years. I was practically an old-timer. 'Go on,' I said, unable to fathom what the complaint could be.

McIlvanney picked up a pen and fiddled with it. I resisted the urge to grab it from his hands and toss it into the bin. 'It's been alleged that you're a drug addict,' he said heavily.

I tensed; there was only one person who could have made that complaint. 'Hugo fucking Pemberville,' I said aloud.

McIlvanney winced, confirming it. 'Is it true?'

I waved my hands in annoyance. 'Have I ever done anything during the course of this job that has caused you concern?'

'No, but—'

'Do I turn up on time?'

'Yes.'

'Do I complete all my deliveries?'

'Yes.'

'Do I throw packages around or leave them out in the rain?'

'No.' He finally looked directly at me. 'But are you a drug addict?'

'What I do in my spare time has no bearing on my job.'

'It has every bearing. For one thing, you're privy to people's addresses. You know when homeowners are in and when they're away.'

I glared. 'Are you suggesting that I'm likely to burgle their homes because I can't control myself?'

'No,' he said, although it was obvious that was exactly what he was thinking. 'You're a valued employee, Daisy. I want to help. I've done some research and there's an excellent rehab programme that I can get you into.'

Rehab wouldn't work. I took spider's silk for a reason and, much as I didn't want to be addicted to the damned stuff, I couldn't allow myself not to take it. 'I'm perfectly fine. I don't need any help – and I don't need rehab.'

McIlvanney twisted the pen in his hands, gripping it so tightly that his knuckles turned white. 'The complainant—'

'Hugo Pemberville,' I muttered. 'You can say his damned name.'

McIlvanney began again. 'The complainant is an important person. He's highly placed and he has a lot of influence. SDS has a great deal of competition and we can't afford to piss off the wrong person. We certainly can't afford to piss off someone who can drive away our business. I'm responsible for two dozen employees at this branch alone, Daisy. They depend on their jobs to put food on their tables.'

I didn't take my eyes from him. 'You're firing me, aren't you?'

'If you agree to submit to a drugs test and the results are clear, then no.'

I didn't say anything. McIlvanney didn't hide his disappointment. He ran a hand through his greying hair and tried a different tack. 'I can hold your job for you until you complete rehab. It'd only be a temporary suspension.'

I set my jaw into a tight line. I could try and explain, but McIlvanney didn't have magic. He wouldn't understand.

When it became obvious that I wouldn't agree to rehab, he looked sad. 'Then,' he said, 'you're leaving me with no choice. You'll still receive your holiday pay and your full month's wages, but I'm afraid that this is where we part company. I'm very sorry. It's not personal.'

For the first time, I lowered my gaze and turned my head so he wouldn't see my unshed tears. 'You're wrong,' I said shakily. 'This is nothing *but* personal.'

CHAPTER
FIVE

I could have gone home, buried myself in my duvet with a giant tub of ice-cream and thrown plates at my wall. I could have gone to the Hanging Bat and drowned my sorrows in a vat of heavy-duty gin. I could have called my parents and poured out my heart to their sympathetic ears. But I didn't do any of those things. I am a solution-focused kind of person and the bastards weren't going to grind me down. Neither was Hugo sodding Pemberville.

By the time I walked out of the warehouse, I knew exactly what to do. I couldn't blame McIlvanney for firing me but I did blame Hugo Pemberville, and I certainly wouldn't give him the satisfaction of thinking he'd won.

The van I drove belonged to SDS so I had to gather my things and return the keys, but I wasn't without transport. Living in Edinburgh generally negated the need to own a car of my own; usually I took the bus or cycled.

Without spending any time over-thinking what I was doing, I unlocked my bike from its usual position at the SDS gates and rode it to the nearest train station. The journey would be a proverbial pain in the arse – and potentially a literal one as well, given how far I'd have to cycle – but I reckoned it would be well worth it.

The train time from Edinburgh to Lockerbie was under an hour. Given the lack of news headlines about the recovery of a mysterious lost necklace, I was fairly certain that Hugo Pemberville hadn't found it yet. All the same, I used my time on the train to trawl various news websites and social media to confirm that the search was ongoing and to find out where Pemberville was at that moment in time.

When I discovered that he was deep in the Pentland Hills with his group of stupid Primes, I pumped the air and crowed aloud, startling the family opposite me to the point where the youngest kid dropped his limp cheese sandwich and stared at me while his father glared. I waved a brief apology but my thoughts were elsewhere. Hugo might indeed be a talented treasure hunter with resources I could only dream of, but I knew that part of the country like the back of my hand. He'd not yet been to Devil's Beef Tub – and that was where I was sure the necklace was hidden.

I hadn't actually made any deliveries to Devil's Beef Tub because nobody lived there, but I had been to the nearby town of Moffat on several occasions and I'd seen the road sign. The name had intrigued me enough to look it up and, when I'd passed by in my delivery van, I'd noted the geography of the four hills that surrounded it. From those hills, Devil's Beef Tub appeared to be a deep dark hollow that once upon a time had produced sulphurous water that was carted to Moffat for use in its famed sulphur baths. Based on what I'd seen from those notes in the Neidpath Castle drawing room, apparently it was also a great place to hide treasure. Or at least a stolen necklace.

I carried my bike off the train at Lockerbie station and grinned at the still-disturbed family as I disembarked. I re-checked the route and set off. It was a good fifteen miles to

Devil's Beef Tub but the sun was shining and the sky was clear –
perfect treasure hunting conditions.

I pedalled hard and reached the track that led away from
the main road, and from where the black hole of Devil's Beef
Tub was visible, in better time than I'd expected. I continued
cycling for as long as I could and then, when it became too difficult, left my bike on a grassy verge and continued on foot. I
paused only twice: once to tie back my hair when the breeze
grew too irritating and I kept ending up with mouthfuls of red
curls, and the second time to swallow my day's allowance of
spider's silk. As the drug took hold, my steps became faster
until I was all but sprinting to the deep hollow.

It was all very well knowing the general location of buried
treasure, but once I reached the edge of Devil's Beef Tub I
realised that finding the exact spot would be considerably
harder. Its converging slopes no longer looked like a black
chasm but were a verdant delight of dancing insects, swaying
grasses, low-lying scrubs and rocky outcrops. There were definitely no handy Xs to mark where the necklace was hidden.

I took out my phone to see if I could research further but the
lack of signal stymied that idea. I tucked it away again and
nibbled on my bottom lip. I'd been so determined to get here
before Hugo Pemberville showed up that it hadn't occurred to
me that I might need some tools. I didn't even have a shovel.
Perhaps treasure hunting was more difficult than it looked.

If the story were true, the necklace had been here for over a
hundred years. I didn't look for any marks in the ground that
might indicate where something was buried; it had been too
long and any such marks would have been smoothed over by
the elements long ago. Besides, if the necklace was in a notice-
able spot somebody else would have found it by now.

I swivelled around slowly. There was a vast area to cover
and all I had were my bare hands to work with.

I grinned suddenly. And magic.

I didn't possess the formal magic training or superior powers of a high elf, but I knew enough. I'd taught myself all the basics through a combination of blood, sweat and tears and I was proud of what I was capable of. Unlike true witches, whose skills lie in brewing plants and working with small animals and insects, or sorcerers who rely solely on runes, elven magic harnesses the four ancient elements: air, earth, fire and water. That was how I'd managed to channel water from puddles and set alight scraps of paper. Neither fire nor water would help me here – but I was surrounded by earth. All I had to do was put my natural magic to good use.

The only visible path had been created by previous visitors. High up on one of the hills to my left, I glimpsed a monument to a long-dead covenanter, but nothing else hereabouts was man-made. If I focused, I could use my power to scour the earth for anything that didn't belong. No problem.

I half-closed my eyes and concentrated, rippling out magic in front of me like some sort of heat-seeking missile. In less than a minute, pain jabbed at my chest as the magic faltered. There. There was something to the right, next to an oddly shaped boulder and some scree.

I made a beeline for it, abandoning the narrow path for the uneven ground. Ha! I'd been wrong: treasure hunting was actually a piece of piss.

Slightly out of breath but exhilarated, I reached the boulder. I could push the stone out of the way and the necklace would probably be underneath it. I smiled and crouched down.

'Fuck!' My expletive was whipped away by the wind. I picked up the flattened can of cola from where it was wedged by the side of the boulder and glared at it, silently cursing whichever hiker had left it there. Damned litterbug.

I gritted my teeth and shoved the can into my pocket to

dispose of later then I tried again. Okay. There was something on the slope of the hill opposite me, perhaps five hundred metres away. I drew in a breath and jogged towards it. Come on, baby. Come on, baby. Come on...

Eugh. A used condom? Who the hell was having a sexy time out here? I scowled in annoyance and spun around. I wouldn't be defeated. Third time lucky. I clenched my jaw and flared out magic once again.

~

IT WASN'T third time lucky; neither was it fourth time lucky, or fifth, or sixth or bloody fifteenth time lucky.

Almost three hours later, I'd criss-crossed the deep hollow more than twenty times. I was covered in sweat and dirt, my mouth was dry because I'd not brought anything to drink or eat, and I was certain I'd developed matching blisters on both feet. I'd found five crisp packets, two cigarette lighters, seven cigarette butts, a watch strap, two marbles, three plastic bottles and a piece of wire. I'd even found a small gold wedding ring. What I hadn't found was the stupid necklace that would wipe the stupid smile off Hugo Pemberville's stupid face.

When I'd stomped out of the SDS warehouse for the final time that morning, coming here had seemed like a great idea. Now it only felt foolish. Perhaps this wasn't the right place. Perhaps I wasn't quite as clever as I thought I was.

I sat down cross-legged on a hump of prickly grass and wiped the sweat from my brow. It was incredibly tempting to give up and pretend that I'd never come – but what was the alternative? I could go home with my tail between my legs and start the arduous task of job hunting, but I doubted McIlvanney would give me a reference. I certainly didn't fancy signing on the dole, and any meagre benefits wouldn't be enough to pay for my spider's silk pills. I scrunched up my face. I had to keep going. I had to keep trying.

I sighed heavily and willed myself to stand up again. It didn't quite work and I debated reaching for another pill, but I couldn't afford to deplete all my stock. Instead, I cast out yet another net of earth magic from where I was sitting. The irritating pain flared in my chest again as the next spot revealed itself to be somewhere behind me. Great: now I had to climb the steep slope to get to what would doubtless be something as exciting as a discarded sweet wrapper.

I tried to imagine Hugo Pemberville's smug face and how his expression would change when he realised I'd pipped him to the post and found the necklace before he had. That gave me the energy to propel myself to my feet. I turned around and started to climb.

It took fifteen minutes of scrambling, slipping and heavy breathing to reach the spot in question. Digging my feet into the side of the steep hill, I looked around for the litter that had drawn me there but I couldn't see anything. I hastily quashed a flash of cautious hope and knelt down, using my fingers to pull away the tufts of sturdy grass that clung to the hillside. It hadn't rained for a while, but fortunately the ground was crumbly and soft rather than compacted and difficult to dig through.

I scooped away an inch of dirt. Then another. And another. And that was when my fingertips felt the edge of something hard and unyielding. Suddenly, my flagging energy soared into a frenetic spurt of activity. Clumps of dirt and wads of tough grass flew in all directions – and before too long, my efforts revealed a slender wooden box.

I tugged hard to release it from its burial place and lost my footing in the process. I tumbled backwards, rolling several metres down the hillside in an ungainly fashion that would have had my old gymnastics teacher crying with shame – but I didn't lose my grip on the box.

When I finally came to a stop, I paid no attention to my aching bones or the cuts on my skin from the jagged stones and sharp blades of grass. Instead, I hugged the box to my chest and hummed with delight as I allowed myself a moment or two of triumph before I sat up and examined it.

It was a simple affair, roughly made with no adornments, only a small catch holding it closed. It certainly didn't look like it contained valuable treasure. I lifted it up, checked the underside to make sure there was nothing to be wary about then held my breath and opened it to reveal ... a simple silver locket.

I frowned. I wasn't sure what I'd been expecting but it was something grander than this. The necklace was pretty and appeared to be well made, but there were no embellishments, no inscriptions, no jewels.

I thumbed the locket open. Although there was a space on both sides for a tiny photo or perhaps a lock of hair, it was empty. All that trouble just for this? Weird. Still, I'd found what I'd come here for.

Now it was time to return to Edinburgh and use the necklace to get what I really wanted.

CHAPTER

SIX

I stepped off the train at Edinburgh Waverley, held my phone to my ear and affected my best plummy accent. 'Good evening. My name is Gertrude Van Winkle and I'm a researcher with the British Museum. I am trying to locate Sir Nigel Hannigan but he isn't answering his phone. I have some very exciting information for him relating to some Celtic rune-stones we've been translating. I know he'll want to hear what I have to say as soon as possible.'

Marianne, bless her, didn't question my credentials; neither did she recognise my voice. 'I'm afraid Sir Nigel isn't here. He has accommodation in Edinburgh until Sunday.'

That was good news; it meant I had a chance of talking to him without any interruptions from Hugo cumbubbling Pemberville. Assuming I could find Sir Nigel, of course. 'Is that the Balmoral Hotel as usual?' I asked, taking an educated guess.

'No, he's staying at the Royal Elvish Institute.'

Yahtzee. I did a little dance of triumph. I knew exactly where that was, even though I'd never had cause to step through its hallowed doors. I could be there within the hour.

'He's having dinner with Mr Pemberville and the other Primes,' Marianne added helpfully.

My grin changed to a grimace. Oh well, I couldn't have everything.

'Good, good,' I said smoothly. 'I'll call the Institute directly. Thank you so much.' I hung up quickly before she had time to get suspicious then set off at a brisk march in the direction of the Elvish Institute.

Edinburgh is full of dramatic, imposing buildings, most of which appear large enough and solid enough to withstand an apocalyptic event. The Royal Elvish Institute is no exception. Occupying a corner of Charlotte Square in Edinburgh's New Town, it is a grand townhouse with dramatic architecture that demands attention.

Everything I knew about it came from passing its impeccable stone façade or from odd snatches of gossip I'd picked up. I knew that there were state rooms in which high elves and highly-placed officials were permitted to stay when they were visiting the city, and that there was a private members' club that admitted high elves and their guests for a princely annual fee. In short, it was the sort of place – and the sort of organisation – that starkly delineated the difference between those with power and those without.

I wasn't sure how I'd manage to get inside to speak to Sir Nigel, but I was confident that my background as a delivery driver would help considerably. To that end, I took the long way around, passing behind several expensive restaurants and shops until I found the perfect cardboard box to serve my needs. It smelled slightly of old cabbage but its appearance – if not its scent – was good enough to pass muster. I tossed the necklace and its wooden box inside and did what I could to seal the edges. There; that ought to be enough. Then I straightened my shoulders and marched up to the grand entrance.

Two burly elves stood on either side of the door. They were clearly high born, although the bronze clips on their ears indicated that they weren't as well-placed as the likes of Hugo Pemberville. I didn't bother to smile as I approached – I was a bored delivery driver looking to finish my shift as quickly as possible. I wasn't trying to sneak inside to speak to one of their vaulted guests. No, sirree. Not me.

Both elves stared at me as I walked up to the door then the dark-haired one on the right held up his hand to stop me. They didn't appear any more disposed to friendly smiles than I was.

I halted, took out my phone and pretended to consult it then looked up at them. 'I've got a delivery,' I said. 'Parcel for Nigel Harrigan.'

'There's no-one here with that name,' the blond on the left said.

I pretended to check my phone again, this time affecting an edge of irritation. 'Hannigan, then,' I said. 'Nigel Hannigan.' I peered more closely at my screen. '*Sir* Nigel Hannigan.' I jiggled the box. 'I need him to sign for it.'

'We'll give it to him.' He held out his hands.

'Are you Sir Nigel Hannigan?' I asked. 'No? Well then, I can't give it to you. I have to pass it directly to him.' I tapped the phone screen. 'I'm on the clock here. I don't have a lot of time.'

'That's your problem. Not ours.' Blondie folded his arms, probably because he thought it made his biceps look bigger. 'Deliveries are only allowed between the hours of ten and four.'

Damn it. I did my best to look unruffled. 'Look, mate,' I said. 'I don't care what your rules are. I'm only trying to keep my minimum-wage job. I won't be long – you can escort me in, if you wish. I just need to give this to Nigel Hannigan, get his signature and then I'll be out of your hair. Alright?'

I stepped forward to walk past them but, sadly for me, they

were having none of it. These two were better trained than I'd expected.

'You're not getting inside,' said the dark-haired elf.

'And,' added Blondie, 'you're not my mate.' His eyes snapped to someone behind me and his expression transformed. So he *could* stretch to a smile. 'Good evening, Mr Bridger.'

I half-turned my head and clocked a tall man striding past me with a female companion on his arm. 'Good evening,' he said, with a disarming doff of his hat. 'This is my friend, Eleanor Dixon. She'll be joining me this evening.'

I glanced at the woman and suddenly I couldn't stop myself from grinning. I guessed she'd ditched the boyfriend, then. 'Hi, Eleanor,' I said brightly.

She peered around the elf. When she saw my face, she also gave a wide smile. 'Hey!' She thumped Bridger on the arm. 'This is the woman I was telling you about! She's the one who saved me from being killed by that vampire!'

Bridger, who hadn't so much as glanced in my direction, turned to me and bowed. 'My goodness! How utterly fortuitous that you happen to be here,' he said.

I blinked. He was talking as if he'd walked out of the pages of a Regency romance. He bowed again and my mouth dropped open. He was acting that way, too.

'You are a true heroine,' he told me. He took my hand and kissed it, even though my fingernails were still caked with dirt from my earlier digging efforts. I'd done my best to clean myself up in the train loo but I'd only been able to do so much. If Bridger noticed the dirt, he was far too much of a gentleman to react.

I gave Eleanor an approving nod. This guy was good.

'Are you here for dinner, too?' Eleanor asked, despite the

fact that I looked as if I'd been rolling around in grassy dirt for half the day – which was exactly what I had been doing.

'Uh,' I scratched my head. 'No, I'm working. I have to give this to Sir Nigel Hannigan. I need him to sign for it.' I widened my eyes until they were suitably doe-like and pretended not to notice the very obvious glares of the two bouncers. 'These gentlemen won't let me in.' I dropped my voice sadly. 'But I'll lose my job if I don't deliver it tonight.'

Eleanor gasped. 'That's terrible!' She turned to the two men. 'She's an elf, you know. She's a good person. Why won't you let her in to do her job?'

I could tell that both of them were simmering with rage but dared not show it. This was almost too much fun.

'It's policy, ma'am,' Blondie said.

Bridger raised an eyebrow. 'Fiddlesticks! This lady is only trying to do an honest day's work and you're getting in her way. I can't imagine Sir Nigel would be very happy if he learned that he couldn't receive his parcel because of some balderdash policy.' He hooked his arm through mine. 'You can come in with us, dear.' He cleared his throat. 'Humphrey Bridger and guests, Eleanor Dixon and—'

'Daisy Carter.' I bobbed a curtsey.

'Daisy Carter. What a pleasure to make your acquaintance.'

'The pleasure,' I said honestly, 'is all mine.' Then the three of us strolled past the two grumpy elves and into the Institute. It was glorious.

Humphrey Bridger kept up a running commentary as he led us into a grand lobby with a marble floor and expensive looking objets d'art lining the panelled walls. 'I cannot tell you how wondrous it is to meet you in person,' he said. 'Dear Eleanor told me about her horrible encounter and how brave you were. The entire affair puts me in mind of this beautiful painting.' He gestured to a very large – and very ugly – battle scene that adorned one of the panels.

'The Royal Institute purchased it several decades ago and it's hung here ever since,' he continued. 'Of course, it is not the only spectacular painting here. My favourite is the Constable on the second floor. I can show it to you, if you like.'

He reminded me of a golden retriever puppy – a very posh golden retriever puppy. 'That's very kind of you,' I said. 'But I do need to find Sir Nigel and deliver his parcel.'

'You could join us for dinner afterwards, if you like,' Eleanor offered.

'What a brilliant idea!' Humphrey exclaimed. 'The squid here is excellent. The chef does this wondrous thing with foam and tweezers and a blowtorch. The result is exquisite.'

I was starting to wonder if these two were for real. 'I have other deliveries to make,' I lied, unwilling to draw either of them further into my charade regardless of how exquisite the squid was. In any case, I prefer my food without slimy tentacles; I'm more of a burger and chips fan and perfectly content to live my entire life with an unadventurous palate. 'Unfortunately I'll have to decline.'

'We shall have to invite you on another occasion,' Humphrey said. He reached into his waistcoat and took out a small silver case from which he extracted a white card. 'There. You must call me at your earliest convenience. It would be an honour to dine with you when you are free.'

Beside him, Eleanor looked at me earnestly. 'It really would, Daisy. Please say yes.'

I smiled awkwardly. 'Sure. Yes. I'll be in touch.' I tucked the card away, certain that I would never use it.

We turned left and went into the dining room. I tried to appear nonchalant at the extravagant surroundings but it wasn't easy. Every single person here, waiting staff included, was dressed up to the nines and I felt very shabby and dirty in comparison. The tablecloths were pristine white, the silverware glinted in the light shining from the overhead chandeliers and a small orchestra was playing in the far corner.

'Ah, Sir Nigel is by the window with good old Hugo and his chums,' Humphrey said with a satisfied burble. 'I'll take you over.' He glanced at Eleanor. 'You'll like them both. They're good fellows.'

I managed not to snort aloud and maintained a faint, unthreatening smile. I might be both jobless and penniless but I was having the most fun I'd had in years. I was tempted to rub my hands together with glee.

Humphrey wove in and out of the tables that were mostly occupied by other high elves. He paused at several of them, shaking hands and murmuring greetings, but he was gracious enough not to linger and delay my 'work' or interrupt their meals.

Soon we'd passed most of the other guests and only Sir Nigel remained. I scanned the table, noting that all of the faces from the drawing room at Neidpath Castle were present, together with Sir Nigel, Hugo Pemberville and a few others.

One of them, an elf who I recognised from Neidpath, looked at us. He smiled vaguely at Humphrey – then his gaze slid to me and his smile vanished. A second later, he was leaning across the table and gesticulating urgently to Hugo Pemberville.

Hugo's head snapped up and his eyes met mine. The sudden glittering fury in them was a joy to behold. *Just you wait*, I silently promised him. *Just you wait.*

'Dear me,' Humphrey murmured. 'Old Hugs looks rather cross. I cannot possibly imagine why.'

I knew I'd have to get in the first word before Pemberville had me thrown out of the building. I carefully removed my arm from Humphrey's, strode forward until I was standing in front of Sir Nigel Hannigan and thrust the cardboard box in his face. 'Sir Nigel,' I said loudly, 'I have a special delivery for you.'

To give them their due, Hugo and his Primes reacted quickly. I'd barely finished my sentence when the box was yanked away and two of them had grabbed me by the arms.

'I say!' Humphrey blustered. 'Whatever is going on?'

'Keep him back,' Hugo ordered and another underling jumped to do his bidding. Humphrey and Eleanor were hastily ushered several feet away. 'Call the police,' Hugo snapped to the blonde by his side.

I remained calm, despite the pincer-like grip from the elves on either side of me. 'Open the box,' I said, my attention wholly on Sir Nigel, who was looking more entertained than alarmed.

The elf next to him reached for it but Hugo got there first. 'Don't touch it, Rizwan.' He glared at me as if I'd deposited a bomb in the middle of his dining table. 'Is it dangerous?'

I grinned cheerfully. 'You tell me. I don't know what's so special about an old silver necklace, but you guys were the ones who were looking for it.'

Sir Nigel jerked. 'You found it?' he breathed. 'You found the necklace?' He pulled the box towards him and, ignoring another warning from Hugo, opened it up. He frowned. 'Why does it smell of cabbages?'

'Daisy?' Eleanor asked shakily. 'What's going on?'

'Who is she?' Hugo snarled at Humphrey.

HUMPHREY MIGHT HAVE RESEMBLED a puppy but he was no push-over. He straightened up and glowered. 'I'll ask you to remain civil, Hugo. This is Eleanor. She is my companion for this evening and will be joining me in the hunt for the Arkaig treasure.'

Hugo's lip curled. 'How does she know this ... creature?'

'You're a very rude man,' Eleanor said in a remarkably snippy tone. 'This wonderful woman saved my life the other night. A vampire would have killed me if it hadn't been for her.'

'How very convenient,' Hugo muttered. His expression suggested that I'd been in cahoots with a mindless vampire and somehow ordered it to attack Eleanor so as to get inside this dining room on this very evening.

'I guess life is full of coincidences.' I shrugged.

Hugo's jaw clenched. 'Get her out of here. Now.'

The two burly doormen were marching over to us from the dining-room entrance. Every face turned towards me and the elves who were trying to drag me backwards. I dug in my heels. I had a definite sense that things were about to take a turn for the worse.

'Wait.' It was Sir Nigel. He'd taken out the small wooden box and opened it to reveal the silver necklace. 'You found this?' he asked me.

I lifted my chin. 'I did.'

'Where?' he asked. 'How?'

I met his eyes. 'If you want the necklace and the story behind it, you'll have to stop treating me like a criminal.'

Hugo bared his teeth. 'This woman cannot be trusted. She's a junkie.'

Sir Nigel looked me up and down. 'Have we met before?'

Hardly. 'No.'

He tugged on his moustache. 'Hmm. You look incredibly familiar. What's your name?'

'Daisy Carter.'

'Well then, Daisy, would you like to join me for dinner?' he asked.

CHAPTER
SEVEN

To give the staff of the Royal Elvish Institute their due, as soon as Sir Nigel gave the word they sprang smoothly into action without a single flicker of judgement in their eyes. The tables were separated so that we could sit together. Hugo and his cronies were moved several metres away, though that didn't stop him glowering at me with undisguised hatred. I smiled sweetly every time I caught his gaze.

I sat down, unfolded the delicate white napkin, placed it on my lap and leaned forward to speak to Sir Nigel. 'I'm not missing a trick, am I? You're human and not a high elf?'

Sir Nigel didn't take offence. 'You mean why am I treated with such deference in a place that probably shouldn't allow me through its doors?' he asked. I nodded. 'Well, it helps that I know the likes of Hugo. He's well-thought of around here.'

I managed to stop my lip from curling, but only just.

'But I've also been a friend to the elvish community for a very long time.' He raised his glass and took a sip of his wine. 'The fact that I'm a wealthy philanthropist from a well-established lineage who enjoys throwing both my patronage and money around is also a contributing factor.'

I gave a bark of surprised laughter – I hadn't expected such honesty. I was already starting to like the man. 'Fair enough.'

'Your turn,' Sir Nigel said. 'Why did you come to me with the púca necklace instead of selling it on the black market? You could have earned a pretty penny from it.'

Púca necklace? I frowned. 'It wouldn't be an easy object to sell, and I don't know the sort of people who would buy it. But mostly I went looking for the necklace because I wanted to piss him off.' I jerked my thumb at Hugo Pemberville who was ignoring the food that had been placed in front of him in favour of continuing to glare at me. He would be a terrible poker player, that was for sure.

Sir Nigel's eyebrows shot up and he chuckled. For some reason, he appeared impressed by my answer. 'Why?'

I helped myself to bread and smeared butter liberally onto a crusty piece of sourdough. 'He called up my boss and complained about me. I lost my job.'

'I see. So this about revenge?'

'It's petty, I know, but incredibly satisfying.'

He gave me a long look but I didn't get the sense that he was judging me. 'You're a drug addict.' It wasn't a question. He gestured to my eyes. 'I wouldn't have noticed if Hugo hadn't mentioned it, but I can see the silver rings now he's pointed them out. Spider's silk is a nasty substance.'

I chewed the bread slowly, using the delay to work out my answer in a way that didn't sound overly defensive. 'I don't steal to fund my habit and it doesn't make me violent. I'm not a scourge on society. The only person I harm is myself.'

'You're an elf, so you must have some magic. Surely you are aware that spider's silk affects that magic.'

I hadn't expected him to know so much about it. 'That's why I started taking it,' I said quietly.

Sir Nigel stared at me for what seemed like a long time. His handlebar moustache quivered slightly but otherwise he didn't react. Finally he said, 'Ah,' then changed the subject and gestured to the necklace on the table between us. 'How did you find it?'

I'd told him nothing but the truth so far and there was no reason to lie now. 'Before I was fired, I spotted some notes when I was making a delivery to Neidpath Castle. I wasn't snooping – they were right in front of me.' I recited the words. '*Black abyss. Four hills. Sulphur*. I saw the pair of you on television afterwards and made the connection. I've travelled the countryside around here a lot during the course of my job and I reckoned I knew where the notes were referring to. So I went there, dug around a bit and found it.'

'Dug around *a bit*?' He looked at my grubby hands.

I grinned. 'Maybe dug around quite a lot.'

A starched-shirted waiter appeared at the table with bowls of steaming green soup. Sir Nigel thanked him and dipped his spoon into his bowl. I sniffed the heavenly aroma and my tummy grumbled loudly. I was desperately hungry; if I hadn't been in polite company, I'd have lifted the bowl to my lips and drunk the soup in three gulps rather than using my spoon. Even so, I guzzled it with far more gusto than Sir Nigel was probably used to.

'It's been a long day,' I said when I finished. 'And I'm hungry.'

'I can tell,' he murmured. He'd barely taken three mouthfuls. He leaned forward. 'So, Daisy, you've succeeded in annoying Hugo but I imagine you're also hoping for something in return for the necklace.'

Now we were getting down to brass tacks. 'Some monetary compensation would be appreciated.'

'How much would you like?'

I thought about it. The necklace was old, which was positive, and it had some sort of interesting history, which also helped. In terms of its face value, though, the plain silver wouldn't fetch much – I wouldn't expect to pay more than twenty quid for it if I saw it in a shop window. I could do better than that, however; Sir Nigel would probably be prepared to pay a lot of money for it, maybe as much as £500. That much, together with my last wage, would see me through another two months and I could find another job in that time.

I made a decision and high-balled, preparing to negotiate hard. 'Eight hundred pounds,' I said.

'Eight *hundred*?'

I nodded. 'Yep.'

Sir Nigel eyed me. 'I have a counter-offer.'

I smiled. 'I'm sure you do.'

'I'll give you £800 if you agree to take part in the hunt for the Loch Arkaig treasure. I'm organising a competition to find it. I think you'd be an excellent addition to the teams that are already participating.'

Of all the things I'd been expecting him to say, that wasn't one of them. 'You realise I'm a low elf, right?'

'If you say so.'

'And the only reason I found the necklace is because I copied Hugo Pemberville's homework.'

'You told me that already.'

'I only went looking for it to annoy him.'

Sir Nigel smiled. 'I'm running this competition because I'm a bored old man who wants to inject a little excitement into proceedings. It's not the treasure that excites me, it's the hunt.' He jabbed his finger at me. 'I think *you* will add even more excitement, and I suspect you will prove to be a more competent hunter than you think.' His eyes gleamed and his smile was mischievous. 'Besides, Hugo could do with the competition, don't you think?'

We both glanced at him. He was leaning back in his chair watching us. Although he'd managed to rid himself of his glower, I had no doubts as to what he was thinking.

'I'm a drug addict,' I said.

'As you've already pointed out, your addiction only affects you. I think you'd be the perfect addition to the search for the lost treasure of Loch Arkaig. The worst that can happen is that you fail, and there is nothing wrong with that. We all fail sometimes.'

I gazed at him; he was genuinely serious about this.

'Take a week to think it over, Daisy. We are convening at my estate in Northumberland next Sunday when I will give the teams the information I've uncovered so far and set out the parameters for the competition. Whoever finds the Arkaig treasure first will receive £50,000. I suspect that you needing the money rather than the glory of winning, as is the case with most of the other teams, will encourage you to go further.'

Fifty thousand pounds? Fifty fucking thousand pounds? For once, I was genuinely lost for words.

'Of course,' Sir Nigel went on smoothly, 'if this hunt is of no interest to you, then I'm glad we met and I still wish you well. I shall transfer £800 to your bank account – that is yours, no matter what you decide.'

It was a no-brainer. 'I'll do it,' I burst out.

'I'm pleased to hear that.' Sir Nigel smiled and pushed the necklace towards me. 'You should keep this, too. As a memento.'

My brow furrowed. 'But you've paid for it. It's yours.'

'It's worthless.'

'Pardon?'

'You opened the locket, didn't you?'

'Yes, but there was nothing in there.'

Sir Nigel pulled a face. 'Mmm. I think you'll find that there *was* something in there. It's too late now that it's been opened – it's of no use to anyone. If I can offer any advice at all, I would caution against interfering with old treasure in the future. If you hadn't opened the locket, it would have been worth twenty grand.'

My mouth dropped open.

Sir Nigel glanced over my shoulder. 'Ah, the main course is arriving.' He patted his belly. 'I do hope you enjoy squid.'

I THANKED Sir Nigel after the meal. He had been entertaining company, and I couldn't deny that taking part in another treasure hunt – one that sounded far more complicated than the search for the necklace – had me fizzing with excitement.

I said goodbye and waved to Eleanor and Humphrey, neither of whom tried to hide their curiosity about what had transpired between Sir Nigel and me, then tripped out of the Institute with a full belly and a busy mind. The squid had been tastier than I'd expected and the dessert so masterful that even the twin snarls from the doormen as I bade them goodnight didn't dim my pleasure.

I wandered down the road in the direction of the train station where I'd left my bike. Before I reached the corner, a dark shape stepped out of the shadows and blocked my path. Hugo Pemberville. Of course it was.

This was no chance meeting. He arched an eyebrow, put his hands in his pockets and tilted his head. 'What are you playing at?'

I sidestepped; he mirrored my movement and repeated his question, this time with more bite. 'What are you playing at?'

I sighed and gave up trying to get away. 'I'm not playing at anything. I'm trying to get home.'

'Sir Nigel doesn't need the likes of you sniffing around his drawers.'

I lifted my chin. 'Sir Nigel's drawers are his own business. He invited me to have dinner with him. You might remember – you were there.'

Pemberville's mouth twisted. 'You sneaked in under false pretences. And you'd never have found that necklace on your own. You looked at our notes when you came to Neidpath Castle, didn't you?'

There was no point trying to deny it. 'Sure.' I shrugged. 'But you had the information longer than I did, so it's hardly my fault that you didn't act on it.'

'Where did you find it? Where was the necklace?' He was very demanding for somebody who'd already lost.

'What's the information worth?'

His eyes glittered, then he took out his wallet and removed a wad of notes. 'Here, take this. Tell me where you found the necklace and promise never to come near me, Sir Nigel or any of my friends again.'

Wanker. I eyed him for a moment while I pretended to consider his offer. Finally I said, 'Nah. I don't think I will promise to do that – and I couldn't, even if I wanted to. I've already promised Sir Nigel that I'll take part in the search for the Loch Arkaig treasure.'

Hugo stared at me. 'You what?'

I smiled. 'I guess you don't have to be a pompous high elf with a stick up your arse to be a treasure hunter.'

'For fuck's sake,' he muttered. 'What did I ever do to you?'

He was kidding, right? 'You got me fired!'

'And you sent a damned troll with a chip on her shoulder to my home! She's moved in, claimed bridge-squatter rights and is refusing to leave!'

Ah. So he'd nipped home to his fairy-tale castle and spoken

to Duchess. 'Maybe that will teach you not to be so rude to strangers.'

'You're a spider's silk addict!'

I shrugged. 'And how does that have anything to do with you? At least I'm not a bully.'

He glared at me, his expression simmering with rage, but suddenly I couldn't tell whether his anger was directed at me or at himself. Twisting emotions flitted across his face; he seemed to be wrestling with some sort of internal argument.

He closed his eyes briefly. When he opened them again and spoke, his voice was calm. 'It might sound glamorous, but treasure hunting is dangerous. You got lucky with the necklace – although I will admit that you did well to find it. But finding the Loch Arkaig treasure won't be the same. It will be exhausting and you'll be putting your life at risk. You could end up seriously hurt – or worse. I'll call your boss and tell him I was wrong, get you reinstated. I'm sorry you lost your job but I can make it right.'

I understood he was making concessions and I appreciated the apology, but his assumption that he had ultimate control over what happened to my job – and therefore me –irritated me even more. 'Don't tell me that Hugo Pemberville is afraid of a little competition from a pathetic junkie like me? I'll prove to you that finding the necklace wasn't a fluke, so don't be upset when I find the Loch Arkaig treasure before you.'

He laughed mockingly. 'You don't seriously think that you can beat me? I've got a team of people and years of experience. You've got nothing.'

I stepped forward until we were so close that our noses were almost touching. 'Well, we'll have to see about that.'

'I guess we will,' he said softly. 'But don't come crying to me when you're facing down an ogre and you've not slept for three days.'

'Not going to be a problem.'

His velvet-blue eyes gazed into mine. 'Tell me, Daisy Carter,' he said softly. 'Did you open the locket on the necklace?'

When I didn't answer, he sniggered. 'And that is why you'll never succeed as a treasure hunter.'

'Watch this space, posh boy,' I returned. 'You might be surprised.'

The corner of his mouth lifted slightly as he moved back. 'I doubt it.' His smirk grew wider. 'Game on, princess. Game on.'

EIGHT

I have never suffered from insomnia; I fall asleep at the drop of a hat, and I don't lie awake at night fretting over past mistakes or future anxieties. Those sorts of thoughts only worry me during waking hours. Normally my head touches the pillow and I'm out for the count until my alarm goes off the next day.

Even the tumultuous day I'd just experienced didn't change that. I got home, scrubbed myself clean in the shower and fell into bed without a second thought about my lost job, treasure hunting or Hugo Pemberville. Thirty seconds later, I was fast asleep. So far so normal.

Unfortunately, when the clock hit midnight, everything changed.

It was the tiny jabs in my cheek that woke me; it felt as though somebody was pricking me with a needle over and over again. It wasn't painful but it was uncomfortable and seriously annoying.

In my sleep-fogged state, I wondered if I was getting toothache and was due a dreaded trip to the dentist. I raised my hand to my cheek to sleepily prod for any tender spots. That was when I heard the voice. 'Oi! Watch it!'

I sat bolt upright, suddenly wide awake with my fists clenched and my eyes searching the dark room for the intruder. Nobody was there; my little bedroom looked the same as it always did.

Then there was a second voice. The first one had been female but this was definitely male. 'Look what you've done! You've woken her up. For goodness' sake, she needs her sleep.'

'I'll say,' muttered the female. 'Have you seen those bags under her eyes? If they get any bigger, she can use them to pack for a weekend away.'

What the actual fuck? I kicked off the duvet, leapt out of bed and spun around. 'Who are you?' I snarled. 'More to the point, *where* are you?'

'She's not too bright,' the female voice said.

'That's mean, Hester.'

I heard a faint buzzing sound in my right ear, and a second later a tiny figure appeared in the air in front of my face. I jerked with shock and instinctively swatted it away. There was a high-pitched squeak from somewhere near my left ear, then peals of laughter. I swore, reached for the bedside lamp and turned it on to get a better look at my assailants. Even so, it took me a moment to find them.

The second one, the male, was sitting on my pillow rubbing his head. He was wearing red trousers, a cap at a jaunty angle, a striped shirt and a tie. He was also about two inches tall. My jaw dropped an inch. When a second figure flew off my shoulder to join him, I saw that his female companion was dressed in a black mourning dress akin to something Queen Victoria might have worn. She was also about two inches tall. My jaw dropped even further. 'Wh – what?'

The tiny female flicked her hair. 'I'm Hester. This is my brother Otis.'

Otis gave me a weak wave.

I stared at the pair of them. Hester rolled her eyes. 'Hello? It would be polite for you to tell us your name – or are you as dumb as you look?' She nudged her brother. 'What kind of grown woman wears night clothes with bunny rabbits all over them?'

I looked down at my pyjamas. 'They're very snuggly and warm. Besides,' I retorted, glad that I'd found my voice, 'you can hardly talk. You're dressed like an emo teenager.'

She frowned. 'What's an emo?' She nudged her brother again. 'She might talk like a fool but at least she's got attitude. Maybe this one won't be too bad.'

I glared at her. 'Who the fuck *are* you?'

Hester sighed impatiently. 'I already told you – I'm Hester, this is Otis. I take back what I said. You might be the worst one yet.'

Otis shook himself and pulled himself up to his feet. I caught a glimpse of tiny wings attached to his back as he took off his cap and bowed. 'Don't worry about her.' He smiled at me and tiny dimples appeared in his chubby pink cheeks. 'We're brownies. It's a real pleasure to meet you, uh—'

'Daisy,' I said faintly. 'Daisy Carter.' My eyes flicked to the necklace and locket, still in its original wooden box on top of my bedside table, and my shoulders sank. I hadn't understood what Sir Nigel had meant when he'd called it a pùca necklace but I was starting to. Brownies were also known as pucks – or, presumably, pùca.

Bugger. 'You were in the locket.'

'Well,' Otis demurred, 'yes and no. Our essence was in there so when you opened it, in effect you called us back into existence. We were dormant souls but now we're awake and ready to serve you.'

I sat on the edge of the bed. This was unexpected, to say the least.

'I don't understand why you look so surprised,' Hester said. 'You're an elf. All elves know that they must check over any object very carefully before opening it. A simple burst of water magic would have told you everything you needed to know.'

'I was adopted when I was a baby and brought up as a human.' I rubbed my eyes. 'I didn't grow up in the elvish community. There's a lot I don't know.'

She snorted. 'I'll say.'

'Look,' I said, 'it's lovely to meet you and all that, but you don't have to hang around here. You're free to go. Enjoy the big wide world and all it has to offer. I'm not looking for anyone to ... serve me.'

Otis wrung his little hands. 'That's not how it works. We're brownies – we live to serve. And we now serve you.'

Hester nodded. 'You're our person. You're not the person I might have chosen but you're what we've got. We're going nowhere.'

'What happened to your last person?' I asked, still befuddled.

'Murdered,' she said cheerfully.

'Not by us,' Otis added, with a quick worried glance in my direction.

Hester sniffed. 'The sorcerer who killed her conjured our essence into the necklace to stop us from taking revenge.' She pouted. 'Which is a shame because I excel at revenge.'

I was starting to think that I had a lot to learn. I pushed my hair away from my eyes. This was too much to take in and I still wasn't convinced that it wasn't a dream. The urge to burrow under my duvet and hide from the two tiny absurdities was overwhelming. They obviously didn't present any danger, but that didn't mean I wanted them in my bedroom.

'I'm going to sleep,' I announced firmly.

'Good idea,' Otis said. 'You need your rest.'

'You can sleep when you're dead,' Hester protested. 'Let's go out and see what this place has to offer. We're in Edinburgh, right? There must be some decent parties to go to. What year is this?'

'2024.' I got into the bed and pulled the duvet over me. 'Go and party, if you wish. If you're not here when I wake up, then good luck with your new life. Have a great time and enjoy the twenty-first century. The door is over there.'

I gently shooed them off the pillow and lay down. 'Good night,' I said, then more firmly, 'Goodbye.' I closed my eyes.

For some ridiculous reason, I thought that would be last of them.

'GET ONE OF THOSE TAXIS,' Hester said in my ear when I alighted from the train at Morpeth a week later.

'I can't afford a taxi,' I muttered.

'Yes, you can. You've got more than enough money to pay for one.'

'She will need that money later,' Otis said. 'It's wise to hold it back until it's absolutely necessary. In fact if you invest the money, Daisy, this time next year you'll be in a much more stable position. You've already spent more than you should have on those nasty illegal drugs.'

I pinched off a headache. The pair of them had made themselves scarce while I was with my parents, sensing that their presence would be a bridge too far for my unmagical mum and dad. Since then, however, they'd barely left my side – and they never seemed to shut up. It didn't help that almost everything they said was an unsolicited opinion about how I should live my life.

I hefted my backpack onto my shoulders. It hadn't seemed too heavy when I'd packed it yesterday but I was already thinking that I ought to take out half the items to lighten the load. I was also wishing that I'd brought along my bike. I'd decided it would be too cumbersome, especially since I didn't know where this treasure hunt would take me or what distances I'd have to cover. Now, with a five-mile hike to Sir Nigel's mansion, I was already regretting that decision.

'Give me an hour or two's peace, guys. Please!' I begged the brownies.

Hester muttered in my ear and even Otis seemed slightly put out but at least they both lapsed into blessed silence.

I turned left and headed for the road out of town. Of course it started to rain less than ten minutes after I'd left the train station. It wasn't exactly an auspicious start to my new career. I pulled up my jacket hood, glad that at least it was waterproof, and reminded myself that I'd have to get used to being out in bad weather. As a delivery driver, the worst I'd usually experienced was a mad dash from my van to a doorway. As a treasure hunter, I'd be spending a lot more time outdoors.

I tilted my head up to the sky, briefly enjoying the sensation of cool raindrops on my skin. It wasn't so bad – though it was incessant in the way that British drizzle always manages to be. By the time I finally arrived at the grand gates of Sir Nigel's Northumberland estate, I was feeling much less refreshed and much more bedraggled.

I was buzzed in without too much bother then trudged up the long driveway towards the massive house. The more time I spent hanging around grand palatial homes like this one and Neidpath Castle, the more baffled I was about the lifestyles they offered. Their heating bills had to be enormous and the cleaning would be never ending. I wondered if Sir Nigel spent so much time at places like the Royal Elvish Institute and the British Museum because knocking around his own home was too lonely. Maybe that was also the reason why Hugo Pemberville was such an arse.

'Tiny violins,' I muttered aloud. 'Tiny violins playing sad songs for the poor millionaires, Daisy.'

I wandered through the main doors of the mansion and found myself in a lobby that my entire flat would have fit in three times over. It wasn't its size that surprised me, however, it was the number of people milling around. They all looked like they meant business. For a good long minute I stood and gawked.

There were four large human men gathered around a marble statue of a naked nymph. I didn't think it was the statue that had drawn their attention because none of them were looking at it; instead, their attention was focused on the shiny tablets in their hands. They were dressed in tight black clothes, had earpieces, walkie-talkies and mobile phones. If this were a competition for who had the most communication devices, they'd win hands down.

To the right of the men were two elvish women, both with silver cuffs in their ears and identical features. Twins, then. Their perfectly straight glossy hair and immaculate make-up made them look out of place; when I examined them more closely, however, and noted their toned bodies and alert expressions, I understood. These two were serious competitors but they wanted to appear otherwise, to be underestimated. I vowed to watch myself around them.

Humphrey and Eleanor were deep in conversation on the opposite side of the room. I tried to catch their eyes but neither of them noticed me. Another couple were near them, obviously eavesdropping. From the faint green tinge to their lips, I was certain they were witches. I watched, amused, as they sidled closer to Humphrey. If they were trying to be subtle, they weren't doing a very good job of it.

I swung my gaze further around and squinted at a camouflaged trio – shapeshifters of some description, judging by their loose clothing. I mouthed a silent greeting to a tall, bearded man who appeared to be on his own. He nodded without smiling, but there was a friendly look in his eyes. Deciding he might be a good person to talk to, I shifted my weight and prepared to walk over to him.

I was halted in my tracks by a voice murmuring in my ear. 'Sizing up the competition?' Hugo Pemberville asked. 'I hope you're finally starting to realise that you don't have a hope of succeeding.'

Arsehole. I turned towards him, irrationally irritated that he remained so good looking. If there were any justice in the world, surely he could have broken out in acne or hives or, at the very least, contracted flesh-eating leprosy.

'Quite the opposite,' I assured him smoothly. 'In fact, I suspect it's you who's concerned otherwise you wouldn't be trying so hard to psych out the competition.' I waved an airy hand. 'But go ahead, keep trying to intimidate me. It says far more about you than it does about me.'

He laughed. 'I don't have to intimidate you. As soon as you're stuck up a mountain, your drugs have run out and the withdrawal symptoms are kicking in, you'll be running home in even more of a quivering soggy mess than you are now.' He glanced down at the grubby puddle that had formed around my feet and smirked, then he strolled away with his hands in his pockets to join his Primes.

I glared at his departing back. Then my eyes drifted down to his tight arse.

'Go on,' Hester whispered. 'Kick it.'

'She's taking the higher ground,' Otis said.

I grimaced. 'I thought you two were going to leave me in peace.'

'We did,' Hester said. 'Now we're back to give you the moral support you need.' Her wings buzzed as she gazed after Hugo. 'He is kind of sexy though, isn't he?'

I rolled my eyes. 'No.'

'Liar.'

I stuck my tongue out at her. But I didn't argue.

CHAPTER
NINE

You could have heard a pin drop as Sir Nigel walked to the front of the room to address us – but then I shifted in my seat. My wet jeans made a squeaky, squelchy sound; it not only sounded as if I'd had a little accident but also made half the room turn around and glare at me.

At least Sir Nigel had the good grace not to react. 'Welcome, one and all. I am honoured to have so many esteemed and experienced treasure hunters here.'

Being neither esteemed nor experienced, I sank down an inch in my seat.

'I understand that this will be an unusual experience for you all,' he continued. 'There is no record in modern history of a competition such as this, but I strongly believe that the Loch Arkaig treasure merits it.

'Almost three hundred years ago, seven caskets of gold coins were sent to the Jacobites from Spain and France. The coin was intended to help Bonnie Prince Charlie's bid to claim the throne. Alas for the Jacobites and Charlie, it arrived after the terrible losses at the Battle of Culloden and was too late to make any impact on the war effort. The Jacobite rebellion collapsed and Bonnie Prince Charlie fled, never to return.

'The gold, however, remained in Britain. One casket was stolen and the remaining six were passed to a series of clan chieftains for safe keeping in the hope that they could be used to help more Jacobites escape from Scotland. They ended up in the hands of Ewen MacPherson, who hid the treasure in a cave known as The Cage, at Ben Adler in the Scottish Highlands. Nobody has seen the gold since.'

One of the black-clad communications experts raised his hand. When Sir Nigel pointed at him, he stood up. 'Ben Adler is miles from Loch Arkaig so why is it called the Loch Arkaig treasure?'

'Because, John, Loch Arkaig is rumoured to be the last place where the treasure was hidden after being removed from Ben Adler. Both locations have been picked over by treasure hunters for hundreds of years and only a small number of coins have been discovered. Most of the contents of those six caskets have never been found.' He smiled. 'Until now.'

There was a murmur of excitement around the room. The buzz affected me, too; the tragic romance and bitter history of the Arkaig treasure was compelling.

'If you know where it is,' the bearded man called out, without bothering to either stand up or raise his hand, 'why don't you retrieve it yourself?'

Good question.

'I don't know where it is.' Sir Nigel gave a wry grin. 'I only know how to find it. Colleagues of mine have been deciphering some documents that were found rotting away in an old, locked box deep in the bowels of the British Museum. I am confident that these documents are genuine and that they will lead to the Arkaig treasure.'

We all leaned forward.

'It appears,' Sir Nigel continued, 'that there was considerable friction and mistrust among the clan chieftains who knew of its existence. They were concerned that one of them might decide to keep it for themselves. To guard against such an eventuality, a sorcerer was employed to help conceal it and three chieftains were nominated to take responsibility for it. The sorcerer created a key, which was divided into three equal parts and given to those chieftains. Only when the key is fully formed again and placed at the northernmost tip of Loch Arkaig will the treasure's location be revealed and the treasure itself, wherever it is hidden, be magically uncovered. So far I've found clues to locations for two parts of the key and I'm working on the third as we speak. Whoever finds any of the key parts will be in the running to find the treasure itself.'

One of the glossy elvish twins seated in front of me muttered, 'Find three separate key parts and only *then* find the caskets of gold? It might be easier to go looking for the lost Lady Rose.'

Her sister snickered quietly in agreement. I had no idea who Lady Rose was, but even so I didn't agree. What could have been a diverting interlude before I returned to the real world to find a real job was starting to feel like the beginning of a thrilling adventure. My heart was almost leaping out of my chest with excitement. I was ready – *more* than ready.

'What's it worth?' Humphrey asked. 'How valuable is this old gold?'

'In modern currency, around ten million pounds.' A ripple ran around the room. 'But,' Sir Nigel added, 'as you all know, treasure-trove law does not permit you to keep it for yourself. The British Museum will take ownership of the Arkaig treasure on behalf of the country. The person who finds it will receive £50,000, together with the unofficial title of the Britain's greatest treasure hunter.'

I glanced around. It appeared that most of the people in the room wanted the title far more than the prize money. They could have it; I wanted the dosh.

Sir Nigel's eyes gleamed. 'To keep the hunt as fair – and as competitive – as possible, the locations of the parts of the key will only be revealed one at a time. You will be issued with satellite phones. Once the first part has been found and verified, all competitors will receive information about the location of the next part.'

Hugo cleared his throat. 'But one team could find all three parts, right?'

Sir Nigel nodded. 'In theory. Only the teams – or team – that possess a part of the key will proceed to the final location, wherever that may be.'

I would be one of those teams. Even though I didn't have an actual team. Or any real clue about what I was doing. I smiled, then looked at the other contenders. Most of them were apparently thinking the same thing. I sneaked a look at Hugo Pemberville; he appeared to be as eager as the rest of us.

He must have felt my glance because he turned his head and his eyes met mine. My skin prickled in a not entirely unpleasant manner. We gazed at each other for a long, drawn-out moment until, to my surprise, he raised his eyebrows and winked at me.

'Samuel is waiting by the door,' Sir Nigel said. 'He will give you your phones and the information we have gleaned about the first location. The rules are quite simple: you are not permitted to physically harm any other team, and you must find part of the key to participate in the final stage of the hunt.' He spread his arms wide. 'Everything else is fair game.' He grinned. 'Good luck to you all.'

~

I STOOD up and prepared to shuffle down the aisle. As I stepped forward, at least four people hastily moved away. I moved closer to the camouflaged trio and they also hurried away. I tried stepping in the opposite direction, towards two of the black-clad men, and they swerved away too. My eyes narrowed. So I wasn't imagining it: I was obviously persona non grata. I probably had bloody Hugo Pemberville to thank for that.

Unwilling to appear cowed, I raised my left arm and ostentatiously sniffed my armpit, then did the same to my right one. 'Nope,' I said loudly. 'Not smelly.'

Nobody looked at me. How rude. I tightened my lips and glanced ahead. The others were forming a polite queue to receive their phones and instructions. I watched them for a moment. This was a competition and my fellow competitors had already made their feelings clear, but I could play games too.

I marched past all of them to the front of the line, ignoring the outraged gasp from one of the twins. 'Whatever happened to manners?' I heard her sister say.

I turned around and curtsied in her direction, then did the same to Samuel. I took my packet from him and, for no other reason than to be perverse, curtsied for a final time.

'That was quite impolite,' Otis said in my ear.

Hester clapped her hands with delight. 'It was brilliant! We might have some fun with you after all.'

I smiled. The back of my neck itched as everyone behind me stared in what I imagined was disgust. I couldn't figure out why they cared; I was only living up to their expectations. In any case, I'd learned a lot from what Sir Nigel had said about the one and only rule of the hunt – do not physically harm any other team. It meant he was already expecting under-handed shenanigans and sly double-dealing. I had no doubt that each and every one of them was prepared to cheat to win. It was just as well I wasn't there to make friends.

I scurried off to a quiet corner and sat down cross-legged on the floor to open the zip-locked bag. Some others did the same, but I noted that Hugo Pemberville and his Primes made a beeline for the exit. So did the men in black, who marched out with their walkie-talkies jiggling at their sides.

I gazed at the bag's contents. As promised, there was a satellite phone that was heavier and chunkier than expected and a map of the British Isles. There was also a sheet of paper with a note clipped to the corner explaining that it was a transcribed version of an old letter found at the British Museum. It had been translated from its original Gaelic.

I skimmed through it to find the relevant information.

WE HAVE PRESSED FAR *into England but the retreat has been called. I am in two minds whether to retrieve the item from Doctor Talbot or leave it in situ. I suspect the latter is the safest option for now.*

SERIOUSLY? Was this it? I turned the piece of paper over to see if there was anything written on the other side then I checked the bag in case I'd missed something. It was definitely empty.

Frowning harder, I stood up and went over to Samuel, who was preparing to leave. 'My packet has some missing information.'

'Everyone has everything they need to locate the first part of the key.'

I waved the letter at him. 'But this is all I received.'

He bowed stiffly. 'As I said, everyone has everything they need. And everyone has the same information.'

'This doesn't tell me anything! Only something about a doctor who must have been dead for three hundred years!'

Samuel gave me a patient smile.

'This can't be it,' I protested.

'Sir Nigel is confident that it will lead to the location. The rest is up to you.'

I ground my teeth. I hadn't expected the treasure hunt to be easy – but I hadn't thought it would be impossible. 'Can't you give me a hint about where to go?'

He bowed again. 'Good luck, ma'am.'

I cursed. 'Nobody's looking,' Hester said in my ear. 'You could smack him over the head and drag him outside, then beat him up until he tells you everything he knows.'

I couldn't tell whether she was being serious; I sincerely hoped not.

Fortunately, Eleanor and Humphrey took that moment to pass by and waved in a friendly manner as they strolled towards the doorway. I smiled in return.

'My throat is parched!' Eleanor complained. 'Why don't we head for that little pub we passed on the way here?'

'A champagne cocktail would be delicious,' Humphrey agreed. He glanced at me. 'Would you like to join us, Daisy? You'd be very welcome.'

While the pair of them were kind to think of me, especially given the wide berth I'd received from the others, I didn't want a drink. I wanted to find the damned treasure before anyone else did. And I seriously doubted that a Northumbrian village pub sold champagne cocktails. 'Uh, maybe another time.'

Humphrey smiled genially. 'Your loss.'

As I watched them go, I saw that two of the other teams were also heading out the door. From their optimistic expressions, they had a good idea where to go.

I read the letter again. What was I missing? My brain wasn't computing the information clearly enough. I felt my fingers tremble and I reluctantly delved into my pocket for a spider's silk pill. Most of the money I'd received from Sir Nigel had gone on replenishing my supply, but I'd still need to be careful and ration what I had. All the same, the thrill of pleasure that shivered through my veins as I swallowed the pill was enough to stop me worrying and start focusing.

My eyes strayed to the top of the paper. The letter was dated December 6th, 1745. I sucked on my bottom lip. 'How old are you?' I asked the brownies.

Hester flicked her wings towards me in horror. 'How old am I? You should never ask a lady her age!' She raised her tiny fist and shook it. 'Take another one of those magic pills and stop being rude!'

Otis flapped towards her until his tiny body was also facing me. Ignoring his sister, he hovered in the air. 'It depends if you mean lived years or you want to include necklace years,' he said.

I knew next to nothing about brownies or their lifespan. 'Specifically, I want to know if you were alive in the eighteenth century.'

Hester shook her fist again. 'How old do you think I am?' she screeched.

'I don't know. That's why I asked.'

Otis smirked. Hester's eyes darted towards him and he instantly smoothed his expression. 'We're not *that* old,' he said. 'I was born in 1868. Hester is older by a year.'

My shoulders sagged a little. 'Do you know anything about the Jacobites? Or how far they got when they invaded England in 1745?'

They exchanged glances; I guessed the answer was no, then.

'Perhaps Sir Nigel can tell you,' Otis offered, in a bid to be helpful. 'Or he might have a library that will provide the answer.'

My phone was already in my hand. 'Sure,' I said. 'Or I can ask Google.'

'Who's Google?'

I barely heard him as I squinted at the screen until I'd located the answer. Excellent. It was a shame that I couldn't find anything relating to a Doctor Talbot, but at least I had a location now. I wouldn't be beaten by an enigmatic old letter after all. 'Derby,' I said, satisfied.

Otis flew towards my phone, stared at it and then at me. 'You're a sorcerer,' he breathed.

'Nope.'

He started to shake while Hester's eyes widened with terror. 'You've trapped a brownie in there, haven't you?' he demanded. 'You've taken their essence in the same way that sorcerer took ours and you've stuck them behind that glass and ... and ... and...'

'I knew there was something off about you!' Hester yelled.

Clearly their entrapment had affected them far more than they were willing to reveal. 'I haven't done anything like that,' I soothed. 'Come on. I'll explain along the way.'

CHAPTER

TEN

'Show me another one!' Hester demanded.

Otis shook his head. 'No. Let's watch the one where the mum hugs its kitten again.'

'You've already watched it five times.'

'But it's so cute! The kitten is having a nightmare and its mum calms it down.'

'There are other ones we still have to see.' Hester blinked at me anxiously. 'There are more cat videos, right?'

I'd created a monster. *Two* monsters. 'Thousands more.' I pulled my phone away from Oscar. 'But there's only so much battery life and we're about to arrive in Derby.'

'But—'

'Later.' I pulled down my backpack from the luggage rack and moved towards the door. The train was already slowing to a stop. 'We're already behind everyone else because they all drove here. For all I know, one of the other teams is about to dig up the first key as we speak.'

'My money is on Hugo Pemberville,' Hester said. I glared at her and she smiled innocently. 'What?'

The train doors whooshed open and I stepped out, forestalling any further conversation.

I had no connections here in Derby and it was my first visit, so I didn't know the lay of the land. But I wasn't without a plan. Although Hester and Otis had commandeered my phone to watch cat videos for most of the journey, I'd managed to wrestle it from them long enough to do some research. I wasn't any wiser as to where the first key part might be hidden – but I did have an idea about where I could go for help.

Outside the station, I ignored the queue of taxis and turned right, away from the town centre. I'd barely turned the corner when I spotted the four men in black at the entrance to a small park, frowning at the screens in their hands. Ah-ha. So I was in the right place!

Perched on my shoulder, Hester lowered her voice as if she were afraid somebody might listen in. 'I bet they know where the first part of the key is. Sneak up to them, Daisy, then you can listen in.'

As expected, Otis immediately protested. 'Eavesdropping is wrong! Daisy is perfectly capable of finding the key without resorting to underhand tactics.'

She sniffed. 'Do you want her to win or not?'

None of the men had looked in my direction; they still hadn't realised I was there. I made a quick decision.

Skirting around the park railings, I entered through a small gate on the opposite side to where they were standing. Less than a minute later, I was skulking behind a large oak tree and straining my ears. Hester was right – I wanted to win. And was it underhand to eavesdrop on their conversation? After all, they were standing in the open to have a tactical discussion. What did they expect?

Unfortunately, it soon became apparent that the discussion wasn't going well. 'That road didn't exist in the eighteenth century, you plonker!' one of them protested. 'There's no point going that way.'

The man nearest me ground his teeth so vigorously that I heard them crunching. 'We have to go somewhere! We know it's not in the city, it's somewhere to the north. There are several locations along that road where it might be hidden.'

A third man piped up; despite his thick muscles and height, he had a high-pitched voice that sounded cartoonish. 'Pemberville went that way. We should have followed him when we had the chance.'

'Come on, John. You saw the way his team was moving. They don't have an exact location either. We won't find the key part first if all we do is follow other people around. We have to be smarter than that.'

'Then where the fuck do we go, Boris? Where do we start?'

I didn't wait to hear what Boris thought. It was obvious that the four men in black, for all their sleek communication technology, didn't have a clue what they were doing or where they were going. If nobody else knew exactly where to look, then I still had as good a chance as anyone of finding the first part of the key.

I slipped away before they noticed me. They'd been right about one thing: following other people around wasn't the way to success. I had to forge my own route.

I wasn't like them – and I certainly wasn't like Hugo Pemberville. I wasn't a connected high elf and I didn't even own a car. But I wasn't without resources. Less than twenty minutes after I'd nipped away from their argumentative huddle, I walked into the Derbyshire franchise of Swift Delivery Services.

I ordered the brownies to stay out of the way; delivery drivers were almost exclusively human and I didn't want my tiny companions to scare them off.

It was surprising how similar the warehouse was to the one

in Edinburgh – they could have been carbon copies of each other. As soon as I strolled through the main doors, I knew exactly where to find the manager's office, though I couldn't risk talking to anyone in management. If I did, they'd probably contact Mr McIlvanney and I was pretty certain he'd tell them to steer clear of a dangerous junkie like me. However, not everyone at SDS would be a slave to the system; life didn't work that way. All I had to do was find the right person.

With that thought in mind, I gave the offices a wide berth and made a beeline for the staffroom towards the rear of the warehouse next to the battered vending machine. If the Derbyshire franchise kept to the same timescale as the one in Edinburgh, the evening shift was only just starting. When I heard the murmur of voices from inside the staffroom, I smiled; some drivers hadn't set off yet. I wasn't too late.

I pushed open the door and stepped inside. Three faces turned towards me – two women and a man all wearing SDS uniforms. I grinned and waved. Confidence was key here; I couldn't afford to appear awkward. 'Hi, there! My name is Daisy. I worked for SDS in Edinburgh.'

All three of them smiled at me. Good. They were friendly.

'I'm Jamila,' the older woman told me.

'Anne,' said the other woman.

'And I'm Mark.' He stood up briefly to shake my hand. 'You've transferred here?'

'Nope.' I sat down on the chair next to him. 'I'm here because I need some help and I reckoned that you guys might be the ones to ask.' I didn't try to tell them that we were all part of the same team or fall at their feet with a sob story; if this lot were like my ex-colleagues, they'd prefer straight-talking.

Mark's expression suddenly looked wary but Jamila and Anne appeared intrigued so I focused on them. 'I'm taking part in a treasure hunt. It's a competition and I'm losing.'

Anne snapped her fingers in delight. 'I told you, Jamila! I knew that was Hugo Pemberville I saw in the street!'

I told my face to continue smiling despite my irritation at his name continually cropping up no matter where I happened to be. 'I'm trying to beat him,' I said. 'And a bunch of others. I only managed to snag my way into the competition by chance because of my deliveries near Edinburgh, so I know that drivers like us have bags of local knowledge. I'm taking a punt and hoping you can help me with a clue.'

'This is so exciting! What's the clue?' Anne demanded.

Emboldened by her enthusiasm, I leaned forward. 'I'm looking for someone called Doctor Talbot. I know he's been dead for hundreds of years so—'

I didn't need to finish my sentence. The three of them replied in chorus, 'Doctor's Gate.'

Bingo. I sat up straighter. 'What's Doctor's Gate?'

'It's not a gate, it's actually an old road that's been around since Roman times. You can't drive along it but you can walk most of it. It goes from Glossop to Brough-on-Noe. Some old folks still call it Doctor Talbot's Gate because he was responsible for improving the road in the fifteenth century.'

So Doctor Talbot was considerably more dead than the Jacobites were. I hoped that meant the other teams hadn't learned of his existence yet – or of this old road. A thrilling fizz ran through my veins; it was almost as satisfying as a double helping of spider's silk.

Jamila read my expression. 'I wouldn't get too excited. It's got to be fifteen miles long. If you're looking for buried treasure, that's a lot of distance to cover.'

Her caution didn't dampen my enthusiasm. I already knew a lot more than I had five minutes earlier. There had to be some sort of landmark that would lead me to the treasure because the Jacobite who'd buried it would have needed something to guide him back to it. It wasn't as if he could have used sat-nav.

'How do I get to it?' I asked eagerly.

They exchanged glances and suddenly I sensed something unspoken and dangerous passing between them.

Mark cleared his throat. 'The closest point is about forty miles away. It's a straight route if you're driving.'

Jamila choked slightly. 'Mmm.'

'What?' I asked. 'Is there a problem?'

'Doctor's Gate starts at the summit of Snake Pass.' There was an air of grim finality about her words.

My eyes flicked from one to the other. 'Let me guess,' I said slowly. 'It's called Snake Pass because...'

'Because of the monstrous snake that lives up there and likes to eat people.' Mark shrugged. 'We get paid double whenever we have to go that way.'

'Is the snake worse than a grumpy troll with a penchant for drenching drivers in her own snot?' I demanded.

'Only if it sees you.'

I pursed my lips; I could work with that. I leaned forward. 'I just have one more question.' They looked at me. 'Are any of you heading that way now?'

I HOPPED into the driver's seat next to Jamila. 'Thanks again for this.'

She smiled. 'No problem.'

'Yes,' Otis piped up out of nowhere. 'Thank you.'

Jamila jerked in shock and recoiled. 'What the fuck...?'

'He's a brownie,' I said quickly. 'He won't do you any harm.'

'He will if you listen to him,' Hester butted in. 'Otis is full of good intentions and bad ideas.'

Jamila's skin had turned pale and I suppressed the urge to loudly berate both brownies. The last thing I needed was for her to change her mind and boot me out of her van. I sighed. 'I sort of … acquired the pair of them just before I was invited to join the treasure hunt. They seem determined to stick around. They're annoying, but I promise they're not dangerous.'

She gave Hester and Otis a wary look. 'I suppose they're kind of cute,' she said doubtfully.

'Trust me,' I told her. 'The cuteness wears off pretty damned quickly.'

Hester aimed her tiny leather-clad foot at my cheek. I grimaced.

'You know,' Jamila said, starting the engine before driving the van out of the SDS car park and onto the main road, 'for a moment there I was kind of jealous of you and all that you had going on. I'm over it now.'

Funny that. 'Hey,' I said lightly, 'maybe one day you can also be insulted by a minor elf celebrity, sacked from your job, driven mad by two brownies and thrown into the deep end where you'll be competing against people with more power, more riches and more knowledge than you have.'

She sent me a sideways glance.

'Those are all the reasons why I'm desperate to win. I've got a lot to prove,' I added, only realising it for the first time,

Jamila grinned suddenly. 'Delivery drivers for the win.'

Amen to that.

'But you won't have much success if you keep hitch-hiking across the country,' she went on.

She had a point. I was reluctant to use my money to buy an old car because even a clunky banger would wipe me out financially. My fingers strayed to the pills hidden away in my pocket. I'd told Jamila most things – but I hadn't told her about my addiction.

'How are you with motorbikes?' she asked suddenly.

I frowned. 'Uh...'

'My little brother is off travelling for six months. He left his bike in my garage. You can borrow it, if you like.'

My mouth dropped open. I hadn't expected anything like that.

'You'll have to pay for petrol and sort out the insurance, and if it's not returned in perfect condition he'll bear a grudge for the rest of his life. But if you want to borrow it, it's yours. You can pick it up once you're done at Snake Pass.'

My jaw worked uselessly as I tried to fathom her generosity. She offered me a crooked smile. 'Lending you the bike isn't costing me anything. In fact, it's getting in my way so you'd be doing me a favour.'

'You don't even know me,' I managed.

Jamila shrugged but her eyes were warm. 'A little bit of kindness goes a long way. Besides, you'll probably be eaten by a giant snake in the next hour or so.'

I laughed. Then I gulped.

Jamila's gaze strayed to the rear-view mirror. 'At least you won't be alone.'

'What do you mean?'

She jerked her thumb backwards. 'We're being followed.'

CHAPTER
ELEVEN

I didn't have to see the driver's face to know exactly who was in the SUV behind us. The black paint job matched all four men's clothes perfectly, and I already knew from my brief eavesdropping session that they'd been considering following Hugo Pemberville. If they'd spotted me when I was walking away from them, they probably figured I knew where I was going and decided that I was worth tailing. They must have tracked me to the SDS warehouse and waited until I emerged with Jamila. Apparently I wasn't so tainted that they wouldn't follow me.

Jamila didn't appear bothered; I guessed that if the likes of Hester and Otis didn't faze her, neither would four black-clad men in a speeding SUV. In fact, the gleam in her eyes suggested quite the opposite. She grinned. 'Let's have a little fun.'

I opened my mouth but before I could say anything she put her foot down and her little van sped up. In a normal car race, the SUV would have won hands down because Jamila's delivery van didn't have the horsepower to compete. But she knew this city and the nippy vehicle could weave in and out of the traffic far more effectively than the SUV.

She veered around a grimy lorry, overtook it at speed and smacked her lips in satisfaction. I glanced back and saw the SUV do the same, but Jamila was already prepared for that. She twisted the steering wheel and, wheels screeching, turned into a side street.

I clung on while Hester and Otis went flying into the side window. Their little bodies slammed into the glass with a painful thump. I reached out and cupped them in my hands. 'You guys okay?'

They nodded, eyes wide. I drew them towards my body to keep them safe while Jamila accelerated even harder. 'I've always wanted to do this!' she said, turning down an even narrower side street.

'I bet you always finish your shifts early,' I said. The woman was a driving demon. Then I paused and glanced at her; it was entirely possible she possessed some supernatural blood. It certainly wouldn't have surprised me.

'You bet right!' She swerved again, sending a cloud of dust in our wake. The SUV was still following us but it was falling further and further behind with every turn that Jamila took.

'What's that smell?' Hester asked, popping her head up.

'Something is rotten in the state of Derby,' Otis agreed.

I sniffed the air. They were right; there was a definite tinge of deep rot tingling my nostrils. I stiffened: was one of the men behind us part-witch and using magic in some nefarious way to hold us back?

As we approached the next crossroads, I realised that the answer was far more prosaic: it was bin day and a large slow-moving lorry was nudging out in front of us. If we got trapped behind it we'd be stuck but, if we could get ahead of it, it would trap the SUV and we'd be free.

Fortunately, Jamila had the same thought. She closed the

gap to allow us to move in front of the lorry. Fifty metres. Forty. I clenched my jaw.

'Shit,' she swore. 'I don't think we're going to make it.'

We'd make it – all we needed was a nudge in the right direction. I half-closed my eyes and concentrated hard, forcing magical energy into the air behind us, then held my breath for a split second. There was a loud whump as the energy exploded and the air propelled us forward with greater speed.

Jamila yelped, shot past the bin lorry with barely an inch to spare and hit the brakes. 'That was a little closer than I'd have liked,' she admitted, wiping her brow.

It wasn't a manoeuvre I was keen to repeat. I exhaled as the screech of a loud angry horn beeping from behind the bin lorry filled the air. The men in black were going nowhere.

'That was very risky,' Otis scolded. 'You could have caused an accident. Don't do anything like that again.'

Jamila winked at him. 'We don't need to. They'll be there for five minutes while the bins are collected. They won't see us for dust.' She changed gear. 'Time to vamoose to Snake Pass.'

THE REST of the journey passed without incident. We soon returned to the main road and left Derby heading north. As soon as we hit a long hill and started climbing, I knew we were reaching the drop-off point.

'This is as far as I can take you.' Jamila pulled into a layby near the top of the slope. She pointed to her left where a steeper hill dominated the skyline. 'You need to go the rest of the way on foot. The snake will probably be asleep in its cave. As long as you walk quietly past it, you'll be fine.' She looked up at the sky. 'It'll be dark in a few hours though,' she warned. 'There aren't lights up here so you might struggle to see.'

'I can camp out till dawn if I need to. It'll be fine.' It was summer, the nights were short and I wasn't afraid of roughing it. I turned to face her. 'I can't thank you enough for all your help.'

'Daisy, it's been fab. I haven't had this much fun for weeks. I've got the day off tomorrow so come by my house when you get back to Derby and I'll get that motorbike sorted for you.'

The kindness of strangers. 'Thank you,' I said fervently.

'I always like to root for the underdog. Find that treasure and show the rest of them how it's done.'

'I'll give it everything I have,' I promised. 'If I win, you'll get a share.'

'That's not why I helped you,' she protested.

'I know,' I said quietly. I swallowed the lump in my throat. 'Hopefully I'll see you tomorrow.' I gave her a quick hug and then, with Hester and Otis flapping beside me, I got out of the van. I waited until she was driving away so I could wave her off.

'Nice lady,' Otis commented.

And then some, I thought.

I swung my backpack onto my shoulders and turned around. It was possible that I'd have the first key part in my grubby paws by dawn. I grinned and set off along the narrow track with a spring in my step.

Although the light was starting to dip, there were still a couple of hours to go before nightfall. It was no longer raining and there was a freshness to the air. I found I was genuinely enjoying the walk.

I knew from what Jamila and the others had told me that it was a two-mile hike to the top of Snake's Pass where the old Doctor's Gate road began. I eyed the dark opening of the cave to my right where the snake resided. There was no sign of it; all I could hear was the evening chorus from a few birds flapping overhead.

I wasn't particularly worried but neither was I foolish enough to drop my guard. I wouldn't do a damn thing to risk waking up the beast. It would only take thirty minutes or so to sneak up to the summit. Once I was there, I could relax.

I placed a finger to my lips to remind Otis and Hester to be quiet. The usually chatty brownies nodded solemnly, obviously as unwilling to become a monster snake's teatime snack as I was. I slowed my steps, taking care where I placed my feet to be as quiet as possible. By the time I drew level with the mouth of the cave, I was on tiptoe and moving at snail's pace.

Dark rock overhung the cave entrance, casting black shadows across the ground and making it impossible to see anything inside no matter how much I strained my eyes. The cave mouth was roughly two metres wide, although I reckoned the tunnel opened out once you were inside. Not that I'd be slipping past the entrance to check. Yes, there were occasions when curiosity got the better of me – but this was definitely not one of them.

The faint, rhythmic rumbling inside suggested that Jamila had been right and the snake was indeed fast asleep in its dark den rather than slithering around the hills searching for tasty treasure hunters to munch on. There were no signs of any carcasses or bones, so it probably dragged its prey inside and finished them off in there.

I shuddered slightly and held my breath until I was several metres past, then I moved more quickly to put as much distance as I could between the cave and myself. Soon my thigh muscles were aching and my breath was coming in short gasps, but my wariness had subsided. It was no longer the snake I had to worry about; now it was merely my own fitness and my ability to locate the key.

'What's wrong with you?' Hester asked. 'Why are you breathing like that? You sound like a horse.'

90

'You do sound strange,' Otis agreed. 'Are you alright, Daisy?'

I didn't deign to reply but reached into my pocket for a little pill of heavenly relief and tossed it into my mouth, enjoying the familiar bitter taste. Within about three seconds, I started to feel better. My breathing eased and my blood fizzed as renewed energy zipped through every artery and vein. I cracked my neck and sighed with deep satisfaction as I strode up the final few metres and paused to look around.

Behind me, the black cave mouth remained still and silent; ahead, Doctor's Gate stretched out for several miles before curving away behind a distant hill. I lowered myself to a cross-legged position and carefully scanned the scene.

'Keep your eyes peeled,' I told the brownies. 'There must be some sort of landmark that points to the key's location. Search along either side of the old stone road – we could be looking for anything man-made or natural.'

'There's an old, ruined farmhouse at the foot of that hill,' Otis said, pointing to his left. 'Behind those trees.'

He had sharp eyes. I squinted but could barely make out a stone wall and what might have been a chimney stack. Hmm; it was a possibility because the house could have been there since the eighteenth century, but it felt too obvious. I couldn't picture a Jacobite chieftain hiding such an important object inside a farmhouse.

'Okay,' I nodded. 'Keep searching.' I leaned forward, gazing hard through the failing light at a misshapen shadow. I tilted my head to the left and then to the right before realising it was nothing more than a bush. Given how much low-lying scrub there was, I doubted that was the landmark I was looking for.

'A waterfall?' Hester asked doubtfully. 'There's a small one over there.' She was pointing at a narrow stream of water tumbling down one of the rock outcrops, maybe three or four miles away from the stone track. It had potential but surely it was too far from Doctor's Gate to be the spot we were searching for.

I looked to the right; there was something else between the old road and the waterfall. 'What's that?' I asked.

The brownies twisted around to look. 'It's a little cairn,' Hester said.

'They usually mark burial sites,' Otis added, helpfully.

'I know what they're used for,' I told him. 'But don't you think it's a little strange that somebody was buried halfway up a rocky hill?'

We stared harder at the distant lump of stones. 'Winner, winner, chicken dinner,' I breathed.

Hester scratched her head. 'I'm all for some food, Daisy, but shouldn't we get that treasure before we eat?'

'It's a figure of speech,' I said. 'It—'

Otis interrupted. 'Look,' he said urgently. 'Over there. There's a group of people coming around the hill from the other side.'

I peered ahead, squinting until I saw them. My back stiffened. Although they were too far away to make out their faces, I recognised them from their clothes: it was Hugo cumbubbling Pemberville and the rest of his Primes. Naturally he was leading the way, his long-legged stride obvious even from this distance.

I flicked my gaze towards the cairn. We were closer, we could beat them. A slow, satisfied smile spread across my face. This was brilliant; I'd get to the section of the key first. I couldn't have planned it better.

'He must have gone the long way around to avoid the snake,' Otis said.

Hester snorted. 'I didn't think he'd be such a scaredy-pants.'

I smirked and licked my lips in anticipation. 'Come on.' I shouldered my bag. 'Let's make our move and beat him.'

I'd barely taken three steps forward to descend into the

valley below when I heard the roar of an engine behind us. I turned my head in time to see the men in the black SUV pull up.

All four of them jumped out. One of them spotted me on top of the hill and started yelling, waving and pointing. That was quickly followed by more yelling as all four of them ran towards me, clearly determined to catch me.

'We should go,' Hester said. 'They're fit and they're fast. If we don't hurry, they'll overtake us.'

I nodded but I didn't move.

'Daisy!' Hester muttered. 'Come *on*!'

The men's shouts and heavy footsteps were amplified by the hills around us and I looked at the dark hole where the snake resided. The men didn't know it was there and they were making no attempt to be quiet. 'Fucking idiots,' I muttered, then I waved frantically at them to be careful. I didn't dare shout – that would only increase the risk of waking the snake – but I couldn't let them make so much noise.

Hester grabbed hold of my earlobe and pinched it. 'Let's go!'

'She can't go,' Otis told her. 'They'll wake up the snake if they don't start taking more care.'

'All the more reason to get out of here,' she retorted.

'We can't leave them to be attacked and eaten!'

'Of course we can,' Hester snapped. 'It's their own fault for following us here.'

The men were closing in on the cave mouth – they'd be level with it in a minute. And their voices were getting louder.

'Otis,' I said urgently, 'can you fly down and warn them? Tell them that if they don't stop making so much noise then—'

I didn't get the chance to finish my sentence. There was a sudden rumble, like ominous grumbling thunder, and the ground beneath my feet trembled. There was no longer any point in attempting to stay quiet; the snake was already awake. 'Run!' I screamed at the men. 'Get out of the way!'

That was when the snake's giant head darted out from the cave at lightning speed. It lunged towards the nearest man in black and snapped its jaws twice in quick succession, then it grabbed hold of him in its massive mouth and chomped down hard as if he were nothing more than a tasty *amuse-bouche*. But then, of course, the snake still had starter, main course and dessert to go.

CHAPTER
TWELVE

I flew down the path in the direction of the men, my feet sending clouds of dirt into the air. The snake hadn't fully emerged from the cave yet, but it was already a terrifying thing to behold. Its girth was massive, spanning at least a metre, while its glittering black eyes displayed nothing but malevolent, hungry intent. As its dappled emerald scales caught the fading sunlight, there was a terrible beauty to it; in any other circumstances I might have admired it. But the bloodied body of its first victim was lying across the path and the shocked reaction of the three survivors, who clearly had now realised that they were in a fight for their lives, negated any such sensibilities.

'What are you doing?' Hester screeched in my ear. 'You're supposed to run away from the monster, not towards it!'

I ignored her and concentrated on reaching the three men. The snake hadn't noticed my approach; it was focused on the men, hissing and spitting at them before lunging at one and then at another. It was toying with them like a cat might toy with a mouse. For all their sophisticated gadgetry and sleek appearances, the men in black didn't stand a chance.

But I was less than a hundred metres away. They weren't alone.

One of the men – I was pretty sure he was called John – reached for something clipped to his belt and motioned to his two companions to do the same. When he held the device in front of him, I realised it was a taser. It probably wouldn't do more than annoy the snake even further, but it might buy a few seconds of precious time. I prayed that it would and veered to my right to check on their fallen comrade.

He was lying on his back, blood bubbling from his mouth as he struggled to breathe. There was a gaping hole in his side where one of the snake's fangs had punctured his body. His skin was pale and waxy and his glassy eyes told me that he was beyond pain.

My magic didn't extend to healing powers. I knew there were witches who boasted that their potions were strong enough to heal any wound, but even if there had been one around I doubted any potion could help this poor guy.

I yanked out my phone to call for help but a glance at the screen told me that I had no signal. I hissed and started to peel off my jacket, then glanced up at Hester and Otis. 'Can either of you do anything to help him?'

Otis wrung his hands while Hester only stared; I guessed that was a 'no' then.

I dropped my bag, knelt over the man's body and wrapped my jacket tightly around the wound; it would staunch the flow of blood, if nothing else. I had a small first-aid kit but nothing inside it would be effective against a wound of this magnitude. Besides, we were running out of time.

'You need to go and fetch help,' I told the brownies. 'Fly out to the road, find a way to stop the nearest vehicle and get the driver to call 999. Make sure the emergency services know that the snake is free. The last thing we need is more potential victims coming here.'

Neither of them moved. I drew in a sharp breath. 'Otis! Hester! Go and get help!'

My words finally seemed to register. 'Yes,' Otis said. 'We will.' He tugged at his sister.

'We have to get out of here,' Hester whispered. She raised her eyes to mine. '*You* have to get out of here.'

'I will,' I said firmly. 'I'll be right behind you.' I gave Otis a long look. He nodded, tugged Hester again and they flapped away, staying as far from the snapping, vicious snake as possible. Luckily they were too small to draw its attention, and slid past in seconds.

'Alright, buddy,' I said to the man in black. 'You stay right here whilst I help your friends.' Wishing I could do more than offer platitudes, I patted his shoulder. 'Don't go anywhere.'

I stood up and returned my attention to the snake. The other three men had fired their tasers and, as I'd expected, they'd had little effect. Its head continued to whip around and snap at each of them in turn. The only thing I could do was try to distract it and give them a chance to run. If they could get inside their SUV, they might have some protection against the snake's jaws.

I waved frantically at the desperate trio. 'I'll distract it. You need to get out of here!' I shouted.

John wasn't daft enough to take his eyes from the snake as he replied. 'You're an elf, right?' he yelled. 'Use earth magic and collapse the cave!'

That was a stupid idea; it would piss off the snake and bring it further out from its home instead of trapping it. We needed it to retreat inside, not have another reason to stay in the open. Besides, regardless of the circumstances, it was against the law to harm magical creatures in their own habitats.

I didn't waste time explaining all of that. 'Be ready,' I called.

He grunted as he raised his arms to fend off yet another lunge. The snake was starting to get bored with play time and it wouldn't be long before it chomped another of the men. I had to act now – and, as far as I could tell, there was only one option open to me.

Reaching into my backpack, I pulled out the length of rope that thankfully I'd thrown in at the last minute. I coiled it tightly around my right hand, sucked in a breath, tightened my muscles and ran towards the snake's glittering green body. All I needed was momentum and a tonne of good luck. Easy-peasy.

I flung my left hand backwards, using both it and the natural swing of my arm to propel me upwards. A second later, I was scrambling up the snake's scales until I was perched on its back twenty metres from its head.

The snake's body jerked and I fell to my hands and knees as I scrabbled to get a grip on something to avoid falling off. I managed to hook my fingers underneath the edges of two of the sharp scales. It was as well that I did because the snake had obviously registered that I'd landed on its body and it definitely wasn't happy about it.

It jerked its head around and fixed its beady eyes on me. I slid forward until I was straddling its wide girth as it writhed and bucked in an attempt to throw me off. I clung on with all my might.

I lifted my head and yelled at the men, 'Run, for fuck's sake! Get out of here!'

I didn't waste time checking to see whether they took off; it was taking all my energy to stay on the snake's back. Its head was curving towards me and I knew I'd be a goner if its fangs reached me. I had to move.

I released my grip on the scales and stood up shakily, keeping my body low to maintain my centre of gravity. A breath later, I started running the length of the snake's long spine towards its huge head. As long as I kept my balance, I was in with a shot. Speed was key, so I moved quickly, taking care to watch the rippling muscles so I knew in which direction the snake was jerking and could adjust my weight accordingly. At the same time, I uncoiled the rope and stretched it out between my hands. I was no cowgirl but I reckoned I could wrangle a giant snake. Maybe.

The snake bucked to the left and then to the right. My foot slipped and I almost fell, but providence smiled on me and I managed to cling on. Then its massive, forked tongue flicked out towards me and I was forced to duck to avoid it. The rotten stench of its breath was almost enough to knock me over, but I threw myself forward another four strides until I was too close to the snake's head itself for it to twist and reach me.

Heart hammering, I swung the rope out to loop it around the snake's head. The first time I missed, but I stayed calm and tried again – and the second time the rope caught beneath the snake's jaws. I pulled tight, forcing its head backwards. It gave a loud grumbling complaint as I yanked as hard as I could, directing its head away from the fleeing men.

'I'm sorry that we disturbed your sleep,' I said, though I had no idea if talking to the creature would do any good. 'But you can't eat them, not today. Anyway, they're all muscle. They won't make much of a meal.'

The only response I received was a vicious hiss. I looked towards the black-clad trio and saw that they had almost reached their SUV. Ignoring the pain as the rope chafed against my hands and rubbed my flesh raw, I prayed. Five more seconds. Just five more seconds.

Unfortunately for all of us, the snake had also realised that its opportunity for a meal was sliding away. Its head jerked against the rope I'd looped around it, and it made a last-ditch effort to lunge for the men. Its long body slid further from the cave until it was fully outside, its tail lashed from side to side in a renewed bid to knock me off, and its head thrust forward to snap at the three men.

I strained against the rope, hauling it backwards as best as I could, but I was losing my grip. I could feel it slipping through my hands. Between the sweat running into my eyes and the snake's head blocking my view, I lost sight of the men. When I heard the roar of a car engine a second later, I knew they were inside their vehicle and already escaping. I exhaled. They were taken care of – now I only had to worry about myself.

Unable to cling on a moment longer, I released the rope. Immediately, the snake lashed its tail towards me yet again – and now I had nothing to grip onto. The tip of the tail smacked into my ribs and I felt a piercing jab, then I was flying through the air until I landed in a clump of sharp gorse up the hill to my left. Now, as far as the snake was concerned, I was easy pickings.

I wheezed, doing my best to ignore the acute pain throbbing through my body. As I scrambled to my feet, I tried desperately to think of any magic that would help me. Water wouldn't be any use: snakes like water. Fire could set the undergrowth alight and cause more problems than it would solve. And the snake belonged to the earth, so commanding the ground to open up wouldn't be a good idea. All that was left was air, but there was barely a wisp of a breeze to work with. This would be touch and go.

The snake swung around until it was facing me. Its head rose up and swayed from side to side and its tongue flicked out in anticipation. This wasn't simply about a snack now; it wanted revenge.

I shivered and tore my gaze away. If I could manipulate the

air currents sufficiently, I could use them to push me further up the slope out of the snake's reach. *Come on*, Daisy. *Come on*.

I turned and concentrated on the air, coalescing as much of it behind my body as I began to half run, half stumble upwards. All I had to do was release my control at exactly the right moment – but the snake was right there, right behind me. I had to move.

I tightened my stomach muscles and, with a whoosh, threw all the magic I possessed. Within a heartbeat, a massive gust of cold wind propelled my body upwards. Now my feet were barely touching the ground – but I still had to put as much distance between myself and the snake as possible.

There was a narrow crevice to my right. Maybe I could squeeze inside the gap and keep away from the snake's fangs. It might work...

I jumped, using the last of the air magic to throw my body forward between the sharp, black rocks. Pressing my spine against the rear of the shallow fissure, I raised my hands instinctively to ward off the snake's next attack.

Its glittering eyes drew closer and I felt its hot breath against my bare skin. Huge, yellowing fangs dipped towards me, testing to see whether they could reach inside and snatch me out. Realising it couldn't get to me that way, it hissed – but its tongue remained a danger. If it coiled that around any part of my body, it could drag me out. Hell, that tongue alone probably had enough power to break my neck if it struck in the right place.

A voice drifted up from below. 'Oi! Bella!'

The snake's eyes narrowed a fraction. It flicked out its tongue then stretched beyond the edge of the rocks surrounding me to scrape it against my legs.

'Bella!' Whoever was yelling sounded sterner now. 'Back off.'

I stared at the snake and the snake stared at me.

'I will count to three,' the voice shouted. 'One, two—'

The snake flicked its tongue towards me again, but this time I had the strange feeling that it was simply trying to get in the last word. My stomach twisted as I tried not to retch at its breath. Then its head vanished and I felt the ground shake as it twisted around and slithered away.

I held my breath. When it didn't reappear, I poked my head out and peered down. At the foot of the hill, next to a battered Jeep and what appeared to be the carcass of a sheep, a man was patting the snake's head and murmuring what might have been endearments or a gentle admonishment – from this distance it was impossible to tell.

The snake – presumably Bella – looked irritated but, after a long moment, she lowered her head, snatched up the dead sheep and retreated to the dark maw of her cave. A second vehicle appeared and made a beeline for the fourth man in black who was still prone on the ground where I'd left him. Two uniformed paramedics jumped out and ran to his side.

It was over.

Hester appeared in front of my face, her tiny wings flapping. 'We found help,' she burbled cheerfully. 'That man's the ranger for this area. He's not very happy that you woke the snake up, so we should probably get out of here before you're arrested or something.'

I grunted and wiped my forehead.

'Ew.' Hester peered at me. 'Is that sweat? Ladies aren't supposed to sweat.' She sniffed. 'You should glow.' I scrunched up my face. 'What?' she asked.

'I'm trying to remember when exactly I told you that I was a lady,' I said.

Otis floated into view. 'You'll always be my lady, Daisy.'

Yeah, yeah. I forced myself to smile: it was either that or collapse into a blubbering heap.

'Your body is vibrating in a most bizarre manner.' Otis waved his tiny hand at my waist.

I frowned as I pushed myself out of the crevice. Dusting myself down, I reached for the satellite phone that I'd clipped to my belt and gazed at the screen. Fuck.

'Problem?' Hester inquired.

'Hugo's found the first key part,' I muttered.

Of course he had. I sighed, then turned to the red-faced ranger who was storming up the hillside to confront me. Apparently this entire debacle was my fault, whether I liked it or not.

CHAPTER

THIRTEEN

S ir Nigel had thoughtfully arranged for a local hotel to accommodate the remaining hunters for the night now that the first key part had been found. It was the wee hours of the morning before I dragged myself through the doors and heaved my aching, fractured body up to the empty front desk.

I dinged the bell, hoping a night porter would appear quickly; I was in desperate need of a shower and a decent sleep. I slumped untidily across the desk like a rag doll. I was so damned tired I could probably sleep right there.

'We'll go and see if we can find a member of staff.' Otis sounded worried. 'You need a bed before you collapse.'

I raised a hand in acknowledgment, impressed that I could muster up even that much strength, and the brownies flapped away. Hester went right while Otis flew left. Hopefully, they'd find someone to check me in before I passed out.

'Well,' drawled a familiar voice behind me, 'I expected you to be ruthless but I didn't think you'd go so far as to lead four men to their deaths.'

I didn't have the energy to be annoyed. 'Nobody is dead,' I

mumbled. It was true; before they released me, the police had told me that Alan Vargas, the man in black who'd been the recipient of Bella's worst attack, would survive.

'Not for want of trying,' Hugo said. 'You knew they were following you and you deliberately led them to Snake Pass without a word of warning.'

I hauled myself upright and turned to face him. The bastard was freshly showered and shaved; from the look of him, he'd happily head out for a ten-mile jog before bedtime. I gazed at his handsome, annoying face for a long moment. There didn't seem any point in denying his accusation. He would believe the worst of me no matter what I did.

'Were you charged?' he asked.

'Would I be standing here if I had been?' I demanded. 'I was questioned and then released.' I didn't mention that I'd been arrested, questioned and was now being fined an eye-watering amount for disturbing the snake. Hugo Pemberville didn't need to know that part – and I didn't want to think about it.

The only saving grace was that the police hadn't searched my belongings very thoroughly and discovered my hidden stash of spider's silk. If they had, I wouldn't be facing Hugo Pemberville right now, I'd have been a quivering wreck with serious withdrawal symptoms. And a guaranteed criminal record.

Hugo continued to watch me. 'So you'll be free to continue with the treasure hunt then.' It wasn't a question. 'That's a shame because I suppose we'll have to watch our backs. But you won't win, no matter how much you cheat.'

Unbelievable. 'You think that *you'll* find all the parts of the key?'

He shrugged. 'Of course.'

What must it be like to possess so much arrogant confidence that you never felt a moment of self-doubt? I sighed and turned away. I couldn't deal with this conversation any longer – and I certainly couldn't continue to look at his smug expression.

Hester reappeared, preening herself as she zipped around my head before settling on my shoulder. 'Found someone. They're on their way.'

She sounded happy. Knowing Hester that probably meant she'd frightened them out of their wits by appearing out of nowhere and demanding their attention. She was often blind to the fact that most people had never seen a brownie before. Forget giant snakes; before too long Hester and Otis would give someone a heart attack simply by opening their mouths.

'Goodnight then, killer,' Hugo called out.

I paid him no attention but Hester stiffened. Before I could say or do anything, she took off from my shoulder and flew at him. 'What did you say?' she demanded. 'What did you call my Daisy?'

'Leave it, Hester,' I said tiredly. 'He's not worth it.'

'Maybe not,' she snorted. 'But *you* are.' She addressed Hugo again. 'It's not Daisy's fault that those idiots followed us. We thought we'd lost them during the drive. They're the ones who woke up the snake. Daisy could have left them to be eaten and she'd have found that key before you did but instead she helped them. They're only alive because of what she did. You need to show her some respect.'

Otis emerged from the other doorway, glanced towards me and then gave his sister a worried look. 'Is there a problem?'

'Yes,' Hester yelled, her tiny voice echoing around the hotel lobby. 'There's a problem. There's a *big* problem. This idiot seems to think that Daisy was trying to kill those men by leading them to the snake.'

Otis's mouth fell open. 'What? We didn't know they were still following us!'

'That's what I told him!' Hester replied.

'She saved them!'

'I told him that too!'

Otis curled his tiny hands into fists and flew past me, also prepared to confront Hugo on my behalf. I raised my eyes heavenward. 'Guys,' I said. 'Can we please just leave it? It doesn't matter.'

'Of course it matters! Your honour is being impugned!' Otis protested.

'Hit him, Daisy,' Hester urged. 'Challenge him to a duel. Or stab his eyes out.'

'She doesn't need to use physical violence.' Otis put his hands on his hips. 'But a stern word is definitely merited.'

'A stern word?' Hester shrieked. 'He should be hung, drawn and quartered.'

'That's probably a bit extreme, Hes.'

'Is it? *Is it*?'

I passed a hand over my eyes as they continued to bicker, then I glanced at Hugo. He wasn't watching their antics, he was watching me with a strange look on his face that I couldn't decipher.

'Why didn't you tell me that before?' he asked, his voice considerably softer. 'Why didn't you defend yourself?'

My body swayed with exhaustion. 'What's the point? You've already made your mind up about me.'

I could have been wrong but I thought I saw him flinch. I didn't care and to prove my point, I reached into my pocket and took out another spider's silk pill. Holding his gaze, I tossed it defiantly into my mouth then raised my eyebrows, daring him to comment.

'Good evening, ma'am,' said a polite voice. 'Do you need to check in?' The man behind the front desk was studiously avoiding looking in Hester and Otis's direction.

'Yes,' I said. 'I do.' I gave him my details. When I moved

away a minute later, keycard in hand, Hugo Pemberville had vanished. Frankly, I was so tired that it was possible I'd imagined the whole scene.

'Come on, you two,' I said to the brownies, who were still yelling at each other. 'I need to hit the sack.'

'You shouldn't be hitting sacks!' Hester told me. 'You should be hitting *him*!' She frowned at the spot where Hugo had been. 'Where did he go?'

Otis clapped his hands. 'We scared him off with our stern words,' he said. 'See, Hester?'

I was already at the bottom of the stairs. They could argue all night if they wanted to but I was going to my damned bed. I didn't care what Hugo Pemberville thought of me. I didn't care about anything beyond getting some fucking sleep.

THE BABBLE of voices inside the breakfast room silenced as soon as I stepped across the threshold. I could feel several pairs of eyes burning into me with hatred; so everybody *did* think I'd tried to lead the black-clad men to their deaths. Hugo had obviously done nothing to dissuade them of that despite Otis and Hester's sterling defence of my integrity the night before.

I looked around but I couldn't see any evidence of him or his Primes, so I helped myself to a glass of fresh orange juice and did my best to act nonchalantly. Loudly protesting my innocence would only make me look more guilty. Besides, none of the people in this room were my friends before this treasure hunt had started, and none of them would be my friends after it. I shouldn't let their silent censure get to me.

I sat at one of the empty tables in the centre of the room and ordered a full English from the waiter. The hotel was on Sir Nigel's dime and, after receiving the fine from the police last night, I needed to save every penny I could until I found the Arkaig gold. If I ate enough now, I wouldn't need to spend money on food later.

I checked the satellite phone, noting that that the last message from Sir Nigel told me to await further instructions about the location of the second part of the key. With any luck, the next stage of the hunt would be monster free. I could only hope.

As a steaming pot of coffee was placed in front of me, I noticed the twins at the next table eyeing me with undisguised malevolence. I poured myself a cup and smiled at them cheerfully. They glowered in response.

'I'm going to say something,' I heard one of them mutter.

'Don't,' urged her sister. 'She might strike you dead where you stand.'

'She can't. It's against the rules.'

'Those rules didn't stop that bitch yesterday.'

I lifted my chin. They must know I could hear them, right? 'If you have something to say to me,' I called across, 'go ahead.'

They exchanged glances, then the first twin pushed back her chair and got to her feet clearly prepared to storm across and tell me what an evil being I was. Before she could move, however, a murmur rippled across the rest of the room.

I turned my head as Hugo and the rest of the Primes walked in. The other treasure hunters got to their feet as well, obviously acknowledging Hugo cumbubbling Pemberville's success.

When they started to applaud, I rolled my eyes. Nobody was glad that he'd found the first key part – I could practically smell the jealousy emanating from every corner of the room. Obviously, I didn't give him a standing ovation; I took a sip of my coffee and let my arse stay firmly on the chair where it belonged.

The cluster of Primes moved like an amorphous group to

the centre table, smiling, waving and acknowledging the others' adulation. You'd have thought Hugo and co had saved the world from an apocalyptic disaster instead of simply digging up an old key part.

Hugo glanced around the room as if searching for something. When his eyes landed on me, I stiffened. Instead of joining his cronies, he marched over to my table. Here we go again, I thought, and prepared for another argument.

'Is this seat taken?' he enquired, gesturing at the chair opposite my own.

I blinked stupidly. 'Huh?'

He smiled patiently. 'May I sit here?'

I was too taken aback to refuse. 'It's a free country. Knock yourself out.' I paused. 'Actually, if you could knock yourself out, that would be awesome.'

He smirked, pulled out the chair and sat down. 'I'm not going to do that,' he said. He reached for the napkin, unfolded it and placed it primly in his lap, while I – and everyone else in the room – stared at him. 'Where are your two companions?' he asked.

I couldn't begin to fathom what was going on. 'Why do you want to know? Do you want to knock *them* out?' I added pointedly,

'I'm only making conversation.' His tone was disconcertingly pleasant.

'They're still sleeping. If you want to attack me again for trying to murder four men, you can do so without their interference.'

Hugo didn't miss a beat. 'I'm sorry about that. I didn't have all the facts and I jumped to conclusions.' He smiled again and the dimple in his cheek was disarming. 'My sincere apologies.'

My skin twitched. This had to be a trap of some kind but I couldn't quite work out what it was.

The waiter placed my breakfast in front of me and I murmured a quick thank you before tucking in. The quicker I ate my food and left, the less chance Hugo would have to belittle me.

I glanced up and saw that the twins were gazing at Hugo with fascination. 'Did we get it wrong?' one of them whispered in a voice still loud enough to carry. 'Did she *not* try to get them killed?'

I shovelled sausage into my mouth. Yep; the faster I got out of here, the better.

'You seem hungry,' Hugo commented.

'Uh-huh.'

'I'm not surprised. It must be hard work taking part in the hunt without a team behind you.'

I swallowed and shrugged. 'At least I don't sound like I'm leading a seventies' pop group.' Hugo gave me a quizzical look. 'Hugo Pemberville and the Primes,' I said. 'Appearing live at a stadium near you!'

He barked an unexpected laugh. 'That's fair.' He leaned across the table. 'We can perform a medley of our greatest hits for you later, if you like.'

I furiously cut up my bacon. 'I'm good. But thanks.'

He pulled back. 'As you wish.'

His eyes were on me but I kept my head down and concentrated on my plate. Eat and run, that was my plan.

'Listen, Daisy,' Hugo said. 'I want to—'

'Good morning! May we join you?'

Thank God: two people who genuinely seemed to like me. I waved an enthusiastic hand towards Humphrey and Eleanor. 'Yes! Please do!'

They offered identical smiles and took the two remaining empty chairs. 'I hear congratulations are in order, Hugs,' Humphrey said. 'First key part in the bag! I'm afraid Eleanor and I missed all the action because we didn't get here until late last night. We didn't know this was where we were supposed to be until the news came over the satellite phone.'

I sneaked a look at Hugo's face. Whatever curious, indecipherable expression he'd been displaying earlier had been replaced by a bland mask. 'Perhaps treasure hunting is not for you,' he said smoothly.

Humphrey was far too jovial to take offence. 'Perhaps, old chap.' He chuckled. 'Perhaps.' He grinned at Eleanor. 'We should lay off the cocktails in the next leg.'

Eleanor touched her head and groaned. 'I think that would be a great idea.' She turned to me and added with mock sternness, 'And you, Daisy – from what I've been hearing you should stay away from monsters.'

Chance would be a fine thing. I felt a warm glow that there was no trace of suspicion from Eleanor; I liked her a lot and I didn't want to lose her good opinion, whether I merited it or not. 'Do we know anything about the next location?' I asked, keen to change the subject.

Humphrey flicked a hand towards the far wall where two of the hotel staff were setting up a projector. 'I suspect we're about to find out,' he said.

CHAPTER
FOURTEEN

S ir Nigel's face flickered into view. 'Is it working?' he asked somebody offscreen. 'Can they see me?' He listened to the response then beamed at the camera. 'Good morning, treasure hunters! Congratulations to Hugo Pemberville and the Primes for locating the first part of the key so quickly! Almost all of you solved the clue and worked out where to go, proving your worth and indicating that this will be a fabulous competition.'

Several heads turned towards Humphrey and Eleanor. Neither of them appeared fazed, but I reckoned they were the only team that hadn't deciphered the first part of the clue we'd been given in Northumberland. To be fair, with hindsight some might think that drinking cocktails in a country pub was the better move; it beat lassoing giant snakes followed by an inter-rogation from the local police.

The screen flickered and the sound took on a tinny quality. 'John Thurgood's team have sadly pulled out due to injury, so there are fewer of you than before, but I am confident, that the remaining teams are evenly matched. You are all still in the running to find the Arkaig treasure!

'I also wish to add that both the police and I have investigated the events involving Thurgood and his team mates yesterday and no rules or laws have been broken.' His voice hardened slightly. 'Nobody deserves to be disqualified and nobody *will* be disqualified. Not at this point.'

Oh. Clearly, at least one of my fellow treasure hunters had contacted him to request my removal. I grimaced but Eleanor took my hand underneath the table and squeezed my fingers. She was more intelligent than she let on.

I gave her a brief smile to let her know that I genuinely appreciated her support, then I sat straighter. With Hester, Otis, Humphrey, Eleanor and Jamila, I'd already gained my fair share of allies – everyone else could take a running jump.

I felt Hugo's eyes on me and I tilted my chin towards him defiantly. His expression remained the same but he raised his coffee cup to me before taking a sip. Cumbubbling arse. Maybe he'd decided that the best way to trip me up wasn't to attack me verbally but to confuse me. I resolved to pay him no more attention.

Sir Nigel continued, 'There are eight teams still in the running and they all have an equal shot at finding one of the remaining key parts. It is important to me that the competition continues to be as fair as possible. The next part is in a particularly remote location and you will all receive the same help to reach it.'

At least half the people in the room started to murmur. I didn't; something about Sir Nigel's words made me suspect that this key part would be extraordinarily difficult to find.

'The British Museum has tracked it to Smoo Cave near Durness in the Scottish Highlands,' he said.

Out of the corner of my eye, I spotted the twins grabbing their phones so they could search for the cave. Next to me, Eleanor frowned. 'I've been to Smoo Cave,' she whispered. 'It's a tourist attraction. I don't see how the key part could have remained hidden for almost three hundred years when people have been traipsing through there in their thousands.'

Humphrey nodded. 'You're right, my dear. I suspect there's more to this than meets the eye.'

Across the table, Hugo raised an eyebrow. 'Smoo derives from the Old Norse word for hiding place,' he said.

I tried – and probably failed – not to look too interested at this titbit of information.

Sir Nigel was still speaking. 'Many of you will have heard of Smoo Cave and will know that, while it is a sea cave, it is also partially submerged thanks to freshwater streams that trickle in from overhead. One of these freshwater passages, believed for decades to have been permanently blocked, leads to a far larger network of caves that I do not think anyone has explored in more than two hundred years. The only way to access the secondary cave network is by unlocking an old sorcerer's underwater rune that bars the way.'

He pulled a face. 'That is what we *think*, but it is not a theory that has been tested and we don't actually know what lies on the other side of the magical blockage. Divers have located the rune but it has not yet been opened.'

He paused. 'I'm sure I don't need to tell you that this section of the hunt could prove incredibly dangerous. The secondary cave system may be underwater or blocked by debris that has fallen in the centuries since the Jacobites walked there. There might be dangerous creatures dwelling in those dark reaches.' He raised his shoulders expressively. 'We simply do not know. There is no dishonour in not proceeding into the cave – nobody's life should be lost in the pursuit of old gold.'

I shuddered. I suffered occasionally from mild claustro-phobia – but I'd almost been eaten by a giant snake so I couldn't let a dark cave worry me. In fact, despite the frisson of anxiety, I felt a ripple of excitement at the thought of treading where few others had ever been. This was what treasure hunting should be about – the perilous thrill of the unknown.

Goosebumps rose on my arms and I realised that my fear of confined spaces hadn't dampened my excitement at seeing this hidden cave network. I glanced around the table. Humphrey and Eleanor both looked nervous, but Hugo's expression mirrored mine. It was a shock to think that we felt the same. This wasn't about the key or the gold, it was about exploring somewhere new and mysterious. I shivered in anticipation.

'If you decide to continue into the unknown,' Sir Nigel said, 'we shall convene at the entrance to Smoo Cave in twenty-four hours' time. I have engaged the services of a skilled sorcerer who will unlock the rune so all the teams can proceed. Everyone will be on a level footing when they enter the cave network but,' his eyes gleamed, 'only one team can gain the next part of the key. The competition is still on – and it is heating up.'

Somebody coughed on the other side of the room. The solo hunter – the bearded man whom I'd almost approached on the first day – had stood up. 'Do we have to wait twenty-four hours?' he asked. 'Or can we try to get in on our own?'

I gave him a closer look. If he thought he had the ability to unlock an old rune, he must be a sorcerer. My stomach tightened. Those sorts of skills could lead him to the key part before the rest of us got anywhere near it.

Sir Nigel grinned. 'I thought you might ask that, Boonder. You are certainly welcome to try and break the rune, but it's taken me a while to find a sorcerer capable of doing it. You might find it harder than you think.'

Translation: you can try but you won't succeed. I exhaled. Good. I had nothing against the sorcerer but I wanted to be the next person to find part of the key. Hell, I *would* be the next person to find it.

I felt Hugo's eyes on me and glanced at him. He looked amused; no doubt my thoughts were written all over my face. I tried to school my expression into something blander before I remembered that his opinion meant nothing to me. I didn't care what he thought; I was supposed to be ignoring him.

I leaned back in my chair, stretched my legs out underneath the table and inadvertently kicked him. 'Are you playing footsie with me?' he asked archly.

Wanker. 'Actually,' I sniffed, 'I was attempting to break your leg to take you out of the running.'

Humphrey's mouth fell open. A tiny smile played around Hugo's lips. 'You'll have to try harder next time.'

I folded my arms. 'Challenge accepted.'

Hugo laughed, then got to his feet, nodded and wandered off to join his Primes. I forced myself not to watch him go.

The screen displaying Sir Nigel's face flickered and turned black. He'd given us our marching orders and presumably had nothing more to tell us.

I checked my watch; it was just after 9am. There was plenty of time to meet Jamila, borrow her brother's bike then get up to Smoo Cave before nightfall. Unless Boonder did have the skills to unlock the sealed rune, there was no need to rush.

I eyed him as he dabbed at his mouth with a napkin then strode out of the breakfast room. 'Do you know him?' I asked Humphrey. 'Boonder?'

He beamed at me. 'I do. He's a good fellow.'

Humphrey seemed to think that everyone was a good fellow; there didn't appear to be anyone he disliked. 'Is he a powerful sorcerer? Can he unlock the Smoo Cave rune himself?'

'I doubt it,' he said, after thinking about it for a moment. 'Boonder has excellent skills but Sir Nigel wouldn't have employed another sorcerer if he thought that Boonder could open the rune on his own. Sir Nigel's primary concern is the competition aspect of the hunt.'

Humphrey might like everyone he met but that didn't mean he wasn't canny. 'You're not just a pretty face,' I told him.

He grinned. Eleanor nudged me with her elbow. 'Speaking of pretty faces,' she said, 'what's the deal with you and Hugo? There was definitely some flirting going on there.'

'What? No, there was not!' I shook my head vigorously.

'That was definitely flirting,' Humphrey agreed. 'Are you secretly courting?'

'No!'

'Hugs is a good fellow.'

No, he wasn't.

'You could do worse.'

Not much worse. I reminded myself about what the house-keeper at Neidpath Castle had told me about the 'bone zone' at Hugo's ancestral home. 'There is nothing going on apart from mutual dislike,' I said firmly,

Humphrey and Eleanor exchanged looks. 'If you say so, Daisy.'

'I do.' I sniffed. 'Now if you'll excuse me, I have to retrieve my brownies, check out of this hotel and get to Scotland.'

Humphrey offered a mock salute. 'We'll see you there.' His brow creased. 'Probably. I have some friends close to Durness that we might visit on route. I've not seen them for months.' He smiled at Eleanor. 'They'd love to meet you.'

'That sounds wonderful,' she said. 'We should visit Ullapool, too. There's a lovely café there.'

I left them to it. Cafés and long-lost friends were all very nice but I wanted to find some treasure – before anybody else got to it.

ALTHOUGH I'D RIDDEN a motorcycle before – I'd even used one for deliveries in Edinburgh on a few occasions when time had been an issue – I'd never ridden one any distance. I wasn't entirely stupid; I took a lot of breaks and made sure that I walked around and stretched my legs every time. Even so, by the time I finally arrived at the little carpark on the outskirts of Durness, my arse felt like it was on fire.

I climbed stiffly off the seat and tried to massage myself. The oversized leathers that belonged to Jamila's brother, and which she had kindly lent me, didn't make it easy. In the end, I plonked myself down on the verge and stripped them off until I was sitting in my underwear in full public view. My tender bottom required more attention than any sense of misplaced shame, which by this point was non-existent anyway.

I was not the first treasure hunter to arrive; the car park was already packed. I recognised most of the vehicles. I wasn't surprised to see that Humphrey and Eleanor were missing. I was particularly pleased to spot Boonder grumpily setting up a tent on the grassy field at the other side of the car park. Judging by his wet hair, he'd already tried and failed to break the under-water rune.

'Guess who just stepped out of their tent and saw you parading around in your underwear?' Hester asked slyly.

'I'm not parading around,' I protested, but I still looked up. My eyes met Hugo's; he was staring at me. I couldn't tell what he was thinking; I didn't want to know. Probably.

'You *should* parade around. Do some strutting,' Hester advised. 'Show him what he's missing.'

'Hester!' Otis gasped. 'Don't be so scandalous!'

I zoned out their bickering as I gently rubbed my bum to loosen the muscles and ease my pain. The blonde woman who was one of Hugo's Primes appeared and spoke to him. He said something to her and she glanced in my direction; no prizes for guessing what – or rather whom – they were talking about then.

I reached into my bag and pulled out a pair of loose-fitting trousers and a T-shirt that smelled only slightly musty. By the time I was dressed, the blonde was standing directly in front of me. Her eyes crinkled as she smiled. 'Hi there.'

I grunted, 'Hi.'

Otis flapped up and performed a bow in mid-air. 'Good afternoon, Miss.'

She curtsied, making an effort to look serious rather than mocking, and went up an inch in my estimation. Only an inch, mind you. She was still a Prime. 'I'm Becky.'

I looked at her again. Yep. She had good hair.

'Otis. This is my sister, Hester.'

Hester curled her lip.

'And my owner, Daisy.'

I winced. 'I'm not your owner, Otis.'

'Leader, then.'

I pursed my mouth. 'Can we use friend? Is that allowed?' Otis looked delighted.

Becky followed our interaction with bright-eyed interest. 'I've never met a brownie before,' she admitted.

Hester snorted. 'That's hardly surprising. We already know you don't move in the right sort of circles.'

Becky didn't miss a beat. 'You're talking about Hugo. I can't blame you for being wary of him. That's why I've come over. He has his reasons for acting as he did but he knows he's been something of an arse.' That was an understatement.

'You've been something of an arse too,' Becky went on.

Justifiably so. But whatever.

'We'd like to make amends. Why don't you join us this evening? There's a small pub nearby that has a good menu and we're heading over there for something to eat. It'd be lovely if you could join us.'

My skin prickled. There was a catch somewhere. 'Does dear old Hugs know you're inviting me?'

'Of course.' She waved a hand around. 'I'm inviting everyone. Just because we're in a competition doesn't mean we can't enjoy each other's company.'

Before all this started I'd have agreed with her, but I'd been persona non grata so far.

'We can exchange war stories,' she added. 'And I know that Hugo wants to talk to you some more.'

'Does he indeed?' I murmured.

Hester floated up to my right ear. 'You should say yes then we can spy on them and find out more about all these other sneaky bastards.'

Otis headed for my left ear. 'You have to agree, Daisy. This is your chance to smooth the waters and make new friends.'

It was rare that both brownies agreed with each other, even if their motivation was markedly different. 'I've got to put my tent up,' I said to Becky. 'But once that's done, I might join you.'

She grinned. 'Excellent! We'll have fun.' She looked over her shoulder and I realised with some discomfort that Hugo was still watching. 'He sent you over here,' I said. It was like being at a school disco.

'Yeah,' she admitted. 'But only because he knew you'd refuse the invitation if it came from him. He's a good guy, Daisy. Honestly. The two of you just got off on the wrong foot.'

That's not how I would have described it. Becky was a little too zippity-doo-dah in her approach to life, but I managed a weak smile. 'We'll see.'

She beamed. 'We can't ask for more than that.'

FIFTEEN

I heaved myself and my bag over to the grassy field next to the car park and pulled out everything I needed to set up my tent. It was a tiny thing and wouldn't take long to assemble. As I laid out the gear and examined the ground, the other treasure hunters went off towards the pub; Becky had clearly used her shiny personality to persuade them to join her. I wondered if she was related to Humphrey; they certainly possessed the same outlook on life.

'Why don't you put the tent up later?' Hester said. 'Let's go to the pub and have some fun!'

'Work now, play later, Hes,' Otis chided.

Her lip curled. 'Boring.'

'Hugo Pemberville is still checking his team's tents,' Otis said pointedly.

I looked up. He was right: Hugo was wandering around and using a mallet to drive tent poles deep into the soft earth. I frowned and tapped the ground with my foot. It was somewhat water-logged and squidgy. Hmm.

'All the more reason to go to the pub now,' Hester replied. 'We don't want to be like him.'

'Why don't the two of you take my phone and watch some videos until I'm finished?' I suggested. 'I'll be quicker if I can get some peace and quiet.'

They both looked thrilled. I pointed towards my bag and they immediately flew to it and tugged out my phone. I concentrated on the patch of earth in front of me and used a flash of magic to draw out the water to make the ground less soggy.

'That's a clever use of magic.'

Startled, I yelped. 'Don't sneak up on me like that!' I said to Hugo and glared at him.

He ran a hand through his tawny hair. 'Sorry. I didn't mean to scare you.'

'I'm not scared.' I sniffed. 'I was just surprised.'

'Sorry,' he said again.

I frowned. He sounded like he meant it. 'Well, alright then,' I muttered. I reached for my tent.

'I didn't realise that low elves could use elemental magic in the same way that high elves can.'

Was he being deliberately patronising or simply making awkward conversation? I flicked him a look. It appeared to be the latter. 'Low elves have magic.' Duh.

'Obviously,' he replied. 'But I've never seen a low elf wield it without a lot of preparation first.'

What was there to prepare? The ground was too wet, I drew the moisture away to make it dry. It wasn't rocket science. A thought occurred to me. 'Do you want me to do this for the area around your tents?' Hugo Pemberville was perfectly capable of drying out a patch of earth without my help, but perhaps there was more to this conversation than I'd realised.

Hugo grinned suddenly and something about the combination of the dimple in his cheek, the sparkle in his eyes and the flash of white teeth made my stomach flip. 'You seem to have the knack for it, so yes, I would appreciate it. You already know what you're doing so you'll probably be more efficient than me. In return, I'll set up your tent for you.' He held out his hands, palms upwards. 'I won't sabotage it. You have my word.'

'I'll turn the ground around your tents into a swamp if you do.'

His grin didn't waver. 'I have no doubt.'

I was about to turn away but I didn't. 'Why are you being nice all of a sudden?'

He gazed at me, a glimmer of honesty in his eyes. 'I may have judged you unfairly.'

My eyes narrowed. '*May* have?'

'Okay,' he conceded. 'I *did* judge you unfairly and I apologise sincerely for being prejudiced. I've known one or two spider's silk users in the past and they've caused ... problems.' His mouth tightened. 'I'm not trying to make excuses for my behaviour, I just want to explain. I should apologise.'

I waited. When nothing else was forthcoming, I raised an eyebrow. 'Go on then.'

'What?'

'Apologise.'

He gave a sharp laugh. 'You don't take any prisoners, do you?' He bowed deeply. 'Miss Carter,' he said formally. 'I apologise wholeheartedly for my behaviour towards you. It was unnecessary and impolite. I acted unfairly. Your addiction to spider's silk is none of my business and I should not have judged you. I was ungentlemanly and you deserve better.' He straightened up and looked me in the eyes.

Bloody hell, I couldn't fault that apology. I wasn't sorry I'd sent Duchess to his castle – I wasn't prepared to go that far – but I acknowledged the fact that he was trying to placate me.

'Daisy,' I said, suddenly wishing I didn't sound quite so grudging. I cleared my throat. 'Call me Daisy.'

Hugo's grin returned and he held out his hand. 'Hugo. It's nice to meet you.'

Against my better judgement, I took his hand and shook it. His grip was warm and firm but without the pressure that some people employed when they were trying to exert their authority.

'We won't ever be best friends, Daisy,' he said. 'But for the purposes of the competition, I'd like to get along as much as we can. I'll understand if you don't want to take the olive branch I'm offering, but it is genuine.'

I wasn't wholly convinced I could trust him and I certainly didn't want to be his friend, but a truce would be good. And I could always be a better person. I sniffed. 'Alright.'

His eyes held mine for a long moment. 'Good,' he said finally, his tone surprisingly soft. 'I'd like us to be able to get along.'

'Daisy,' Hester said plaintively from a spot by my feet. 'Your magic telephone isn't working.'

I ripped my gaze away from Hugo and glanced down to see that Otis was jabbing furiously at the screen but nothing was happening. 'Here,' I told the brownies. 'Let me unlock it for you.'

I reached for it as Hugo turned away and knelt down to start assembling my tent. As I did so, I saw that there were three missed calls from my mum and my blood immediately froze. I'd told my parents I'd probably be out of touch for a few weeks. Mum would only call repeatedly if there was a problem.

I straightened up, gripped the phone more tightly and marched towards Hugo's cluster of expensive tents. With my stomach churning, I called my mum, praying that nothing disastrous had happened. Please be well. I crossed my fingers. *Please.*

When she answered on the fourth ring, I gasped aloud in relief.

I gestured to Otis and Hester, who were flapping along beside, me to stay quiet. 'What is it?' I demanded. 'Has something happened?'

'Daisy, darling!'

'You've called three times,' I said. 'Is something wrong?'

'Wrong? Not exactly. Both your father and I are well. It's just that something's happened that I thought you should know about.'

I stiffened. 'What?'

'There's been a strange man asking questions about you. He's been around all the neighbours and he's knocked on our door to talk to us. It's been disconcerting and I'm concerned about his intentions.' She paused. 'I think he's an elf. Like you.'

Mum and Dad had adopted me when I was a baby. They were human and they didn't know any elves apart from me. 'You *think* he's an elf?'

She sighed. 'I *know* he's an elf. Maybe he's a friend of yours?' She sounded doubtful and I didn't blame her. I scarcely knew any elves. A prickle of discomfort itched at the skin between my shoulder blades.

I swivelled round and gazed at Hugo, who was already hammering tent pegs into the ground. 'What does he look like?'

'Pointed ears, dark hair. I asked for his name and he wouldn't tell me, but he spoke to June down the road and she said he was called Rizwan Matcliffe.'

My gaze hardened instantly. There'd been an elf called Rizwan with Hugo at the Royal Elvish Institute. I'd noticed him at Neidpath Castle as well but, now I thought about it, I'd not seen him with the other Primes since the start of the treasure hunt. No prizes for guessing who had sent him to dig up the dirt on me. So much for Hugo Pemberville's olive branch. That fucking bastard. I should have trusted my instincts.

'I know who he is. You don't have to worry about him,

Mum.' The last thing I wanted was to worry her. 'He's an old friend who's been trying to get in touch,' I lied. 'I'll give him a ring and tell him to stop bothering you. Let me know if he comes around again, though.'

'I will. How are you doing? Are you eating properly? Are you looking after yourself?'

'I'm doing fine. How's Dad?'

'He's good. I'll tell him you were asking after him.'

'Thanks, Mum.' I continued to glare at Hugo. 'Love you.'

'Love you too, Daisy Pop.'

I hung up. 'Can we have the phone now?' Otis asked.

'Sure.' I laid it on the ground, facing upwards so they could watch all the cat videos they wanted. Then I drew in a deep breath and marched back to Hugo.

'Almost done,' he said cheerfully, his attention on the canvas.

I crossed my arms over my chest and cleared my throat loudly until Hugo looked up. 'Is everything alright?' he asked.

I tapped my foot. 'It's interesting that you seemed to think I was a criminal because I take spider's silk when *you're* the dodgy elf around here.'

His brow furrowed slightly and he got to his feet to face me. 'Pardon?'

'What gives you the right,' I spat, 'to send one of your goons round to my parents to investigate me?'

Hugo's face smoothed into a blank façade. 'Oh. That.'

'How dare you!'

His expression didn't alter. 'It was a perfectly reasonable action to take under the circumstances. I couldn't allow my team – or anyone else taking part in the treasure hunt – to be endangered by one of the other participants.'

Unbelievable; he actually thought he was in the right. 'You

disturb my parents, invade my privacy and you think you did a good thing?'

'You'd already proved yourself untrustworthy. There was a very real chance that you tried to get John Thurgood and his team killed. Plus, you stole information from me at Neidpath Castle—'

'I saved John fucking Thurgood. And I didn't steal anything! That information was out there in the open! I only used it after you got me fucking fired!'

Hugo didn't pause for a second. 'Well, you got your own back for that one. You deliberately made me look like a fool with the way you swooped in and used my research. You got that necklace after sending the most cantankerous troll in the country to my damned home! You started this vendetta against me. You can't blame me for being wary.'

I hadn't started it, he had. 'Are you upset because I dented your pride?' I sneered. 'Is that why you've become this massive thorn in my side?'

Hugo growled, '*I'm* a thorn in *your* side? After all you've done to me?' He stepped towards me.

I matched him and took a step towards him. I wouldn't let him intimidate me. 'All I've done to you?' I scoffed. 'You can't stand a bit of real competition.'

'You're no competition for me. I'm the one who's standing here with part of the key. You've got nothing.'

'I'd have beaten you to it if I hadn't stopped to help those idiot men from being eaten by a snake!'

'So you say.'

We glared at each other. The man was nothing but a cumbubbling pain in my already sore arse. He was a stuck-up high elf with too much arrogance and annoying blue eyes that were the colour of the ocean and a cinnamon scent that belonged in a bloody bakery and ... and ... and...

Goddamnit. Suddenly I was strangely, painfully aware of our proximity to each other. I pulled back but Hugo grabbed my right hand. His eyes dropped to my mouth as his thumb caressed the flesh of my palm. 'Are you attracted to me?' he asked roughly.

I gritted my teeth. 'No.'

He moved his head closer, until his mouth was hovering over mine. 'Are you sure about that?'

'I don't know how you usually get women into your bone zone but sending someone to interrogate their parents isn't a seductive move as far as I'm concerned.'

Hugo blinked but stayed where he was. He loosened his grip on my hand until his touch was feather light. 'Step away, then,' he said.

'This is my tent pitch,' I replied. 'You step away.'

'If you insist.' But he still didn't move.

I could feel his warm breath on my cheek. He swayed forward and his chest brushed against mine. I met his gaze. 'You're a manipulative, judgmental bastard,' I told him softly.

'And you're a hot-headed junkie.' His eyes glittered darkly. 'So I guess that makes us even.'

And that was when he kissed me.

My senses swam. He tasted of spice and salt and I couldn't stop myself from reaching up to draw him closer. Hugo groaned – and I abruptly realised where I was and what I was doing. I sprang back, breathing heavily. 'No,' I said. 'No way.' I wouldn't allow this to happen. Not with him. This was a terrible mistake.

Hugo wiped his mouth with the back of his hand. 'I couldn't agree more.'

I saw the regret flickering in his blue eyes and drew in a breath. My traitorous heart was still hammering against my chest. 'It tastes nice though, doesn't it?' I said. He frowned. 'The spider's silk. It tastes nicer than you expected.'

His nostrils flared and he backed further away. There: at least now I'd guaranteed he wouldn't kiss me again, whether I wanted him to or not.

'It's time,' he said, his breath catching slightly, 'that we returned to the original plan and stayed the hell away from each other.'

I tilted my chin defiantly. 'I couldn't agree more.' I gestured to his feet. 'You're still standing on my pitch.'

Hugo's eyes briefly met mine once again. Then he spun around and left.

CHAPTER

SIXTEEN

The following morning when we all gathered in front of the entrance to Smoo Cave, I made every effort to stay as far away as I could from Hugo. I didn't look at him, I didn't strain my ears to hear what he was saying, and I definitely wasn't painfully aware of his every move. Or the fact that the wetsuit he was wearing displayed every inch of his taut, muscular body. Nope. Not me. I was focused on getting into the cave and finding the next key part before he did.

The sorcerer engaged by Sir Nigel didn't look particularly powerful. He was gangly, tall and nervous, as if he were not used to being out in public. I'd been tempted to sidle up to him and make conversation, to persuade him that I was a good guy and maybe even encourage him to allow me into the cave first. But when I saw the elven twins try that very thing and registered the way that the sorcerer bristled with discomfort, I decided against it. He didn't want to make small talk with anyone; I could respect that.

At exactly half-past nine, the sorcerer cleared his throat. He appeared both gratified and embarrassed when everyone fell silent and looked at him expectantly. 'Hi there.' He shifted his feet. 'I'm Gordon.'

Beside me, Boonder sucked in a breath. 'Gordon Mackenzie?'

Gordon's cheeks coloured. 'Yes.'

The trio of shapeshifters stared. 'Sir Nigel's pulling out the big guns,' one of them whispered.

I looked at the sorcerer with greater interest. I hadn't heard of him but he was obviously someone important. Hester buzzed in my ear. 'Is he famous?'

I shrugged. 'I guess so.'

Whoever he was and whatever he'd done, he didn't seem to want to talk about it. He scratched his neck awkwardly and looked at the ground. I risked a fleeting glance at Hugo; interestingly, his eyes were avoiding the sorcerer. In fact, none of the assembled Primes were looking directly at Gordon.

'Two people are missing,' he mumbled. 'There should be eight teams and twenty-six people. I only count twenty-four.'

Humphrey and Eleanor were absent. I wasn't surprised but I did feel slightly disappointed. I liked having them around.

One of the twins called out, 'There's no need to wait. We can start without them.'

It was clear that whatever brief camaraderie had existed the evening before had vanished now. All of us wanted to be the next to find a key part and the atmosphere was rippling with the tension of the competition.

Gordon obviously agreed. 'We will head into Smoo Cave. Towards the back of the third accessible cavern, there's a large pool of water. Within that pool is the rune and the blocked-off entrance to the secondary network of caves where the object that you seek is believed to be hidden. You will draw lots to decide the order of entry, then I will unlock the rune and open the way. The rest is up to you.'

'Lots?' one of the human treasure hunters asked. 'We should enter by alphabetical order.'

I stifled a smile. His name was Aaron Allen: of course he wanted alphabetical order.

Gordon was introverted but he wasn't a pushover. 'You will draw lots to decide the order of entry,' he repeated in a firmer tone of voice, although he continued to look at his feet. He turned around and, without glancing at any of us, trudged into Smoo Cave.

The entrance was massive. There were slate-grey cliffs on either side of us and a sandy beach behind us. Although it was nothing like the dark hole at Snake Pass, I couldn't prevent a tiny shudder rippling through me. But I told myself that there were no giant reptilian monsters here – at least not in this first section.

I trudged after the others, taking care to avoid the rocky debris on the ground and the narrow stream flowing to my right. Given I was about to submerge myself underwater, I didn't know why I was worrying about getting my feet wet but I wanted to stay as dry as possible for as long as possible.

We headed in single file along a wooden walkway. Soon the roar of water from the small waterfall inside Smoo Cave made it impossible to hear what the others were saying. Otis flew ahead of me, his tiny wings flapping furiously as he investigated. When he returned to tell me what he'd seen, I could barely hear him. I squinted in an attempt to lipread but the most I gleaned was 'dark' and 'pretty'. He was certainly correct about the dark part.

We turned a corner and the natural light from the opening behind us receded. With each step the darkness became more oppressive and it felt as if the cave walls were pressing in on me.

I saw the glow of light ahead as Gordon flicked on a torch and a few of the others did the same. I resisted calling on a spark of fire magic to light my way; I would wait until I was away from the others before I used my powers again. They didn't need to benefit from my magic, and their torchlight was enough for all of us. Besides, in spaces like these it was crucial to keep magic to a minimum.

I concentrated on staying calm and putting one foot in front of the other. Several minutes later, we came to a stumbling halt next to a dripping cave wall and a murky pool of water.

Gordon angled his torch up to his face. 'I have a bag here with numbers inside it,' he said, his quiet voice suddenly booming out as it bounced off the damp cave walls. 'Each team will take a number to decide the order of entry.' He pointed at the pool of water. 'That's where you will go.'

I gazed at the black water; it certainly didn't look particularly inviting. 'This is kind of scary,' Otis whispered. I agreed.

From somewhere behind us, another voice called, 'Wait! We're coming!'

I grinned; Humphrey and Eleanor had made it after all.

'They should be disqualified for tardiness,' one of the twins muttered.

'She should be disqualified for rudeness,' Hester said in my ear.

Humphrey and Eleanor bustled forward. 'Apologies,' Eleanor said with a vaguely embarrassed smile. 'We slept in.'

'And we had second helpings at breakfast,' Humphrey added. They'd obviously stayed in a hotel instead of camping out like the rest of us. Lucky them.

'Take a number and pass the bag around,' Gordon said.

Humphrey blinked owlishly. 'Gordon Mackenzie?'

'Good morning, Mr Bridger.' Gordon passed the small velvet bag to Hugo who pulled out a number. I watched his expression as he glanced at it. Damn: a tiny smile was playing around his lips so he'd probably drawn a favourable one.

He must have felt my gaze on him because he looked up and his eyes met mine. There was no denying the challenge written in their blue depths. I looked away.

'You know him?' Eleanor asked Humphrey in a low voice. 'The sorcerer fellow?'

'His name is Gordon – we were schoolboys at Eton together. He's human, but he often works with the elvish community. I didn't expect to see him here – he's been employed exclusively by the Assigney family for several years to find Lady Rose. He's a...'

'...good fellow,' I whispered.

'...good fellow,' Humphrey finished.

I smiled.

'Who's Lady Rose?' Eleanor asked.

'She's a high elf who—' Humphrey stopped abruptly and looked at Hugo. 'Never mind.'

I raised an eyebrow. Interesting. I didn't know who Lady Rose was either, but this wasn't the first time I'd heard a treasure hunter mention her name. Was she the reason why Hugo and Gordon were avoiding eye contact?

'Here.' Boonder thrust the bag into my hands and interrupted my thoughts. 'Your turn.'

I reached inside the bag and pulled out the first thing I touched, then passed the bag to the shapeshifters next to me. I glanced at the number inscribed on my counter then held it up for Otis and Hester. Hester frowned, but Otis shrugged. Number five: we'd be the fifth team to pass through the blocked passage. It was neither the worst nor the best scenario.

The shapeshifters passed the bag to Humphrey, who held it towards Eleanor. 'There's only one number left,' he said.

Eleanor dipped her hand inside. She let out a tiny squeal when she pulled out the final counter out and looked at it. 'Number one!'

'Unbelievable,' one of the twins muttered. 'They arrive last and they get to enter the cave first.'

At least that meant that Hugo wasn't first. When I looked at him again, he held up two fingers. The Primes would be second, then. I rolled my eyes.

'I will give you five minutes to prepare,' Gordon said. 'Then I will unlock the rune and open the passageway.' He paused. 'If anybody changes their mind and does not wish to go through, you can still back out.'

I was already pulling my T-shirt over my head to reveal my bathing suit underneath. Back out? No chance.

'I DON'T UNDERSTAND,' Hester said plaintively as I beckoned her and Otis towards my waterproof bag, where I'd also stuffed my clothes, some food and a bottle of clean water. 'Why can't you use magic and create an air bubble to travel through the passageway? Then nobody will get wet and nobody will drown.'

I might not have enjoyed a formal magic education but I'd picked up enough to know exactly why I couldn't do that. 'Cane toads,' I said.

'Huh?'

'In the 1930s, Australia imported about a hundred cane toads to deal with an infestation of cane beetles. The theory was that the toads would adapt to the countryside and keep the beetle population down so the farmers wouldn't need to use pesticides. Not only did the toads not eat the beetles, they multiplied by their millions, began to spread disease and depleted dozens of other native species.'

Hester cocked her head in confusion. 'I still don't get it.'

'You don't introduce something to a new environment unless you know exactly what effect it will have,' I told her.

'I'm not suggesting you turn us into frogs, Daisy,' she protested. 'I'm only saying that a bit of magic would help.'

I tried a different example. 'Twenty years ago, some enterprising miners in Wales hired a few elves to shift the earth around and make it easier for them to get at a large coal seam. Using earth magic underground unsettled the earth and triggered an earthquake. The mine collapsed, killing everyone inside it, and there were millions of pounds of damage above ground as well.'

I pointed at the pool of black water. 'We don't know what's in there or what's on the other side of it. We don't know what using a burst of air magic might do to the atmosphere, which has probably remained undisturbed for at least two hundred years. Until we know what we're dealing with, magic isn't a good idea.'

Otis nodded wisely. 'Prudence is always wise.'

Hester huffed. 'Prudence might get us drowned.'

'It's unlikely.' All three of us turned to Gordon, who had been listening in to our conversation. He blushed at the attention but he continued. 'We've sent out feelers. The water doesn't extend beyond this spot for more than sixteen metres. We don't know what's on the other side of this cave but we know it won't just be water.'

'That's easy for you to say,' Hester muttered. 'You're not jumping into that nasty water for a swim.'

'You don't have to come,' I told her. 'You can stay here.'

She folded her tiny arms indignantly. 'I am not letting you go off and do all the adventuring on your own! What kind of brownie do you think I am?'

Gordon looked amused. 'A very brave one,' he said.

'That's right!' Hester yelled. 'That's goddamn right!' She zipped inside the bag with Otis right behind her. I sealed it and manoeuvred it onto my shoulders, making sure it was securely tied and wouldn't slip off.

Humphrey and Eleanor stepped forward. Despite her earlier pleasure at drawing the first slot, Eleanor was white-faced as she gazed at the murky water. Humphrey didn't look much happier. There were disadvantages to going first.

'Are you sure about this?' Eleanor whispered, reaching for Humphrey's hand.

'No,' he said. 'Are you?'

'Not at all.'

I cleared my throat. 'You've got this. You can do it.'

Eleanor swallowed. 'Thanks, Daisy.'

'If you want to swap numbers,' one of the shapeshifters began, 'we'd be more than happy to take your place.'

'Thanks, old chap,' Humphrey said. 'I appreciate the thought but we will not shirk our task.'

Gordon spread his arms wide and twisted his hands in unnatural directions. His fingertips glowed green and I felt power buzz from his body. The water churned beneath our feet and I felt the ground tremble. There was a loud gurgle, followed by the distant crunching of rock. Then Gordon gasped, dropped his head and intoned, 'The passageway is clear.'

A brief thrill of adrenaline ran through me. We were really doing this. Despite my clawing claustrophobia, I couldn't wait to see what was on the other side.

Humphrey glanced at Eleanor. 'Are you ready?'

Her voice was quiet but firm. 'Yes.'

A moment later, they jumped into the pool and the black water covered their heads. Every one of us stared down, waiting to see if they would re-emerge – except Gordon. Instead, he reached into his pocket, drew out a long artist's paintbrush and knelt down to sketch a small rune in the dirt of the cave floor. While we watched the water, he watched the rune. After several tense moments, he released a long breath and stood up. 'They have made it safely to the other side,' he declared.

Yahtzee. I felt a wash of relief.

Hugo and his Primes moved to the water's edge. 'Don't worry, guys,' Hugo murmured to his team. 'This won't last long.' He slipped in, followed by Becky then the other five team members.

After that, we went in in quick succession; nobody wanted to be left too far behind. When it was my turn to step forward, half of me was screaming to turn around and run away while the other half was yelling at me to get on with the adventure. Obviously, there was no question which half I listened to.

I walked to the edge of the pool and my toes curled over its rocky lip. I gazed into the depths, unable to see anything other than a greenish glow from the right-hand side; presumably that was where I was heading. I glanced at Gordon. He gave me a brisk nod, his earlier shyness abandoned now that the action was underway. I held my breath then I jumped in.

I'd been expecting the cold, but the icy water was still a shock and it made my sinking body shudder and jerk. I twisted around until I was head down then kicked my legs as hard as I could to descend towards the green light. At least, I thought grimly, there were no fish flitting past me to worry about, though pressure was building in my ears as I dived deeper and my bones were already chilled.

The green glow was emanating from the old rune, which had a narrow opening next to it. I grabbed an outcrop of jagged black rock to haul my body closer then swam hard through the dark passageway. After only four or five metres, I emerged into a larger cavern which was lit by a flaming torch at the water's edge.

I silently thanked whichever team had taken the time to make this part easier for the rest of us. My head broke the surface of the water and looked around. The twins, who had entered the water just before me, were already out and pulling on dry clothes.

Only one other person was visible and, inexplicably, it was Hugo. He was standing framed by the craggy mouth of a tunnel on the far side of the water. He stared at me, his brooding face mostly obscured by the flickering shadows. Then he nodded, turned on his heel and disappeared from view.

CHAPTER

SEVENTEEN

I didn't waste time wondering why Hugo had lingered in the first cavern; with four teams ahead of me and three close behind, I couldn't afford to hang around.

I pulled myself out of the chilly water, shaking away the icy drops like a dog, and yanked open the waterproof bag. The brownies flew out immediately.

'Did we make it?' Otis asked. 'Are we here?'

'Yep,' I said, with a satisfied smack of my lips. 'We are here.'

I rubbed myself down with a small towel, put on a pair of loose trousers, T-shirt and socks, and squeezed my feet into my shoes. My body was still damp and my clothes stuck to me, and with the humid air inside the cavern I doubted I'd dry off any time soon. But the mild discomfort didn't compare to the thrill of finding the next key part.

'There's only one path,' Hester said. 'And it's pitch black. Can you use magic now to light the way?'

I inhaled deeply; the air was musty but that was to be expected. I felt a faint breeze blowing towards us, so there must be some narrow cavities that allowed fresh air to leak in. It was safe.

'I can risk a small fire spell now that I can see what's here,' I told her. 'There's breathable air, so fire magic won't have enough of a negative effect to cause problems. Don't worry. As long as I keep it to a minimum, it should be alright. I'll adjust the magic as we move if I need to.'

'No cane toads?' Otis asked anxiously.

'No cane toads,' I reassured him.

There was a splash behind me and I glanced around to see Boonder's head appear from the water. The twins had already disappeared. 'Come on,' I told the brownies. 'Let's vamoose.'

I moved quickly. While Boonder swam to the edge and extricated himself from the water, I focused. It wasn't easy to conjure up fire without appropriate kindling; it had taken me many months of practice when I was younger because it involved pulling delicately on the correct molecules in the air. By the time I reached the start of the tunnel, though, a tiny ball of flame was bobbing in front of me, doing more than enough to light the passage ahead without consuming too much oxygen.

I heard the distant voices of the other teams in front of me, and the trickle of water as it ran gently down the cave walls. This was it. Nobody had walked this path since the mid-eighteenth century; this was what everyone imagined real treasure hunting was like. This was what *I'd* imagined it was like.

'My word,' Hester said. 'This is thrilling.'

Otis was less impressed. 'It's terrifying.'

'Stay close,' I told them as I ducked my head and entered the tunnel.

Nothing here appeared to be man-made. The smooth walls and the way the tunnel dipped and dived, rising in one section before descending yet again, suggested that thousands of years of natural erosion had created the space rather than ancient miners looking for precious metals.

I maintained a steady pace, secure in the knowledge that

the way ahead was safe – at least for now. The four teams ahead of me were testament to that, and that allowed me to take less care than Humphrey and Eleanor who'd gone first. There were benefits to not being at the head of the pack.

I concentrated on the bobbing ball of flame and the distant hum of voices ahead of me and continued to jog. If only my ex-colleagues at SDS could see me now.

My elation didn't last long.

After several minutes the tunnel roof lowered, forcing me to stoop more and more. I turned a corner and my eyes narrowed; now I had to crouch and shuffle instead of running. My claustrophobia returned with a vengeance.

I concentrated on breathing regularly and moving forward, but I knew I would struggle if the cave continued like this. It didn't help that I could hear Boonder coming up behind me; there wasn't enough space for him to pass me, and I didn't like to think that he would be literally nipping at my heels. My mind drifted to the question of exactly how many tonnes of rock were pressing down on me from above, and my chest began to grow tight.

Breathe, I snapped at myself. *This is not a problem. This is new and exciting and exactly what I wanted from treasure hunting. Whatever panic I feel is unwarranted. There is still enough space to move, enough air to breathe. My problems are psychological.*

The narrow tunnel curved to the left and the space became even tighter. Reluctantly, I extinguished my little fireball because I didn't know what was up ahead or if there was enough oxygen to sustain the flame.

I reached behind me for the bag on my shoulders; there was a battery-powered torch in there, though I'd planned to use it only for emergencies. Batteries were a finite resource and I had no way of knowing how long I'd be down here.

I moved my hand away again. I didn't need the torch yet; it

would be wise to leave it where it was, at least for the time being.

'There's an opening ahead!' Hester screeched suddenly in my ear.

Her shout was so unexpected that I jerked upwards and banged my head on the tunnel roof. I gave a sharp moan of pain. 'Argh!'

'Oh,' Hester said sarcastically. 'My apologies. I didn't realise you were actually enjoying this dark, hellish hole. I thought you'd be happy that there's a large space ahead.'

I rubbed the back of my head and winced, then gritted my teeth and dug deep inside myself for a final spurt of energy. It pushed me forward until I all but tumbled out of the opening.

I landed on solid ground and rolled onto my back. Thank goodness: this was a large cavern with plenty of space. I placed my hand on my chest and pressed it against my heart until my pulse slowed. It was okay. We'd made it through.

The tip of Otis's wings brushed my cheek as he zipped away from me and then flew back. 'Everyone else is here! We've already caught up to them!'

That was something. I looked at the lights clustered around a spot thirty metres or so in front of me. Otis was right: all the other teams were here. Then I heard a grunt from behind and turned to see Boonder exit the narrow opening in the same manner that I had.

Annoyingly, he bounded to his feet. He placed his hands on his hips as he looked around. 'That was fun,' he said. 'And this is interesting.' He looked over at me, still sprawled on the cavern floor. 'It was a tight space,' he said kindly. 'But you'll get used to it. Caves are difficult places to explore when they've not been mapped and you don't know what's coming next.'

'Thanks,' I muttered as I got to my feet and dusted myself off. I appreciated his attempts at reassurance.

He smiled awkwardly. 'There'll probably be much worse sections ahead.'

Oh. Great. I gave him a sideways look; was he trying to unnerve me? It didn't appear that way from his expression, but the tight coil of tension in my tummy suggested otherwise.

'I have a spare torch if you need one,' he offered.

I blinked then I gave him a genuine smile. 'I have one, though I'm trying not to use it unless I have to.'

'That's probably wise,' Boonder said.

'You should keep your spare torch for yourself.'

He shook his head. 'In this sort of environment we have to stick together, whether we're competing against each other or not. Especially when we're the only solo competitors.'

I realised he *was* being genuine.

'She's not on her own,' Otis snapped. 'We're with her.'

The brownies were too small to provide physical support, so I understood why Boonder had left them out of the equation.

Boonder glanced at Otis, dipped his head in acknowledgment and bowed. 'My apologies, sir. I was mistaken.'

Otis sniffed, slightly mollified.

'Thank you for that,' I said to Boonder, meaning it wholeheartedly.

'You're not so bad, Daisy,' he told me.

I grinned. 'Neither are you.'

We walked together towards the other teams. Everyone except Hugo was facing away from us. His gaze swung between us, his expression inscrutable. He turned away as we joined the group. 'What's the hold up?' he demanded.

One of the twins replied, 'There are some concerns about the best way forward.'

Humphrey, who was pursing his lips anxiously, nodded his head. 'There's a wide tunnel to the left. Eleanor and I have already investigated it, but it leads to a dead end.'

Eleanor looked extraordinarily pale, even in this dim, flickering light, and she was clutching Humphrey's arm tightly. She appeared to be feeling the claustrophobic weight of the cave even more than I was.

'There's a second accessible tunnel,' the twin continued. 'But it's a small space. Bess wiggled through it for several metres and it seems to lead somewhere.' She looked Boonder up and down. 'I'm not sure you'll fit through it.'

She pointed. When my gaze followed her finger, I couldn't prevent a sharp intake of breath. It was indeed a tiny space. A shudder rippled through me at the thought of entering it; it would be a tight squeeze, even for me.

Hugo and his Primes were already moving right, and my brow furrowed. I stepped sideways to get a better view and felt a flicker of magic emanate from Hugo. A second later, the far side of the cavern was illuminated by a ball of flame similar to the one I'd created earlier.

I squinted, noting the dark entrance to yet another tunnel that appeared large enough to walk through without stooping, then I rocked back on my heels. Oh.

It wasn't Hugo's ability to throw fire magic such a distance that caused my dismay, although that was astonishing enough; it was the thirty-metre-wide chasm between him and the tunnel. There were two routes forward – but both were incredibly perilous.

With a slight nod of my head, I motioned Otis towards the right then I did the same to send Hester left. They understood instantly. As the others mulled their options and the sixth team of treasure hunters – the witches – appeared, I stepped aside and waited as the brownies flew in opposite directions.

The Primes were uncoiling rope from their bags, the shapeshifters had formed a tight discussion group, and

Boonder was kneeling on the ground and gazing at a small book filled with runes.

'I don't like this,' Eleanor whispered to Humphrey.

'Neither do I, my dear,' he replied. He patted her arm reassuringly but I noticed that his hands were shaking. I knew how he felt.

Otis reappeared first, emerging from the blackness of the chasm with a spooked expression. 'It's a long way down, Daisy. If you fell, you'd definitely die. I suppose you could try air magic to manipulate the atmosphere and prevent yourself from crashing, though.' He sounded doubtful.

Only in the worst-case scenario. Using any sort of magic in that dark hole could have dangerous repercussions for us all – and, anyway, none of us knew if crossing the chasm would lead to what we were seeking.

Boonder shook his head. 'You can't risk sending any magic down there. Even fire could be a problem. We don't know what the air is like below us.'

'I know,' I said.

One of the twins – Bess – jerked. 'What?' her voice rose high enough to echo around the chamber. 'She can't use magic in that hole! The consequences could be catastrophic!'

I clenched my jaw. 'I know,' I repeated. As Hugo swung towards me, I was already glaring in his direction. 'I am not planning to use magic down there,' I said for a third time. For fuck's sake.

Hugo returned his attention to his ropes. 'Good,' he grunted. 'We don't know what effect magic might have. Using controlled fire magic in this large space is one thing but using air or earth magic below us is a different matter. You might cause a roof collapse or wake up slumbering beasties that have lived for centuries here in the darkness.'

All the other treasure hunters seemed to think I was an

idiot. I opened my mouth to spit an obscenity at the lot of them, but Hester's reappearance forestalled me. She fluttered from side to side, shivering. 'It's about half a mile long,' she said.

I shuddered. Beside me, Humphrey gasped audibly.

'It gets narrower before it opens into a wider tunnel,' Hester continued. 'If you shimmied along on your belly, you'd probably make it. But,' she added, 'it's very dark. And very difficult.'

I swallowed back the returning claustrophobia. I wasn't convinced that I'd manage it; if panic overtook me in that tiny space, I might hyperventilate and end up truly stuck – forever.

'One team has almost died already,' one of the witches said. 'I'm not risking my life for a chance at some old coins, no matter what reward Sir Nigel dangles in front of us.'

Eleanor looked at Humphrey. 'I know how much you desperately want to find part of the key part but—' She swallowed hard.

Humphrey patted her hand again. 'I agree entirely. We should return to the surface, my dear. This will not be our win.'

But not everyone was giving up. There was an odd slapping sound, then another and another. As I twisted around, I saw that Hugo and the Primes were lassoing their ropes across the chasm, attempting to loop them onto a craggy outcrop on the other side.

Hugo's rope landed first time – of course it did. He pulled it taut before handing it to a moustachioed high elf called Dean. Becky and the other Primes stood beside him.

Suddenly I understood his plan: he was going to leave most of his team here holding the end of the ropes while he made his way across it. It was a dangerous move but, I supposed irritably, if anyone could do it Hugo could.

The second twin sidled up to him. 'Hugs, darling.'

'No.'

She touched his arm gently and I felt a surge of genuine anger. I blinked. What was that about?

'You don't know what I'm going to say,' she protested.

'Yes, I do.' He tugged on the taut rope, testing it. 'You want to use my ropes to get across.'

'Well, if you're offering...'

He turned to her. 'I'm not. This is a competition, Jane.'

'I'll make it worth your while.' She fluttered her eyelashes.

'The answer is still no,' Hugo growled. His eyes drifted to me before he turned away again.

I left them to it. The final two teams had arrived and were looking as doubtful as the rest of us; only the shapeshifting trio seemed to have a plan. They were muttering to each other, then they moved apart and tensed their shoulders.

'If we're going,' Bess said to her twin, 'we have to go now before they change.'

Jane nodded. The two of them darted towards the tiny tunnel and crouched down until they could scuttle into it. I didn't want to go that way; I *really* didn't want to go that way. In fact, I couldn't. I knew my limits and I wasn't afraid to back off when I reached them. There was sometimes as much bravery in stepping back as stepping up.

The air thumped and there was a sudden whoosh followed by a rumble as the ground beneath my feet started to shake. I hissed in alarm and jumped to the side, half expecting the cavern roof to collapse on top of us.

'I don't often wish I were a shapeshifter,' I heard Boonder say, 'but I definitely do now.'

Where the three tall shapeshifters had once stood, there were now three squirrels beside three untidy piles of clothes. No wonder the ground had been shaking. As I watched, the creatures nodded to each other and darted for the narrow tunnel, hot on the heels of the twins.

Three teams had now found a way forward but it looked like the end of the road for the rest of us. I glanced at Hugo; even if I hadn't used all my rope on the snake, I couldn't do what he was doing. He was halfway across the chasm, clinging to the ropes while his Primes held them tightly. He was already some distance away from us but I could see that his muscles were straining and his expression was tense.

'Maybe he'll fall,' Hester said hopefully.

'We don't want him to die!' Otis snapped.

'Don't we?'

I felt their eyes on me, but my gaze was fixed on Hugo. Come on, you cumbubbling bastard. Get over there. I held my breath. Three metres to go... Two metres...

He paused and my stomach flipped over with fear.

'Hurry, Hugo!' Becky yelled. 'We can't hold it much longer!'

Shit. I jerked forward, wanting to help, but then Hugo took a flying leap and abandoned the haphazard rope bridge. For a terrifying moment he seemed to be frozen above the black depths, but a heartbeat later he was flying through the air towards the opposite side of the chasm. When he landed with a thud on the other side, my knees buckled. That had been close. Far too close.

'We don't want him to die,' I whispered. I wrapped my arms around my body and glanced at the brownies. 'We don't want anyone to die,' I said in a firmer voice as I wiped my sweaty palms down my thighs.

Three of the teams, including Humphrey and Eleanor, were preparing to head back the way we'd come. Boonder, who'd abandoned his search for a useful rune, looked at me. 'I'm going to take a wander into the dead-end tunnel and look around.' He shrugged. 'Just in case. Would you like to join me?'

I trusted Humphrey; if he said it was a dead end then I believed it was a dead end.

My palms itched and I desperately wanted to get out of the cave into the daylight and the open air. Even here in this large cavern, my claustrophobia was getting the better of me. But Boonder seemed keen on having company and I didn't suppose it would take long to explore the tunnel. It beat waiting for my turn to squeeze into the tiny space that led back to the exit, so I nodded.

As far as this section of the treasure hunt was concerned, I would have to admit failure – but there was still one part of the key to find. The third part would be mine, come hell or high water. In the meantime, although there was nothing to gain by joining Boonder, there was nothing to lose either.

CHAPTER
EIGHTEEN

With Hester perched on my right shoulder and Otis on my left, I followed Boonder into the tunnel. It was big and airy enough to keep the worst of my fears at bay, and we were able to walk side by side. His eyes flitted from side to side as if he were looking for something specific, while I sniffed the air. I decided that it didn't matter if I used my torch now instead of a magic flame; I wouldn't be down here for much longer.

'I'm sorry that I've not spoken to you properly before now,' Boonder told me. 'To be honest, I was bit wary of you. Lots of people seem to think that treasure hunting is easy – they give it a try and get themselves and others killed in the process. It's usually wise to avoid beginners. And,' he added, 'there was that business with John Thurgood's team.'

'I tried to help them,' I said quietly. 'I didn't deliberately lead them into danger.'

'I know. Hugo made sure we all knew.'

Oh. 'Did he tell everyone I'm a junkie too?' I managed to keep most of the bitterness out of my voice. My feelings towards Hugo were becoming increasingly complicated; it was far easier when I'd simply hated him.

'I heard something about that, but not from Hugo.' He scratched his neck awkwardly. 'I guess word kinda got around.'

My lip curled. Yeah. I guessed it did.

'I get it, though.' His tone was earnest. 'I had a good friend who was a spider's silk addict. He was a nice guy who never did anyone any harm.'

'Was?' I asked.

Boonder was silent for a second. 'He – uh – died a couple of years ago.' I didn't need to ask what had killed him.

I resisted my knee-jerk reaction to dig into my bag for another pill. I'd taken one before I'd left my tent that morning and I'd only brought a couple with me in case I got stuck down here. I didn't need more drugs, not right now. I drew in a deep breath. There was plenty of time before I'd need to dose myself again.

'How did you get into treasure hunting?' I asked to change the subject. 'You're the only sorcerer here. Do the two things go hand in hand?'

He chuckled. 'Not often. Actually, it's not the treasure that lures me in, it's the history.' He waved a hand around. 'I mean, look at this place. Look at *us*. Eight teams of experienced hunters with all that the twenty-first century has to offer and we're finding it hard to follow in the footsteps of men from three hundred years ago who had almost no resources. Sometimes I think we rely too much on technology and not enough on our inner capabilities.'

I tried not to look too surprised at his wise words. Until we'd entered the cave, Boonder had struck me as a grumpy loner. It was far too easy to pre-judge others. I hated the way Hugo had done it to me – but perhaps I was guilty of it, too. 'I like the history, too,' I said quietly. We exchanged mutually approving glances.

Boonder's steps slowed. 'Look. There's something over there. Can you shine your torch that way?'

I pointed it towards the right-hand wall and drew in a breath sharply. Etched into the cave wall was some sort of crude design; if I squinted, it looked like an old rune. It was quite close to the ground so it would have been easy to miss; I'd certainly have walked straight past it but for Boonder's sharp eyes, It wasn't a surprise that Humphrey, Eleanor and the others hadn't seen it.

A sudden surge of renewed optimism flooded my body. Maybe the game wasn't over yet after all. 'You're the sorcerer,' I breathed. 'What is it? What does it say?' More to the point, what did the rune *do*?

Boonder crouched down beside it, brushing away a few clinging cobwebs. 'I wouldn't get too excited. There's no magic attached to it – it won't open a secret passageway like the last one did.'

My shoulders sagged. 'If it's not magical then what's the point of it?'

He reached into his back pocket and took out the book he'd been reading earlier. He flipped through the pages while I held the torch over him. 'Is that a runic dictionary?' I asked.

'Yeah.' He chewed his bottom lip. 'I might not have totally mastered them, but I know a lot of modern runes. What I don't know are the more traditional ones. I brought this along because I thought I might need it, given the age of the treasure we're looking for.'

He turned another page and his back stiffened. 'It looks like I was right.' He sounded grim. 'We should get out of here.'

On my shoulder, Otis quivered. 'Why? What's wrong?'

'It's not a magical rune.' Boonder stood up. 'It's a warning. It says "Beware".'

I met his eyes through the gloom. 'Beware of what?'

'I don't know.' He licked his lips. 'And I don't think I want to.'

It was then that the ground shook again. This time it wasn't because of any nearby shapeshifters – and it was considerably more violent. The vibrations sent me sprawling backwards and knocked the torch out of my hand.

The tremors continued to grow in intensity. I swore. Hester and Otis, who'd only narrowly avoided being squashed by my fall, appeared in front of my face. Even Hester looked scared. Her mouth moved as she said something, but because of the rumbling I couldn't hear her.

I sprang to my feet. Boonder was already stretching his hand towards me to help. I half-turned to grab the torch before making a run for it, but as soon as my fingers grazed the cool aluminium the ground beneath my feet opened up.

I felt my body drop and my stomach rise into my mouth. Shit. My hands automatically reached out, desperate to cling onto something so I didn't fall into the newly formed chasm beneath me.

'Daisy!' Boonder yelled, barely audible above the noise that was enveloping us. He leapt forward and grabbed one of my hands while my feet dangled into dark space and kicked uselessly in the air.

Otis was shrieking while Hester zipped frantically from side to side. 'Pull yourself up! Pull yourself up, Daisy!' she screeched in my ear.

I clenched my jaw. I couldn't pull myself up; there was nothing to pull against, and the cave around us was continuing to judder and shake. Every muscle in Boonder's face and arms was straining with the effort of holding on to me. Our palms were sweaty and, although he tugged and yanked and did everything he could to haul me upwards, gravity was working against us. Sooner or later he would have to let go. I was going to fall – and I was probably going to die.

'Air magic,' Boonder gasped. 'You have to use air magic to propel yourself upwards.'

As I looked into his tense face and his fearful eyes, a strange sensation of absolute calm replaced my own terror. Yes, I could use air magic; I could twist the molecules beneath me to push myself upwards and clamber onto solid ground – but I didn't know what effect that magic would have. I didn't know what was underneath me, and I couldn't predict what that burst of power would do in this confined space. I wasn't the only person inside this cave. Messing with the atmosphere could alter far more than my own fate and I wouldn't be responsible for anybody else getting hurt.

'This isn't your fault,' I whispered. His hold on my hands began to slip. 'Don't blame yourself.' I looked at Hester and Otis. 'Don't come after me. Stay with Boonder. You'll be safe with him.'

'Absolutely not!' Otis protested. 'You can still—'

I didn't hear the end of his sentence because it was lost in a rush of air. Boonder could no longer hold me and I dropped into the depths below to be swallowed up by the darkness of the cave.

Sayonara, sweeties, I thought as everything went dark. It's been fun.

~

I COULDN'T SEE A THING – it was pitch black. Was this what death felt like?

I inhaled, making my body twitch, and jolting pain ripped through me. Fuck. So this wasn't death; I was still alive but it felt like I'd broken every bone in my body.

I must have blacked out or hit my head because the last thing I remembered was Otis, Hester and Boonder staring down at me in horror as I fell. Was I lying at the bottom of a thousand-metre drop unable to move? Would I die here in the darkness, all alone?

I exhaled a long breath and this time the pain was worse. Bloody hell, that hurt. *Everything* hurt.

I wiggled my big toes. Okay, they still worked. So did my other toes. I tested my fingers and they all moved. My tongue darted out to wet my lips and, as slowly and carefully as possible, I turned my head first to the right and then to the left. It was still on my shoulders. That had to be a bonus, right? I wasn't completely paralysed.

I pulled up one knee and the pain was enough to make me moan aloud. The sound echoed around the darkness. I gritted my teeth and did the same with my other knee. Ouch. Ouch. Fucking *ouch*. But I could move my legs and I might be able to stand on them.

I tested my arms, swinging them up in turn. Then, still flat on my back, I patted myself down and searched for injuries. My body was tender and my fingertips came away wet when I touched my face and the bare skin on my arms, but I didn't appear to be gushing blood from any wounds. I had cuts, scratches and a whole lot of bruises but I was in better condition than I had any right to expect.

On a count of three. I would move into a sitting position on a count of three. I swallowed hard and held my breath. *One. Two.* I paused. *Two and a half. Two and three-quarters. Goddamnit. Three.*

I sat up. Huh. That hadn't been so bad. I frowned then I

climbed to my feet, my breath catching as agony flashed through me. The worst of the pain was fleeting, though, and in a few seconds it dissipated into little more than a bone-deep ache. How was that possible?

I tilted my head upwards. Maybe I'd not fallen that far but I couldn't see a glimmer of light above me. I couldn't see anything at all.

'Hello?' My voice was thin and thready, so pathetic that it annoyed me. I tried again, injecting more power and effort. 'Hello? Boonder? Otis? Hester? Are you up there?'

Nothing.

I waved my arms in front of me and took a tentative step forward, wincing as another brief rush of pain assailed me. Then I took another step and another. I stopped and waved my arms around again. There was nothing in front of me except darkness.

The air was still, but it was breathable. Dare I risk a tiny burst of fire magic to get a look at my surroundings? It probably couldn't do much harm. I toed at the ground, double checking for obstacles or anything that might preclude the use of a flame. This appeared to be a reasonably large space. There was enough air to breathe, at least for now. I could—

I froze as I heard something, then tilted my head and listened hard. Was that ... breathing? My stomach dropped. Oh God.

I didn't waste any more time; if I wasn't alone down here, I damned well wanted to know what was with me. I concentrated hard and sparked a small flame though it wasn't strong enough to illuminate more than a metre or so in front of me.

I blinked rapidly, trying to adjust my vision quickly enough to prepare for an attack. There were smooth dark rocks at my feet but I couldn't see anything else. I slowly turned on my heel to check what was behind me.

That was when I saw one round yellow eye staring back at me.

CHAPTER

NINETEEN

Squeaking with both shock and fear, I reacted instinctively and flicked the little fireball towards the owner of the eye. Out of the darkness I caught a glimmer of shadow as a huge, muscled arm rose up and batted it away, extinguishing it so I was plunged into total darkness again.

I raised my hands expecting an assault, but the creature – whatever it was – didn't move. 'Your magic isn't welcome here, elf,' a deep voice creaked. 'And fire will not hurt me.'

I gulped in a breath of musty air and kept my arms in front of me. Just because it hadn't attacked yet didn't mean it wouldn't. 'I can't see anything,' I muttered. 'I wasn't trying to hurt you. I only wanted to get some light so I could look around.' I waved my hands desperately.

There was a long heavy sigh. 'It is dark. What do you expect from a cave?' It was a fair question. 'You,' the voice continued, 'are not very intelligent.'

I was too scared to be offended. 'You're right,' I managed. 'I'm not. So if you could help me out and point me towards the nearest exit, I'll be on my way.'

The creature tsked. 'I have waited a long time for a new

warrior to challenge me. You will not leave until we have done battle.'

There was a lot to unpack there, but before I could say anything there was an odd crackle and I felt a wisp of a breeze. As if from nowhere, a dim green light started to glow, revealing the creature and a large section of the cave.

He was easily more than seven feet tall, looming upwards like some sort of spindly giant. His muscles were tight and wiry, and he was entirely hairless. He was draped in some sort of cloak and one clawed hand held a sword, the edge of which was gleaming in the greenish glow. His other hand clutched my bag. And, yes, he only had one eye.

I glanced from the creature's face to my bag and back again. 'You helped me,' I said in sudden realisation. 'You must have done something to help me when I fell.' I started to relax; maybe things weren't as bad as I'd thought. Maybe this strange cyclops creature was benign.

The tiniest frown marred his smooth forehead. 'Of course,' he said. 'I caught you before you hit the ground.'

I breathed out. 'Thank you for that.'

The frown deepened. 'I cannot fight a corpse. I saved you because you have to be alive if we are to do battle. Only when I beat you may you die.'

Uh... 'Or we could not do battle at all,' I suggested hopefully. 'We could have a little chat then you can show me the way out so I can leave you in peace.'

He looked me up and down. 'Where is your weapon? You should draw your sword now so we can cease these words and begin.'

That wasn't the response I'd been looking for. 'I don't have a sword. I don't have any weapon. I'm not here to fight.'

'Your protestations are beginning to bore me,' he rumbled.

This was not going well. I had to switch tactics – and fast. I stuck out my hand. 'I'm Daisy,' I said. 'It's, um, lovely to meet you.'

The creature stared at my hand, pursed his mouth then handed me my bag. 'Take out your weapon.'

'What's your name?' I persisted as if I hadn't heard him.

The single yellow eye blinked slowly. 'You may call me the Fachan.'

Okay. This was good. I was making progress. 'Have you lived here for long?'

'I have been here forever.'

Right. I nodded slowly. 'Wow. That's a long time.' Think of another question, Daisy. Keep him talking. 'Uh, do you like living here?'

My floundering question wasn't good enough. The Fachan threw back his head and roared, the terrible sound echoing upwards with such volume that I had to cover my ears. 'Enough! No more talking! We will do battle now!'

He was twice my size and he had a sword. I was canny and quick, but even on a good day I couldn't win against a creature like this. This was no mindless vampire or irritated snake; everything about the Fachan screamed skill, power and strength.

I knew when I was outgunned – but unfortunately I didn't know where I was or how to escape. Beyond the wide circle of green light cast by his spell, there was only darkness. I didn't know where the door might be – I didn't know if there *was* a door. All I could do was persuade the Fachan that a fight wasn't a good idea.

I shook my head vigorously as I frantically sought a way out of this mess. 'You said that magic wasn't welcome but you used magic to light up this place.' I gestured around the huge cavern; despite the Fachan's green light, it was so vast that I couldn't see from one side to the other. 'And you must have used magic to catch me when I fell.'

The Fachan's single eye stared at me for so long that my skin prickled. 'So?' he said finally.

'You said magic wasn't welcome here,' I repeated. 'But *you* used magic.'

'No. I said *your* magic wasn't welcome here.'

I nodded. 'Sure. Cool. This is your home and that's your prerogative. But I can't fight you if I don't have magic, so we should call it quits.'

'Quits?'

'Cancel the fight.' I smiled desperately. 'It's the best way forward.'

The Fachan looked even more annoyed. 'Are you suggesting, elf, that I am without honour? That I would use magic in battle while forbidding you from doing the same?'

Uh-oh. 'I ... er ... um ... I...' I stuttered.

'I grow bored. You are both stupid and irritating. We will fight now. Choose your weapon.'

'I don't *have* any weapons.'

'What kind of warrior comes to do battle without a weapon? Are you planning to fight bare-fisted? Do you seek pain?'

'No! And I'm not a warrior! I didn't come here seeking a fight! I only want to find a way out so I can re-join my friends.'

He took a step towards me. 'We will do battle.'

I took a step back. 'I'd rather not.'

'We will do battle.' The Fachan blinked. 'To the death.' He twirled the sword in his massive claw-like hands. 'Now.'

Oh shit. I spun around and ran. Tiny stones of sharp scree flew up around my feet. Maybe I could tire the Fachan by keeping out of his reach for long enough. In theory, it was a good plan; in practice, though, his long-legged stride meant that he caught up to me in seconds.

He swung the sword over his head towards me and its sharp tip caught my shoulder, slicing through my thin T-shirt and my skin. I yelped and turned to face him, holding my waterproof bag in front of me like a shield. 'First blood,' I panted. 'You win.'

'I told you already,' the Fachan said. 'We fight to the death.'

I ground my teeth. Goddamnit.

The Fachan raised the sword again. I ripped open my waterproof bag and pulled out the first object I came to – the still-damp towel I'd used to dry myself off after coming through the waterlogged entrance from Smoo Cave.

I whipped the towel out towards the Fachan. The wet edge slapped against his bare forearm. 'Is that it?' he asked, confused.

I sucked in a breath, turned and started running away again. There had to be a way out of this place. I had to delay him and find it. There had to be *something* I could do.

I was still too wary to attempt either earth or air magic. Given what had happened when I'd fallen, it was obvious that large parts of this massive cave network were unstable and I couldn't risk anything that might further upset the natural balance. But I still believed that fire magic was safe enough – and probably water magic, too, despite the Fachan forbidding me from magicking anything.

I pumped my arms and legs as I continued to run and conjured up enough water from the humid atmosphere to form a cloud over my head. Three seconds after I'd passed underneath it, I released it and dumped a gallon of water on top of the Fachan.

I didn't waste time looking over my shoulder to check if I'd been successful. I didn't have to: his roar of fury was enough. 'Your magic isn't welcome here!' he bellowed.

'You have a sword!' I shouted. 'I need something to defend myself!'

I put my head down and sprinted away from the soaking Fachan. This time, he caught up to me almost immediately, grabbed a hank of my hair and hauled me back. I screamed – it felt as if my scalp were being ripped from my skull. I twisted and kicked but couldn't make contact with him.

He spun me around, his left hand still entwined in my hair while his right hand clutched his sword. He raised the blade and prepared to chop off my head – then abruptly dropped the weapon to the ground with a clatter.

I stopped squirming and gave him a hopeful look.

'You are right,' he said slowly. 'This is not a fair fight. We will do battle as you suggested the first time around.'

I met his one eye. Eternally optimistic, I asked, 'You mean by not battling at all?'

'I mean by using our bare hands.' He released his hold on me and put up his fists. 'I will not use my sword. You will not use your magic. That is fair.'

Not given the size of him, it bloody wasn't. I didn't have time to complain because he was already launching his first punch towards me. I moved to the side but I wasn't fast enough to dodge it completely and it caught me on my ear. I cried out at the pain but did my best to ignore it. I couldn't afford to hesitate.

I ran straight at the Fachan, then veered around him at the last moment and lashed out with my fist. It caught him on the side of his chin but he didn't seem to register the blow. 'Pathetic,' he grunted.

Yup. I twisted and kicked the back of his shins. His legs didn't buckle, he didn't collapse – he didn't even wince. As he slowly turned to face me. I swallowed hard. Time to start running again. I tensed...

The Fachan sent out a lightning quick punch that smacked into my shoulder. Its force sent me sprawling backwards. 'Pathetic,' he said again.

I scooped up a handful of the scree and threw it at his face with all the energy I could muster. 'I am trying my best!' I yelled as I scrambled to my feet. I followed up the tiny projectiles with another punch, this time aiming for the only obviously vulnerable spot – his eye. I had to jump up to reach it and even then I missed by half an inch. What had been intended as a knock-out punch was little more than a glancing blow.

I cursed. *Run, Daisy. Just fucking run.*

The Fachan must have read my mind because he kicked at my ankles, knocking me off my feet yet again and preventing me from sprinting away. His expression grim, he stood over me, pulled back his fist and prepared for another blow.

I tensed and squeezed my eyes shut. This was going to hurt. If I survived this blow, maybe playing dead would work – nothing else could help me. Not that I'd have to *play* dead because I'd most probably *be* dead.

I held my breath and waited. When the killer blow didn't arrive, I opened first one eye and then the other. The Fachan's fist was still pulled back but he was staring down at me with a strange, thoughtful expression. 'Go on,' I said. 'Do it. Hit me.'

'You are pathetic,' he said for the umpteenth time.

Yeah, yeah. I sighed and looked away – and saw the Fachan's sword lying on the ground less than a metre away. Ah-ha. Trying to disguise my movements, I inched towards it.

'You are a high elf,' the Fachan said. 'Why are you not better at combat?'

I shuffled closer to the sword. 'I'm not a high elf.'

'Yes, you are. Do you think I am as stupid as you are?'

'I'm a low elf,' I said. 'Promise.'

The Fachan sniffed. 'I do not smell a lie on your lips.'

'Because I'm not lying,' I said. I snapped out my hand and grabbed the cold metal hilt of his fallen sword, then tried to jump to my feet and swing the blade at him.

The Fachan didn't move; to be honest, neither did the sword. I grunted and pulled at it but it was too heavy and I couldn't even lift the tip off the ground. I tried again using both hands and managed to raise it up by an inch or so, but then I was forced to drop it again. What the hell was it made of?

The Fachan rolled his single eye. 'Pa—'

'—thetic. I know.'

He shook his head, obviously disappointed. 'You are trying hard. You are even resorting to under-hand, unfair tactics and yet you still cannot do more than tickle my skin with your attempts.'

'All right, rub it in,' I grumbled. I dropped the hilt of the sword. There was obviously no reason to continue trying to use it.

'You are no match for me,' the Fachan declared.

It was my turn to roll my eyes. 'Tell me something I don't know,' I muttered.

The Fachan stared at me for another moment. 'Wait here. I shall return.' He spun to his left and marched out of the glowing green light and into the darkness beyond.

I waited for two seconds, then sprinted in the opposite direction. There had to be a way out. I headed straight for the wall of darkness; I didn't know what was there but it had to be better than what was here.

The darkness swallowed me up and yet again I couldn't see anything in front of me. Wary of obstacles, I kept my arms outstretched but I continued to sprint metre after metre – until my hands smacked into a cold, hard wall. I felt my way along it. Come on. There had to be an exit, a door of some sort.

'What are you doing?' the Fachan's voice floated over to me. He didn't sound angry, merely curious.

I would have thought that was obvious. 'I'm trying to escape,' I muttered.

'You cannot go yet,' he said.

I continued my search, moving as fast as I could. 'Because we've not battled yet?' I asked, suddenly feeling very tired.

'We will not battle now,' the Fachan said gravely. 'You are too pathetic to fight.'

I stopped and slowly turned towards the green light. The Fachan had returned and, from the way he was looking at me, he could see me clearly enough.

He sighed. 'I hoped for so much more. There is neither joy nor honour in doing battle with weaklings. Come here, elf. I will show you how to leave.'

I squinted. Was he telling the truth?

'Or,' he said conversationally, 'I could pick up my sword again and kill you instead.'

I threw up my hands in frustration. 'Alright, alright!' I grumbled, wondering if I was doing the right thing but not convinced I had any choice. I trudged towards him.

The weight of the darkness left me as soon as I stepped into the light again. I rubbed the back of my neck. 'Like taking off a bra,' I whispered.

The Fachan looked at me. 'What?'

'Nothing.' I crossed my arms over my chest. 'What are you planning to do?'

He reached behind his back then held out his hand to me. In it was a small, slightly curved blade, something between a dagger and a sword. 'You have no sword,' he said. 'Therefore I shall give you this one.'

Nuh-uh. No way. As soon as my fingers touched that thing,

he'd start the battle talk again. I wrapped my arms more tightly around my body.

'Take her,' he said with more than a little irritation. 'She is a gift.'

I tensed my jaw. 'I don't know how to use a blade like that and I don't want to fight.'

The Fachan sighed again. 'Did I or did I not say that we would not do battle? You are not a warrior. You have disappointed me greatly. I give you this so that in time you may become a true fighter and perhaps one day will return to offer me a real challenge.' I didn't move an inch. 'Take her!' he roared.

I flinched and reached for the dagger-cum-sword thing. As soon as my right hand touched the hilt, I felt a strange warm buzz and I gasped.

The Fachan smiled. 'She likes you. I knew she would.'

She? 'She's *sentient*?'

'Are not all good blades?'

Not these days they weren't. Momentarily forgetting my situation, I hefted the weapon from hand to hand. It seemed to be made of bronze because it was heavier than it looked, and it had an intricate emblem carved into its base. An anxious thought struck me. 'Where did you get this from?'

'She was wielded by the last high elf who challenged me, 467 years ago.' He frowned. 'No – 468 years ago. I haven't been keeping track lately.'

My mouth dropped open. 'That's a very precise number.'

'I am a very precise person.'

'You, uh, beat them in battle? The high elf who owned ... her?'

'I did. He was a strong warrior and fought well, but in the end I killed him. He sought glory. He failed.' The Fachan shrugged. 'He was not the first and he will not be the last.'

I couldn't help asking. 'Is this all you do? Wait here year after year until the next person shows up for a fight?'

He blinked his one eye very slowly. 'No, that would be ridiculous. The battles are my hobby. I do not twiddle my thumbs and simply wait for challengers. I have plenty of other things to do.'

It occurred to me that his English language skills, although perhaps rather formal, reflected modern speech. 'You leave this cave often,' I guessed.

'I am not a mole. I do not wish to spend eternity underground.'

There was no way that he wandered around topside in that body. He had to be some kind of shapeshifter, although I was willing to bet that this was his true form. 'You're truly immortal?'

He gave me a surprisingly wry grin. 'Not if the right warrior appears. One day I shall leave this Earth for good.' He sniffed. 'Of course, that warrior is not you, not today at least. The blade's name is Gladius Acutissimus Gloriae et Sanguinis. Respect her and she will respect you.'

That was quite a mouthful. Gladys for short, I decided. 'Thank you.'

'She will help you to be better.' The Fachan pointed to the right. 'Now come, I shall show you how to leave this place. I do not wish to see your pathetic presence again. Do not return unless your skills improve and you are worthy of a challenge.'

He had no worries on that score. I was never coming back here. 'I won't,' I promised.

There would be no more caves for Daisy Carter. I'd had enough of them to last a lifetime.

CHAPTER
TWENTY

The Fachan was as good as his word, which was just as well because without his help I'd never have found my way out. First he led me up a long sloping tunnel, then through another steeper one before we ended up in a veritable maze of them that swung to the left, to the right and eventually to a rickety ladder that led to a narrow platform.

Once there, I realised we were standing in front of yet another rune. To my uneducated eye, it looked similar to the ancient one that Boonder and I had found just before the ground had literally collapsed from under my feet.

The Fachan traced its shape reverently, using whatever innate power he possessed to unlock its core – and what appeared to be the side of a damned mountain.

The light outside was strong enough to hurt my eyes but the pull of a fresh breeze and the open air were enough to persuade me out of the cave's depths. I hurtled out, stretching my arms wide and tilting my head up to the sky with joy-filled relief.

It was a stupid thing to do because the movement made my head spin and I was assailed with a dizziness that buckled my knees. My skin was clammy, there was an unpleasant oily churning in the depths of my stomach and my hands were shaking. Caves, I decided, did not suit me at all.

When I finally regained some control of my treacherous body and turned to bid farewell to the Fachan, there was no sign of him. There was no sign of the cave, either; it had been smoothed over and refilled with rock. If it weren't for Gladys, which was wrapped in my damp towel and stuffed in my bag, I might have imagined the entire thing.

Despite the Fachan's absence, I raised my voice in case he could still hear me. 'Thank you!' I called. 'I won't forget you. And I won't disappoint you. I will become a warrior.'

Maybe. If nothing else, I'd learn how to wield Gladys properly; I could do that much.

I thought I heard a muffled response from beyond the rock face, though it might have simply been the murmur of the wind. Whatever. I curtsied anyway, almost losing myself to another nauseating surge of vertigo, then carefully turned around. If my bearings were correct, I was around the corner from the Smoo Cave entrance so I'd be back at the campsite in minutes. Now I simply had to pray that everyone else had made it back safely too.

I heaved my aching body up the slope. I wasn't in bad nick considering all I'd been through, although there were a lot of scrapes, bruises and minor cuts, and my trousers and T-shirt were grubby and ripped. I probably I looked more like a walking scarecrow than an elf. My scalp was still throbbing from where the Fachan had grabbed my hair but I dared not check if there was a bald spot. It was quite possible that I was now sporting a tonsure like a medieval monk. I giggled at the thought and a bubble of hysteria choked my chest. Leaving the cave in one piece appeared to be making me delirious.

I started to hum and the notes coalesced until they became a familiar tune. I added the words, grinning trippily all the while. 'She'll be coming round the mountain when she comes, she'll be coming round the mountain when she comes...'

I twisted around the final corner and raised my voice when I saw the campsite. 'She'll be coming round the mountain!'

Nobody rushed to greet me and I pouted, unimpressed at the lack of a welcome. Where was everyone? 'Hellooooo?' I yelled. Still nothing.

My bottom lip jutted out. I'd expected all the tents from the previous night to still be in place but very few remained. My tent was there, and so was Boonder's one-man bivouac. The Primes' collection of expensive tents was also in place – but the others had gone.

'How very rude,' I said loudly. 'Rude!'

I tiptoed to my tent, unzipped it and thrust my head inside. 'Boo!'

Nobody was there. I sniffed, shrugged, spun around – and lost my balance. I fell backwards and landed heavily on the ground, my arms and legs akimbo. I cackled, 'I'm an upturned cockroach! Look at me!'

Nobody was looking. Eventually I rolled over and staggered unsteadily to my feet. Hmm. I suddenly seemed to have four feet instead of two – perhaps I *was* becoming a cockroach. Perhaps the Fachan had cursed me for not doing battle with him.

I held up my hands. Oh: I had four of those, too. My eyes widened. I had *eight* limbs. Not a cockroach, then.

'I'm a spider,' I whispered. Brilliant; that made sense, given how much spider's silk I'd taken over the years. I nodded wisely. Yes, it made perfect sense.

It was important to use my powers effectively. I could spin a web between the tents then when Hugo walked into it I could catch him and hold him there, purely for my delectation. He'd be my tasty prisoner, ready for the taking. I was drooling. Yum.

'Daisy?'

I glanced over my shoulder. Ah-ha – my prey was already here. Hugo was standing less than ten metres away, his skin pale and his eyes wide with shock. 'You!' I said. Then I frowned. Hang on – there were two Hugos. When did that happen?

'Where the fuck have you been?' they both demanded. 'Are you alright?'

I brushed away their angry questions; there were more important things than where I'd been. 'Why are there two of you? Why didn't you tell me you were twins?'

They stared at me. 'What?'

It was a simple question and I tutted loudly. 'Never mind. I'll still catch both of you in my web. Because I,' I gave a dramatic flourish, 'am the spider warrior.'

The two Hugos looked even more alarmed, just as they should. 'What's wrong with you?'

'Come a little closer,' I coaxed. I spun in a circle, narrowly avoiding falling over again. 'You'll soon find out. Mwahaha-hahahaha!'

'You idiot. You're going into sudden withdrawal – and it could kill you. When was the last time you had any spider's silk?'

I thrust my wrists towards him so I could ensnare him in a web but nothing happened. I tried again. Still nothing. That was vexing.

'For fuck's sake.' Both Hugos strode towards me, reached out and snatched my bag off my shoulder.

'Hey! That's mine!'

'Where are the pills?'

I leaned towards them. 'Wow. You smell good.' I smacked my lips.

The two Hugos upturned my bag, strewing the contents across the ground. 'Where's the spider's silk, Daisy?'

'Naughty boys,' I said. 'You'll have to tidy all that up, you know.' I took a step forward to make sure that everything was picked up but my feet seemed to get entangled with each other. Uh-oh.

The ground rushed up to meet me, but a strong arm caught me before I slammed into it. I gazed upwards and fluttered my eyelashes. 'My heroes.' I puckered my lips, ready for a kiss.

'Swallow this.' Something bitter was thrust into my mouth and I recoiled at the fizz on my tongue.

'Swallow it, Daisy!'

Goodness, these Hugos were very tetchy. I sighed but did as they asked. 'There.'

'Your heartbeat is too fast.'

'It's because you're so close to me,' I breathed. 'I can't control myself when you're around. Now there are two of you, it's even harder. I'm so excited to be near you that I might throw up.'

There was a growl. 'Don't you fucking dare.'

'Let's have sex – I've always fancied a threesome. Nobody's around.' I gestured at them both. 'Go on. Take your clothes off.'

'How long do these fucking drugs take to work?'

I tugged at my T-shirt. 'Help me get this off. I want your hot skin against mine and your arms wrapped around me. I want to feel you inside me.'

'Daisy—'

'Call me Spider Warrior.' I smiled at them.

A half second later, I passed out.

AT FIRST, the cluster of voices speaking over my head were difficult to decipher.

'I don't understand. Where was she?'

'How did she get out of the cave?'

'What's wrong with her? Is she going to wake up? Daisy? Daisy!'

My head was pounding but I forced open my eyes. Several people were staring down at me; I saw Becky, Otis, Hester, Boonder, Eleanor, Humphrey and Hugo. Only one Hugo.

Oh. I groaned and sat up.

'You're alive!' Hester flew towards me, burrowing into the crook of my neck. 'I thought you were dead,' she sobbed.

'I'm alright,' I said faintly. It was obvious what had happened: somehow I'd allowed too much time to elapse between doses of spider's silk. But even as I was thinking that, I realised it didn't make sense because I'd taken a pill this morning. I should have been fine for another few hours. In fact, I *had* been perfectly fine until I'd left the cave. Maybe the fresh air and natural light had gone to my head and caused a tsunami of withdrawal to hit me.

Then another thought occurred to me. 'Wait. How long was I gone for?'

It was Boonder who answered. 'Sixty-three hours. You fell sixty-three hours ago.'

My stomach flipped. 'It can't have been that long.'

Next to him, Hugo growled, 'It was.'

I couldn't look at Hugo, not after what had happened, so I kept my focus on Boonder. A huge bruise marred his right eye. 'What happened to your face?'

'Nothing.' He shook his head. 'It doesn't matter.'

'But—'

'Daisy.' It was Eleanor. 'What happened? Where have you been?

'I was in the cave,' I muttered. 'There was a ... man there. He wanted to fight me but then he helped me instead.'

Otis wrung his tiny hands. 'You're still hallucinating.'

'I'm not.' I gave him a tired smile. 'I'm fine. Honest.'

'Give her some water,' Hugo said. 'I'll tell the search parties to stand down.' He disappeared and a little of the tension in my chest eased.

'Search parties?' I asked.

'We've been searching for you for the last two days,' Becky told me. 'But there was no sign of you. We tried to go into the hole after you but it was too deep, so we've been searching for other tunnels and caves to, uh, recover your body.'

That was a sobering thought. 'I'm not dead.'

'Clearly. How did you survive? And how did you get out?'

'I wasn't alone down there,' I said faintly. I cricked my neck then got awkwardly to my feet. Several hands shot out to help me but I waved them off. 'Honestly, I'm okay. I have some cuts and bruises and I could do with a long hot shower, but I'm really okay.'

I swallowed. I was angry with myself for not realising that I was going into withdrawal. I'd had the spider's silk with me and it shouldn't have happened. Being underground had messed with my head in more ways than one. 'Where are the other teams?' I asked.

'The witches and Aaron Allen's team have pulled out. After the Primes found the second key part and everyone discovered what had happened to you, they decided not to continue. Two parts of the key have been found but two teams have almost died. They didn't want to risk their lives so they went home. The others are staying in a hotel nearby. Hugo persuaded Sir Nigel to delay the last clue for a few days until you were found.'

'That's ... kind,' I said, painfully aware that they'd been searching for my corpse.

Humphrey patted my shoulder. 'We couldn't leave you behind. You are one of us now, my dear.'

I wasn't entirely convinced that was true but it was nice of him to say it. Then I paused. 'Wait.' I looked at Becky. 'It was Hugo who found the second key part?'

She nodded and I tried not to scowl. There was only one more to find; the damned Primes were doing too well. 'Six teams left,' I said aloud. 'And only one part of the key to go.'

'Five teams,' Boonder said. 'I'm done. I was only staying until you were found. I'm out.'

I gaped at him. 'What? Why?'

'You almost died, Daisy,' he said. 'I thought you *did* die. It was my fault.'

'No! It wasn't your fault at all!'

'I shouldn't have let you fall.'

I shook my head. 'Boonder, you didn't let me fall. It was an accident that you couldn't have prevented. You can't—'

'The decision is made. This competition isn't for me.'

'What really happened to your face?' I asked quietly.

'Nothing.'

I looked at the others. Every single one of them was avoiding my gaze.

'I made the decision to quit on my own, Daisy,' Boonder said. 'I love treasure hunting and I won't stop doing it, but I don't like competing against others. I work best alone. I have no qualms risking my own well-being but I can't risk others'. I don't want to do this particular hunt any longer.'

'We should withdraw as well, Daisy,' Otis piped up. 'You're in no fit state to continue.'

'Daisy isn't giving up!' Hester snapped.

'She's not well.'

Before the two brownies descended into yet another argument, I held up my hands. 'I'm fine. I don't want to give up.'

Hugo reappeared and my stomach flip-flopped again. As he gave me a long look, a muscle ticked in his jaw. 'Mick in the

Primes is medically trained,' he said. 'I'll get him to look you over. You might need more treatment.'

Mick could look me over all he wanted; I was perfectly healthy and I wasn't going to quit. 'Alright,' I said stiffly, still unwilling to meet his eyes. 'Thank you for the offer.'

He folded his arms across his chest. The knuckles on his right hand were red and bruised. I looked at Boonder's face again and a spark of fury zipped through me. I sucked in a breath, preparing to snap, but Boonder shook his head. 'No,' he said firmly. 'Everything is good here.'

I ground my teeth. I didn't think everything was good at all.

TWENTY-ONE

'Our numbers are depleted,' Sir Nigel said, his face beaming out from the screen in the bar area of the inn close to Smoo Cave. 'But with only one key part still to locate, the competition remains as fierce as ever.'

I stood at the back of the room, my arms crossed. Mick had pronounced me fit to continue, not that it was his call whether I carried on or not. The others, even the twins, had been solicitous when they'd discovered I was indeed alive. Perhaps Humphrey had been right and I was now becoming one of *them*. Stranger things had happened.

There had been plenty more questions about what I'd experienced but, given the state I was in when I exited the caves and the scepticism I'd already been subjected to, I declined to say any more about what had occurred. Only Hester and Otis were aware of the whole truth – and they had only believed it when I showed them Gladys. I didn't know if Hugo had noticed her wrapped up in my towel when he'd upended my bag because I hadn't spoken to him since Boonder had left last night.

Sir Nigel continued, 'I know that there are some safety concerns, given what has occurred in the previous two stages, but I can assure you that the next part of the hunt should not be dangerous.' His moustache quivered. 'It may, however, be slightly illegal.'

I unfolded my arms and stood up straight. Illegal? Suddenly I was even more interested. I'd been under the impression that these treasure hunters, competitive as they might be, took care not to fall foul of the law. The idea that Sir Nigel Hannigan was encouraging criminal activity was intriguing. Frankly, as long as I didn't have to crawl into any caves, I was happy.

Otis buzzed in my ear. 'Illegal? I don't like the sound of that at all. I don't think you should participate.'

'Ha!' Hester scoffed. 'I laugh in the face of the law. I chortle at the concept of justice. The more rule breaking, the better.'

I hushed them both, aware that several of the other treasure hunters – Hugo included – were glancing at us.

Sir Nigel's voice burbled on cheerfully, oblivious to the brownies' muttering. 'I am reasonably certain that the final part of the key is resting in the private collection of Lord Alisdair Greenwood.'

A murmur rippled around the room and my eyebrows rose; even I'd heard of Lord Greenwood. He was probably the most well-known witch in the country, although his celebrity had more to do with infamy than achievement. The curmudgeonly bastard popped up regularly on right-wing television shows spouting views that wouldn't look out of place in a fascist dicta-torship. He seemed to enjoy courting public disfavour. While he had many detractors, he also had a cohort of staunch admirers who agreed with him that witches were superior to all other beings – and that elves, in particular, ought to be ejected from the country.

I'd long suspected that he didn't really believe what he preached, but his strong opinions allowed him to have a successful media career. He was always called on when there was an incident involving witches, elves or both. I was sure he'd be unwilling to hand over a historical object to treasure hunters who included elves. He had a reputation to maintain.

'Unfortunately,' Sir Nigel said, 'Lord Greenwood is reluctant to allow anyone access to his collection. I have approached him several times over the last few days and he has declined to speak to me. The best way forward, as I see it, is to obtain the key part without his knowledge. Once it has been used to locate the Loch Arkaig treasure, I shall ensure it is returned safely to him. I like to think of it as borrowing rather than stealing.'

That sounded like semantics to me; after all, you could argue that bank robbers saw stealing money as borrowing because, once they'd spent their ill-gotten gains, the money was returned to public circulation. Given that part of the reason I'd been fired from SDS was because of my potential to commit crime, it seemed bizarre that I was now being sanctioned to do so.

I would have to be careful – I didn't need any more run-ins with the police. I risked a quick glance at Hugo. Was he willing to break the law to obtain the third key part? His expression gave nothing away.

'Lord Greenwood owns several properties and I do not know which one houses the key part. His collections are vast and it will not be easy to find one artefact amongst the many thousands that he owns. The good news is that he is not enamoured of law enforcement and has many reasons not to contact the police if he discovers any of you creeping around one of his houses. He does, however, pay a considerable amount for private security so you must be careful.'

Translation: if you are caught, you won't be sent to prison but you may well be beaten up by several well-paid goons. I was already sporting more than enough bruises and I would do everything I could to avoid getting any more. Blue had never been my colour.

'As always,' Sir Nigel finished, 'the best of luck to you all.' The screen flickered off.

The trio of squirrel shapeshifters were the first to leave and I felt a touch of green-eyed envy. They were perfectly placed to sneak into a building undetected: they could move quickly, hide easily and scale supposedly unscalable walls that would defeat the rest of us. Even so, I managed a begrudging nod in their direction as they passed me. We weren't exactly friends now, but I supposed we could be described as colleagues. Of a sort.

As soon as they left the room, I followed. I was in no hurry to jump on the motorbike; I had a lot of research to do first. I strolled out of the inn with Hester and Otis flapping their tiny wings next to me and went to the rear where I knew I could find a quiet spot. Stealth was the name of the game in this section of the hunt and I would start as I meant to go on with nobody peeking over my shoulder.

There was a small rose garden at the back of the inn. The flowers were past their best, and there was the faintest tinge of decay lurking behind their sweet fragrance, but it was as good a spot as any to settle down and look for information. I plonked myself cross-legged on a patch of grass, groaning slightly at the ache in my limbs. After all that happened so far, I could do with a damned massage.

Otis was still in a huff at the thought of breaking the law and he zipped off towards a rose bush with pink-tipped flowers. Hester stroked her chin for a moment before joining him. I could hear them murmuring to each other, their voices occasionally raised in argument.

I slid out my phone, checked my internet connection and started searching for anything I could find out about Lord Alisdair Greenwood and his properties. Cumbubbling bollocks – he did indeed own a lot of big buildings.

'Are you avoiding me?'

I jerked and my eyes rose to meet Hugo's. Fuck's sake. Was it too much to ask for some peace and quiet while I planned a heist? The man was like a damned cat in the way he sneaked up on me time and time again.

'Yes.' I lowered my gaze to my phone again. 'I should have thought you'd be pleased.'

'Don't presume to know what I'm thinking, Daisy. You might be surprised.'

I pretended to focus on the screen, hoping he'd either get the message and piss off or my annoyance would dissipate. When neither of those things happened, I placed my phone carefully on the ground and stood up. 'Oh,' I said, 'I've learned all sorts of surprising things about you.'

A gleam lit his blue eyes. 'Go on.'

'You took against me from the very first moment we met because I use illegal drugs, yet now you're embracing the thought of breaking and entering to steal someone else's property. I'm pretty certain that's also against the law. Apparently illegal activities are only a problem when you're not doing them. One rule for you and one for everyone else.'

The smile that had been playing around his lips vanished. 'My issues with spider's silk have nothing to do with its legality – although it's against the law for very good reasons. And I'm not the only one wanting to steal the next key part. You're hardly Snow White.'

'I never claimed to be,' I retorted.

'Neither did I.'

I snorted and Hugo's eyes narrowed but then his shoulders dropped and he seemed to relax. 'I hoped we were past our initial ... difficulties,' he said. 'But I realise that you need to find a way of covering your embarrassment. There's no need for that, Daisy. We both know what you really think of me.' His voice roughened. 'You want my hot skin against yours, my arms wrapped around you. And,' he added, without taking his gaze from mine, 'you want to feel me inside you.'

A flush crept up my neck. 'I wasn't myself when I said those things.'

He gave me a long look, an intense light flickering in his blue eyes, then he stepped back. 'No,' he said finally. 'I don't suppose you were. You should do something about that addiction. It'd make life safer for everyone.'

Yeah, yeah. 'Perhaps you should do something about your temper,' I countered. 'Why did you hit Boonder?'

Hugo's flash of embarrassment surprised me. 'I lost my temper. It wasn't his fault. I was in the wrong and I apologised.'

At least he didn't try to deny it and I saw genuine guilt in his expression. I had to give him credit, albeit grudgingly, for admitting what he'd done and accepting it was wrong. Everyone made mistakes but not everyone could admit to them. Maybe Hugo wasn't a complete bastard – but he didn't understand anything about me. And I didn't understand anything about him.

'Boonder's a good man,' he said quietly. 'A better man than I am. He accepted my apology without a fuss. I tried to persuade him to stay but his mind was made up. He promised that it wasn't me who made him quit but,' he held up his hands, 'I did hit him and I have to own the fact that I fucked up.' He didn't look away but his voice lowered. 'He dropped you. I thought you'd gone because he dropped you and I lashed out.'

My mouth suddenly felt dry. 'It wasn't his fault. It was an accident. There was nothing Boonder could have done.'

'I know. I wouldn't usually react like that – in fact, I *never*

185

react like that.' His jaw clenched. 'Something about you makes me act out of character.'

I couldn't explain why his words made me feel defensive, but they did. 'Because I'm a grubby junkie?' I asked bitterly.

'No,' he said softly. 'Because you're you.'

I swallowed, then I surprised myself by reaching out my hand towards him. Fuck it, I couldn't trust him, I didn't like him – but I certainly didn't hate him. 'You were right before. We won't be besties, Hugo.' I paused. 'But maybe we can be friendly rivals?'

He eyed my hand with a brooding expression. 'I suppose I can accept that.' He took my hand and shook it, and I pretended I didn't feel a jolt of electricity when we touched. 'Only one key part to go, Daisy. It will be mine.'

I pulled my hand away as quickly as possible. 'Game on, princess,' I told him.

Hugo only laughed.

CHAPTER
TWENTY-TWO

I t took longer than I liked to settle down after Hugo left. Something about him made my skin itch – and not in an unpleasant way. I still wasn't sure why he'd sought me out, but the strange frisson between us seemed to grow stronger every time we were alone. To be honest, something about Hugo made *me* feel out of character.

I knew part of me lusted after him whether I wanted to or not, but there was more to it than mere desire. Whatever it was, it annoyed me.

Eventually I shoved him out of my mind. There was a lot of information to sift through, but Greenwood's public profile made it a reasonably easy task and I didn't have to dig far to find what I needed. He liked talking about himself and he'd been interviewed numerous times over the years. He waxed lyrical about his upbringing and his education at Gordonstoun, a posh boarding school for the well-to-do. He discussed his business enterprises; he seemed to believe that poverty was experienced only by those who were weak-willed and lazy, which was easy to say when you'd been born with a silver spoon in your mouth.

Greenwood was so far out of touch, he lived on another planet. Sometimes he said something interesting but not often.

Of the seven properties that Greenwood owned, his palatial country pile over the border in Wales seemed the most likely to house the third part of the key. He spent most of his time there, and I found an old advertisement for a swanky home-insurance company for gazillionaires that included his endorsement on their website. In the blurb, his comments suggested the Welsh mansion required large insurance premiums. It also had a lot of security. It was by far the most probable location for a priceless Jacobean artefact.

I smacked my lips. 'Alright! Saddle up, brownies! I know where we need to go. It's a long way to Wales so we should set off now.' I had no idea how we'd get inside the house but I'd worry about that part later.

Hester's head popped up from behind one of the roses. 'Wales?'

'Yep! That's where the last key part is. I'm sure of it.'

She stared at me but she didn't move and she didn't say anything. Neither did Otis.

'Come on,' I said with a trace of impatience. 'The others will probably come to the same conclusion, so I'd like to get there before they do.'

Hester still didn't fly over to join me. 'We have to tell her,' she muttered to her brother.

'I can't condone theft,' he answered.

'It's not theft, Otis. It's borrowing.'

My eyes narrowed. 'What's going on?'

They exchanged glances. Hester nudged Otis. 'Tell her.'

'You tell her.'

She shook her tiny head. 'It has to be you.'

He pouted then sighed deeply and fluttered reluctantly in

my direction. I waited; I didn't know what was happening but I suspected that a lot of patience would serve me well.

'You need to promise,' Otis said, avoiding my gaze, 'that you will make sure the key part is returned when you are finished.'

'I promise, Otis.'

'It's not that I think you'll deliberately keep it for yourself, or that you're a thief. It's just that I know how these things can get lost when you're busy. Before you know it, several months have passed and you've still not given it back. Then several years. And then...'

I sighed. 'Otis, I promise that I will return it as soon as I can. It will be top of my list once the treasure hunt is over.'

He nodded, although the vigorous flapping of his little white wings made his continued discomfort clear.

I watched him for another few seconds as Jamila's words about kindness flitted through my head. Then I came to an easy decision – one that we all could live with. 'Tell you what,' I said. 'Let's stop this now. We'll sit out the rest of the hunt.' Yes, I wanted to win and yes, I needed the money. But some things were more important.

Hester screeched, 'What? Why would you do that?'

'We're a team. This is making Otis uncomfortable and we have to respect that.' I smiled. 'It's not a big deal.'

'Yes, it is!' Hester yelled.

'She's right,' Otis agreed, his eyes wide and glassy. 'It is a very big deal.'

'Nah.' I waved my hand dismissively. 'Everyone will work out that this house is probably the location of the key part. That's five teams trying to break into the same place at the same time – it'll be carnage. We're bound to get caught by Greenwood's security guards. Walking away is the wisest thing we can do.'

Hester put her hands on her hips and glared at Otis but he

didn't seem to notice. His attention was fixed on me. 'That's not where the key part is,' he whispered. 'It's not in Wales.'

'What?'

Otis dashed away an unexpected tear, then started twiddling his thumbs as if he desperately needed something to distract him from his emotions. 'Our last owner, the one who was murdered by a sorcerer, was a merchant. She dealt in antiquities.'

'Okay,' I said slowly.

'She wasn't very good at paperwork and I have a head for detail, so sometimes I did the books for her.'

'Not easy with tiny hands and massive books,' Hester butted in.

Otis nodded. 'Not easy at all. But that's not what's important. One of the last shipments she sent out was a crate of Scottish antiques. A nobleman had purchased a property up near Dundee and he wanted to furnish it with as much Scottish tat as possible. He already had a Cornish home that was filled with Cornish items, a Welsh home full of Welsh stuff and a London home for his international collections. He liked keeping everything orderly and in its place. He threw a hissy fit when some Wedgwood china was included in the Scottish shipment because it wasn't from Scotland.'

I swallowed. Surely not. 'There was a key part in that Scottish shipment?' I breathed.

'Not that I'm aware of, but we weren't the only merchants he used. He worked with all sorts of dealers.' He paused. 'His name was Lord William Greenwood. He must have been the current Lord Greenwood's great-grandfather or something.'

Suddenly I understood. 'What you're saying is that unless someone in the Greenwood family has moved objects around, the key part will still be at the property in Dundee because it's the only Greenwood home in Scotland and the key part is a Scottish artefact.'

Otis nodded. 'Pretty much. William Greenwood was an avid collector and he had a lot of antiques. A *lot* of antiques. I know it was many decades ago and they could have been shipped around since then but it would be a nightmare to move them all. The antiquities from William Greenwood's time are probably still in the properties they were bought for.'

My heart thumped with the thrill of this new information. None of the other teams would be privy to this; it was insider knowledge on an epic scale. We'd probably be the only ones to head to the Dundee property first and we'd have a chance to grab the third key part long before anyone else realised it was there.

Enjoying the buzz of zippy adrenaline, I clapped my hands – then I suddenly stopped. We were dropping out; we were no longer participating in the hunt. 'It doesn't matter,' I said. 'We're not taking part. Nothing has changed. We're a team and everyone's opinion is important.'

Hester opened her mouth, her tiny apple cheeks turning red with fury.

I shook my head before she could speak. 'Everyone gets a vote and anyone can veto. We're not going.'

Otis stuck his hand nervously upwards.

'What is it?' I asked.

'We should go,' he said. He bit his lip. 'You were prepared to pull out because of me.' He thumped his chest and sniffed. 'You care about what I think and nobody has ever done that before, apart from Hester. You don't know how important that is to me. It means I can trust you to return the key part after we're finished. We should go.' His voice hardened. 'We *need* to go.'

I gave him a long, measured look. 'I've made my peace with

not winning the treasure hunt. I wasn't bluffing, Otis. It wasn't a ploy.'

'I know.' His expression was serious. 'That's why I'm telling you to go.'

'Are you absolutely sure?'

'I am.' Otis flew closer and patted my cheek. 'Let's go to Dundee and get that key.'

WE TOOK OUR TIME. Greenwood's Dundee property was considerably closer to Smoo Cave and Durness than the mansion in Wales, so even with a delayed journey we'd arrive there much earlier than the other teams who I was certain were heading south.

I also managed to avoid getting another sore arse from too much motorbike riding. Honestly, everything about this situation was win-win. I pictured Hugo's face when he realised he'd gone all the way to Wales for nothing and I couldn't hide my smile. Even when we arrived outside the large house and I saw its high walls, CCTV cameras and the unmissable trespass warnings.

I couldn't see any signs of runes, and the only witchy ingredient was a bedraggled clump of monkshood that was growing in a pile of gravel near the northern edge of the wall. I was almost sure there was nothing magical barring our entry.

I considered all the options then asked the brownies, 'Can the two of you sneak in? You don't need to enter the building – that'd be too risky – but it'd be helpful to understand what lies beyond those walls. Any entrance or exit points into the building would be great.'

Hester beamed. 'A spy mission! I won't let you down, Daisy.

In fact, I will be excellent at this.' She pirouetted in the air. 'Just watch me!'

I glanced at Otis, half-expecting him to decline. 'Let's do it,' he said. His renewed enthusiasm surprised me. When I raised an eyebrow, he shrugged. 'There's nothing illegal about a little fly-by.'

'You don't have to do it,' I said quickly.

Hester stuck out her tongue and grabbed him. 'Yes, he does!' she trilled. 'I will make him!'

Before I could say anything else she darted towards the wrought-iron gates that barred entrance to the driveway, dragging Otis behind her. Exasperated, I called, 'Hester! Stop that! Let your brother go!'

'It's fine, Daisy,' Otis shouted. 'I want to do this for you.'

I wrinkled my nose. Was I creating a monster and corrupting Otis? Perhaps this wasn't a good idea but, alas, it was too late to stop them; they'd already passed through the narrow gaps in the gate and disappeared.

I sighed, turned around and wheeled the motorbike around the corner where it would be out of sight but close enough for a quick getaway if we needed it.

I sincerely hoped we wouldn't.

TWENTY-THREE

I wasn't expecting the brownies to be long; they were nimble and spry and, despite their small size, I knew they could flap their way around the exterior of the house quickly. It was a brief reconnaissance mission – nothing more, nothing less.

I wasn't concerned when they'd been gone for five minutes. I wasn't anxious when that stretched to fifteen minutes. But when close to half an hour had passed and there was no sign of them, my anxiety started to get the better of me. There was no reason I could think of why they'd not reappeared – other than that they'd been spotted and snared.

I decided to give them another five minutes before I went after them into the grounds but I only managed thirty seconds. I crossed the road in double time and marched to the gates to peer through them. With a little air-magic boost, I could probably scale the wall on the left-hand side without too much difficulty but I wanted to make sure the way beyond was clear.

There wasn't much to see through the gaps in the wrought iron, just an immaculate driveway that seemed to be free of a single dropped leaf or loose pebble. Only fifteen or so metres were visible as it curved away to the right, and the verdant green foliage of a dozen different trees masked any sign of the grand house that lay beyond.

There was no gatehouse and no sign of life. I sucked my bottom lip; I couldn't see any CCTV cameras or spot any booby traps, but that didn't mean that they didn't exist. But I couldn't leave Otis and Hester alone in there so I'd have to risk it and hope for the best.

'No brownie left behind,' I muttered. 'Hang on, guys. I'm coming.'

I jogged to the furthest corner of the wall; the thick conifers on the other side of it would give me my best chance of making an unobtrusive entry. Before I could conjure up the magic I needed to boost me upwards, however, there was a whirr of electricity. I spun around and my stomach dropped to my feet when I saw the main gates swing open.

I expected to see a troop of uniformed security guards march out waving batons and machine guns, carrying tiny cages containing two imprisoned brownies, but instead an old van trundled out. I glimpsed a woman at the wheel and the words *Hags With Rags* emblazoned on the side. I remained frozen, watching the van as it turned right and moved onto the main road. A second later, I sprang into action.

Throwing all my energy into the attempt, I sprinted for the gates. They were obviously accessed remotely and were already closing. I held my breath and pumped my arms and legs as I hurtled towards them and made it in the nick of time, sliding through the gap the moment before the gates clanged shut.

There. I was in.

I felt a sense of wrongness immediately. I couldn't put my finger on exactly what it was, but the moment I'd passed through the gates I knew in my bones that something about this place wasn't right. Goosebumps rose across my skin and I shivered as foreboding rippling through me.

I did my best to shake it off as I slipped into the line of trees at the edge of the driveway, my senses alert for any signs that my presence had been noted. Despite the unpleasant sensation, I couldn't feel the buzz of any gateway magic in the air, and there was no shouting, yelling or gnashing of teeth either from me or from anyone else.

Unfortunately there was also no sign of Otis or Hester, so I certainly wasn't celebrating yet. I jogged quietly forwards, maintaining a steady speed until the house came into view.

I'd been expecting something big and grand and it didn't disappoint. 'This is your life now, Daisy,' I whispered to myself. 'Flitting from castle to mansion to palace.' My SDS delivery days felt as if they belonged to somebody else; I was no longer that person. I was starting to doubt whether I could ever go back to that sort of life.

I dragged my attention away from the marble arches, statuesque columns with perfectly manicured wisteria creeping up them and the gleaming brass accoutrements on the front door. Where the hell were Otis and Hester? I couldn't see any sign of them, although that was hardly surprising given their size. If I were going to do a thorough search, I'd have to abandon the safety of the trees and undergrowth for the open space in front of me.

Nobody was visible. It was probably fine.

I took a step forward, brushed away a clinging cobweb and avoided the painful looking nettles to my right. Then I hastily jumped backwards as two burly men appeared from around the corner. Shit. That was too close.

'I know Greenwood is anxious,' one of the men said, 'but we have one of the strongest security systems in the country. Nobody's getting into this place unless we know about it first.'

'He wants us to check all the windows.'

The first one rolled his eyes. 'They're all alarmed and they're tested every week. Nobody is getting in through a window.'

'He mentioned the skylights above the dining room, as well.'

'Reinforced glass. With sensors embedded. They'll register if anything larger than a pigeon touches them.'

I exhaled quietly. Brownies were smaller than pigeons; Hester and Otis might still be fine.

'He's antsy. He wants everything double-checked.'

'He needs to chill out.'

The two men walked past less than three metres away from where I was hiding. My left eye began to twitch, then that annoying spot between my shoulder blades felt itchy. I clenched my jaw and forced myself to remain still until it was safe to move again. The twitching and the itchiness subsided.

That was when something in my bag began to hum.

My eyes widened in alarm. I'd left my large bag on the motorbike and only brought my smaller backpack with emergency supplies. There wasn't a lot in there that could make that sound, so what the hell was it? The satellite phone was turned off and my mobile was tucked away in my back pocket.

I waited, frozen like a statue, praying that the two men wouldn't notice. Hopefully they were too focused on their complaints to listen to a muted sound floating out from behind a tree. Even so, I was certain I was about to be clapped in irons and beaten to within an inch of my life until the two men disappeared around the next corner.

As soon as I yanked my bag off my shoulders and peered inside, I realised where the humming sound was coming from. I carefully slid Gladys out and gazed at her. Yes, the Fachan had said she was sentient – but I certainly hadn't been expecting anything like this.

'Shhhhhh!'

The humming stopped.

'What the fuck was that all about?' I hissed, feeling something of an idiot as I stood in a clump of bushes talking to a damned sword Or dagger. Or whatever she was.

I'd barely finished speaking when the tip of her blade started to glow. The hilt felt ice cold and I yelped as I dropped her to preserve the skin on my hand from frostbite. Well, someone was touchy; apparently Gladys didn't appreciate being scolded.

'You deserved it!' I whispered angrily. 'Your humming almost gave us away!'

The spikes of grass and dropped leaves around her began to turn white as frost scalded their edges, despite the relative warmth of the day.

'Stop that!' I muttered. The frost receded. I opened my mouth to tell her that she was a liability and I was going to leave her here, then thought better of it. There was no telling what she might do if I tried that.

I crouched down. 'Listen,' I said in a low voice. 'I don't know why you were making that noise but you need to stay quiet. Hester and Otis are out there somewhere, possibly in a lot of trouble. We have to find them without anyone noticing us. You have to be silent.'

Unsurprisingly, Gladys didn't respond.

I waited for a beat then brushed my fingertips along her hilt; her temperature seemed to have returned to normal. Half-convinced I was going mad, I scooped her up and opened my backpack. Then, in case I'd somehow lost track of time again, I dipped my hand into my pocket and took out a spider's silk pill. I would have to replenish my supplies sooner than I'd anticipated, but I couldn't afford any more hallucinations or withdrawal-induced double vision.

I tossed the pill into my mouth, half closing my eyes in satisfaction as the bitter fizz hit the back of my throat and my heart rate slowed. Okay then. Okay. 'You've got this, Daisy,' I whispered to myself. 'It's all good.'

Rather than return Gladys to my bag, I slid her into my belt. Then, with even greater care, I stepped out from the bushes again. This time the way appeared clear.

I was wary of the windows and anyone inside the house who might pass by and glance out. Thanks to Burly One and Burly Two, I knew that Greenwood's security team was on high alert, so a glimpse of somebody skulking around the property would send them into overdrive. The solution was to make sure I didn't skulk.

Although it went against my every instinct, I pulled back my shoulders and walked around the building in the same direction as the Burlies without making any attempt to hide. Nothing to see here, I projected; just another of Lord Greenwood's worker bees. I even stopped a couple of time to pull up some audacious weeds that were poking through the gravel.

When no alarms sounded and nobody sprinted over to tackle me, I grew bolder. 'Hester!' I hissed. 'Otis!'

There was no answer. I gritted my teeth and continued on my way. The sensation that something was wrong intensified with every step I took, but I still couldn't work out why I felt it so strongly. It was as if there were an aura of evil clinging to every nook and cranny, but that didn't make sense. Buildings couldn't be evil. That particular trait was reserved for people.

I swung towards the rear of the house. There was no sign of the two security men. There was a solid-looking fire exit to my left but it was closed and there was no way to open it from this side. The three steps leading down from it were heavily scuffed, though, indicating that it was used often.

I walked past it and followed the gravel path to the next

corner where it branched off in two separate directions. I swivelled to my left away from the grand house, but my sense of foreboding immediately increased. Whatever was wrong with this place was this way.

With no sign yet of either Otis or Hester, I had no choice but to investigate.

As I crept down the path, I examined the different plants and bushes. From what I'd seen outside the walls, the northern perimeter wasn't too far away. There weren't many trees here; this section of the grounds had more manicured shrubbery that was low to the ground. Consequently, when I heard the voices of Burly One and Burly Two again and the crunch of their footsteps, I knew that there was nowhere to hide. As soon as they turned the corner, they would see me. I bit my lip hard. There was only one thing to do.

I ruffled my hair to make sure my elven ears were hidden, spun around, dropped my bag to the ground and slid Gladys from my belt. Then I crouched beside a rhododendron bush and started to hum as I sliced off stalks and stems and several flowers that were past their best.

Within seconds, the two men reached me. 'Good afternoon,' I murmured, making sure to keep my back turned so that neither my face nor Gladys were visible.

'Afternoon,' Burly One grunted. His arm brushed my spine as he trudged past but I didn't look up; I simply continued snipping.

'Did you catch that film on BBC One last night?' Burly Two asked his companion.

I didn't bother listening to the reply; I was too overcome with relief. It had been a considerable risk but, given that I already knew from the Hags With Rags van that Greenwood employed contractors, I figured that even the alert security team wouldn't question yet another face busy at work in the grounds. That was the trouble with large properties; you needed a lot of staff to keep them running smoothly.

Of course, it helped that I was small, female and didn't look dangerous. Sometimes perception is what counts. Lord Greenwood and his team threw everything they had into high-tech security yet they forgot about their weakest link: themselves. I'd spent enough time delivering boxes and letters to heavily guarded buildings to know that it was easier to slip through a security net than most people realised, whether you were sanctioned to or not.

Once I was certain that the men had disappeared, I straightened up. 'Thanks, Gladys,' I whispered.

Her hilt buzzed in a disgruntled fashion and I stifled a yelp. 'What is your problem?' I muttered. She didn't answer.

Vaguely irritated, I shook my head and returned her to my belt then continued down the path until I reached a pretty summer pavilion. It was immaculately white-washed, with climbing roses along one side and carefully arranged pots of flowers dotted around the porch. It should have been the perfect vision of a simple yet beautiful garden building – but for the now pulsating sense that it was all wrong.

I edged towards it – and stopped dead. Huh. Well, wasn't that interesting? A line of white powder that appeared to encircle the structure lay about two inches from my toes. I bent down, dabbed the tip of my forefinger in it and sniffed. My tongue flicking out, I took a tentative taste. Salt. The pavilion was ringed with an unbroken line of salt.

My eyes narrowed. I stayed where I was but I lifted my head and gazed more closely at the building itself, looking past the pretty façade to see the truth. The windows were shuttered; not a glimmer of natural light could seep inside. There were also many glinting flashes of metal, concealed for the most part by the white, wooden cladding but still visible if I looked closely enough.

I'd bet all the pennies in my dwindling bank account that I was looking at iron – and any fool knew that a building ringed with iron and salt was designed to either keep magical creatures out – or to keep them in.

The harder I looked at the pavilion, the more certain I was that this place wasn't designed for enjoying lazy summer days with a refreshing drink and a good book.

It was a prison.

CHAPTER
TWENTY-FOUR

I didn't feel any more relaxed now that I knew why there was such a discomfiting atmosphere. Instead, my concern for Hester and Otis ratcheted up several notches – and I was starting to realise why Alisdair Greenwood was so unpleasant towards elves. Any elf on this property, low or high, would have sensed the same wrongness. Greenwood was clearly desperate to hide whatever nasty shit he was up to. As far as I was concerned, regardless of what lay inside that summer pavilion-cum-prison, he was no longer a media irritant. He was a complete fucking villain.

I circled the building looking for weak points or any indication that Hester or Otis had been there. Both the salt and iron bindings were unbroken so it would be incredibly difficult for an elf like me to pass through them. I shook my head. Not good. Not good at all.

I tried calling out again, praying that the brownies would hear me. 'Hester!' I hissed. 'Otis!'

Nothing. My anxiety increased.

I opened my mouth to call again – then snapped it shut. I ran to the other side of the pavilion and squinted hard at the large oak leaf that had fallen to the ground and lay between the ring of salt and the iron-clad wall. My stomach clenched. A tiny arm was visible, flopping out from underneath the leaf. There they were.

I didn't stop to think about what had possessed them to pass through the salt barrier. The effort of crossing it had clearly cost them dearly and I couldn't tell if they were still breathing or not. All I knew was that I had to reach them as quickly as possible and that meant passing through the ring of salt.

I tried not to panic and dredged up what little I knew about warded circles. In these supposedly enlightened days, they were considered archaic and cruel. Trolls like Duchess were allowed to take up residence under bridges and had the freedom to come and go as they pleased. Snakes like Bella, whether they were man-eating or otherwise, were not ring-fenced; Bella would only attack when her territory was disturbed. She didn't go searching for people to eat. Respectful co-existence was the name of the game, not unnecessary imprisonment.

But that was often easier said than done – and there were exceptions to every rule. Respect was thrown out of the window when mindless creatures like vampires were involved. You can't co-exist with something that is impossible to reason with and whose only goal is to find you and kill you. In any case, my experience with magical wards was so limited that I knew next to nothing about them beyond the basics. And the basics told me that any magic I threw at them would be nullified immediately.

At my waist, Gladys started humming again, an insistent buzzing sound that did nothing for the clarity of my thoughts. 'Stop that!' I barked. She paid me no attention; apparently obedience wasn't top of the list of priorities for a sentient sword.

I blocked out the sound, squared my shoulders, clenched my fist and thrust it forward through the salted barrier.

The pain was so excruciating that I almost screamed aloud. I staggered backwards, yanking my hand to my chest as tears sprang to my eyes. When I looked down, I saw the angry red blisters already splitting my skin. Fuck: this was going to be harder than I'd thought. And bloody Gladys, oblivious to my agony, was continuing to buzz.

I drew in a calming breath, my gaze focused on the oak leaf. There was still no sign of movement from underneath it and nausea pooled in the pit of my belly, a mixture of fear for the brownies and reaction to the pain.

I waited until the agony in my hand subsided to a dull throbbing and I'd regained control of my thoughts. I reached for Gladys whose hilt warmed as soon as I touched it. At least I'd had the foresight to shove my left hand through the ward and not my right – I was going to need as much dexterity as I could muster.

'Alright then,' I muttered aloud. 'If you think you can do better, Gladys, *you* have a go.' I raised her blade and swiped at the air, as if slashing a hole through the ward.

Not sensing any change in the barrier, I frowned. This was stupid; Gladys was no more effective against the ward than I was.

Apparently sensing my thoughts, she gave a lower-pitched hum and then another, even lower. Huh. I crouched down next to the salted line itself. 'I don't know much about magical barriers,' I hissed at her, 'but I know that this line is the source of the power. It's the strongest part and therefore the hardest to break.'

I couldn't simply scuff away the salt to fracture the circle – if that was possible, nobody would ever bother making a salt ward. But at that moment I saw Hester's arm twitch.

I threw caution to the wind. 'Fine. But on your own blade be it.'

I forced Gladys's tip forward and scratched through the dirt until she reached the salt. There was a flicker of resistance then a puff of yellow smoke rose up from the shiny metal, followed by another and another. I'd have pulled back but Gladys had a mind of her own. She tugged herself forward and fiery sparks joined the smoke. And then her blade sliced through the ring of salt, cleaving it apart.

I waved away the smoke until I could see the line properly. Damn. Gladys had done it. It was only a millimetre wide, but there was a definite line in the salt. The circle was broken.

I stood up and gingerly stepped across. No more blisters, no more pain. Gladys's slice had destroyed any power the salt circle possessed. 'Alright,' I said aloud. I wasn't too big to admit it, even to a hunk of metal. 'You were right and I was wrong.'

I stopped wasting time on chatter and darted towards the fallen brownies. Both of them were underneath the leaf. Although their eyes were closed and their bodies were limp, their chests were rising and falling. They weren't dead. I breathed out, almost overcome by relief, and carefully scooped them up, one in each hand.

The good thing was that they weren't covered in blisters and their skin appeared unmarred, so they hadn't been affected by the salt ward in the same way as I had been. The bad thing was that they were out for the count. I blew gently on their bodies. Hester twitched and Otis's hair ruffled but they didn't open their eyes.

'If you have any more bright ideas, Gladys,' I grunted, 'this would be a great time to tell me.' She didn't respond so I guessed I was on my own this time. Unfortunately, I didn't have the faintest idea how to perform triage on brownies.

Drastic times called for drastic measures. Using a burst of

carefully controlled magic, I doused the pair of them in water. Hester immediately started to cough and splutter before jerking upright. Otis blinked and shot straight up into the air.

'You fiend!' Hester shrieked. She shook her wings, sending an arc of droplets flying upwards, then zipped towards my face and pummelled my nose.

I beamed at her in delight. 'You're alive!'

A barrage of blows smacked my skin. Some of them hurt – sort of. 'Of course I'm alive! No thanks to you trying to drown me!' She changed her punches to slaps, punctuating each one with a shout. 'What,' slap, 'were,' slap, 'you,' slap, 'thinking?' Slap. Slap.

I glanced at Otis; things were definitely bad when even he looked miffed. 'You were unconscious and I didn't know what to do. I figured that water might slough off any residual magic and revive you.'

'It was a stupid idea!'

I folded my arms. 'It worked, didn't it? Besides,' I said pointedly, 'I'm not the one who thought it would be a good idea to fly across a magic ward without a second thought. Why didn't you come back to get me? I could have helped.'

'I did say that we should—' Otis began.

'Because,' Hester interrupted furiously, 'they need us now! We couldn't delay. We still can't!' She pirouetted in the air, abandoning violence to point at the pavilion.

I dropped my voice. 'Who's in there?'

'Can't you sense them?' Otis asked.

I shook my head. 'I can feel that something is wrong, but that's about it.'

'Look through the window,' he said, nodding towards a grubby pane of glass.

I went over and pushed myself on tiptoe. At first I wasn't quite sure what I was looking at, but then I realised and bile filled my mouth. 'I figured it was a prison,' I said as horror rippled through me. 'But I didn't think it would be this bad.'

'Now do you see?' Hester demanded.

Horrified, I nodded. 'We need to find a way in – and a way to get them out.' I rubbed my eyes; the image from inside the pavilion had burned into my retina in all its grim horror.

'It's reinforced with iron,' Otis muttered. 'Pure iron. We can't touch it and neither can you. But there's a door. If we can work out how to get it open...' His voice trailed off and he gazed at me with wide, hopeful eyes.

I didn't know if I was up to this task, but the brownies needed to see confidence. 'Show me,' I said. 'We're not leaving until this building is empty.'

He nodded. Hester addressed me in little more than a whisper. 'Thank you, Daisy.'

We all pretended not hear the anxious wobble in her voice.

I wetted my lips and straightened my spine. I preferred angry Hester; desperate, trembling Hester really scared me. 'We are going to do this,' I said firmly. 'Let's not waste another second.'

The door was at the front of the pavilion, set a metre or so back from the porch and visible to anyone who wandered down the path. I didn't enjoy the prickle of danger at my back, so I sent Otis off to keep watch and warn us if we were about to have visitors.

I examined the door. Alisdair Greenwood, who had presumably commissioned the pavilion, certainly hadn't stinted on the iron. There was a lot of it and even from a metre away I could feel its cold throb. Even so, I suspected that getting past it would be easier than breaking through the salt circle. I certainly hoped so.

Hester fluttered anxiously by my right ear. 'Can you burn it? Melt the iron?'

I shook my head. 'The melting point is too high and I couldn't create a magical fire that would be hot enough. Even if I could work magic against iron – which I can't – the building would go up in flames and kill everyone inside.'

We needed a low-tech, non-magical solution. I tapped my chin thoughtfully, then asked, 'Why did you two throw yourselves through the salt ward? You must have known it would knock you out. You were lucky it didn't kill you immediately.'

'We knew it would be bad but decided it would be worth it,' Hester muttered. 'Sometimes, even when you know there will be painful consequences, you still have to go for it.'

I considered her words as I crouched down and examined the door knob. I didn't touch it. It was clearly made of iron but it had neither a key hole nor a padlock. Unless the pavilion was bolted from the inside – and that seemed highly unlikely – there was no lock at all.

I swung my bag off my shoulders and rummaged inside. 'Do you have something in there that will help?' Hester asked hopefully.

I didn't smile as I pulled out the small ziplock bag that contained my remaining spider's silk pills. 'I do.'

'This is not the time to get high!' she protested.

I didn't take spider's silk because it got me high, I took it because I was addicted. I'd become addicted because it gave me control – and control was exactly what I needed right now. I counted the pills. Another ten days' worth, if I were careful. I wasn't going to be careful.

'Someone's coming!' Otis reappeared at high speed. 'Two men are walking down the path.'

Burly One and Burly Two, no doubt. I guessed they were doing the rounds, treading the same path over and over again. I wondered if they'd noticed that the gardener they'd passed earlier was no longer there. I certainly hoped not.

I had to move. I fished out three pills and tossed them into my mouth, swallowing them dry. The drugs worked fast; in seconds the adrenaline fizz started. I bared my teeth at the brownies, who looked even more alarmed. 'Now!' I hissed. And then I ran at the door.

'Daisy!'

I ignored Otis's panicked plea. I had to act while the triple hit of spider's silk was at its strongest. I pulled my cuff over my left hand to use as a barrier between my skin and the iron door knob. It didn't do much to mask the pain – even the spider's silk didn't seem to do much and the agony was excruciating – but I didn't stop. I twisted the knob, heard the brief click as it turned and burst into the pavilion with Hester and Otis right behind me.

Then I slammed the door shut, just before the Burlies appeared.

Blood was pounding in my ears and my body felt like it was on fire. I wasn't foolish enough to look at the damage to my hand; instead, I simply pretended it wasn't there. I was invincible. I could do anything. *Anything*.

I heard the Burlies' voices drifting in from beyond the closed door. 'He's on his way. Five minutes' tops.'

'We'd better hurry, then,' came the reply.

Indeed. We'd better hurry, too.

I gazed around the pavilion. Now I could see the inside clearly, it looked horrific. There were numerous cages – iron-clad, naturally – of different sizes; one thing they had in common was that none of them was large enough for its occupants to stretch out comfortably.

Eyes stared at me from behind the bars, some fearful, some resigned. Only a few displayed a flicker of hope. I couldn't begin to imagine why Greenwood had imprisoned so many creatures in this place; I didn't *want* to imagine why.

'It's a nightmare,' Otis mumbled. 'It's a fucking nightmare.' It was the first time I'd ever heard him swear and I sincerely hoped it would be the last.

I leaned backwards slightly, listening for the Burlies. By the sounds of things they'd gone. I leapt towards the first row of cages. Here we go. Here we fucking go.

The cages didn't have locks but that didn't make opening the bloody things any easier. They didn't need locks when they were made of iron. I employed the same technique I'd used on the front door, covering my skin with the flimsy material from my shirt and avoiding touching the metal for any length of time.

I focused on the thrill of the spider's silk overdose and started tearing open the doors one after the other. Brownie. Brownie. Brownie. Leprechaun. Brownie. Troll. Each dazed prisoner stared at me but stayed inside their cage as if they suspected some sort of trick.

The troll, who was a third of the size of Duchess and considerably thinner probably because of prison rations, cleared his throat. 'Who are you?' His voice was scratchy and it seemed to cost him a lot of effort to get the words out.

'My name is Daisy. You're free now. You can leave.'

He still didn't move and I cursed under my breath. I went to the front door and gritted my teeth at the renewed surge of bone-deep pain as I opened it again.

'Go!' I flapped my arms. 'Get out of here! If you head around the back, you can climb the wall.' I turned to the next row of cages. Three more brownies. Two goblins. And... Fucking hell. I looked at the final cage, which was larger than the others. A damned unicorn.

There were painful looking sores on its body where it had doubtless brushed against the iron bars of its cage. Even here in Scotland where unicorns were the national animal, it was incredibly rare to see one. I looked into her Mediterranean-blue eyes at the sadness reflected in their depths. There was vicious fury there, too. 'How the hell will *you* climb a wall?' I muttered to myself.

The unicorn dipped her head and stretched the tip of her horn towards me. I ripped open the cage door. 'We'll find a way,' I told her. 'You are all getting out of here.'

Hester flapped her arms as she hovered in the doorway. 'Here!' she called frantically. 'This way! Follow me!'

All the captives gazed at her and for a moment I thought that none of them would move. Then the unicorn stepped forward, her hooves thudding against the wooden floor. I moved aside and she slowly walked out onto the porch. As she tilted her head up to the sky and sniffed the clear air, I swallowed a large lump in my throat. A second later she took off, wheeling around the pavilion and heading for the far wall.

I ran after her, even though I had no idea how I could help her. I needn't have worried. As soon as the perimeter wall came into view, the unicorn picked up speed and started to gallop. I squeaked with terror, convinced she would crash head first into the stone and fracture her skull.

She dipped her head and her horn stretched out in front of her. 'No!' I yelled, no longer caring if the security guards heard me. 'Stop! Don't do it!'

The unicorn galloped harder. I came to a stuttering stop, watching her in horror. 'Don't worry, Daisy,' Otis said by my ear. 'She's got this.'

I barely heard him; I was too busy summoning as much power as I could, combining both air and earth magic to shake the foundations of the wall and make it collapse. But the unicorn was preternaturally fast, faster than the damned magic.

Her horn smacked into the stone wall. There was a tremendous crash and dust filled the air as it crumbled. A split second later, my magic flashed uselessly into the space where the wall had been. The unicorn had destroyed a seven-metre section of it all on her own.

She leapt through the rubble and vanished in an instant, leaving me gaping after her.

Somewhere behind me near the house a shrieking alarm rent the air – but it was already too late. A posse of brownies flew past, then the leprechaun ran forward, his legs and arms pumping hard as he sprinted through the gap in the wall. The troll cantered after him. Even the goblins, who weren't known for their speed, disappeared into the cloud of dust.

It might have taken them a moment or two to pluck up the courage to leave their cages, but as soon as they had they'd moved fast. I reckoned less than thirty seconds passed between the unicorn leaving the pavilion and the goblins making their escape.

'We should go too!' Otis urged. 'Greenwood's security guards will already be on their way!'

Whether it was because of the spider's silk overdose, the adrenaline in my body or simply the joy of witnessing the escape, I felt completely calm.

'No,' I told him dreamily. 'We still have work to do.'

TWENTY-FIVE

I turned back and faced the pavilion. My magic couldn't melt the iron but the rest of the horror-clad building was made of wood. Now that it was empty of living creatures, it was safe to destroy it.

I smiled humourlessly, released the tight control I'd been clinging onto and threw enough fire magic to set it ablaze. The resulting bonfire was the most glorious thing I'd ever seen. The flames glowed red and yellow, their crackling warmth the complete opposite to the sensation that the cold iron had created. 'So pretty,' I murmured. 'So fabulous.'

'Now can we go?' Otis shouted in my ear, struggling to make himself heard over the roar of the fire.

I shook my head. 'We still have to get the key part.'

Hester appeared in front of me. 'We can't get it now! We have to get out of here, you stupid elf!'

I blinked at her slowly. 'This is the perfect time to get it.' I waved at the fire. 'We've created the distraction we need to get into the house.'

'What about your hand?' Otis asked anxiously. 'You need medical attention, Daisy.'

I frowned; I'd forgotten about the pain. I held up my left hand and gazed at it. It was lobster red and oozing blood. I could twitch the tip of my pinkie but my other fingers – and thumb – didn't appear capable of moving at all. I examined each digit curiously before shrugging. 'It'll keep.' I grinned at the brownies. 'Come on.'

I didn't wait for their reaction before veering off the path and into the undergrowth. It was just as well because a few breaths later several panicked-looking people – including the Burlies – appeared hefting buckets of water and a long hose.

Mildly amused, I smiled. That wouldn't work. This fire would burn for days. I'd made sure of it.

I skirted further away but I needn't have worried that I'd be spotted. Greenwood's staff were far too focused on the flames. I wondered if anyone had called the fire brigade before deciding that they'd be under orders not to. Serious questions would be asked if anyone in authority discovered this building – and Greenwood wouldn't have any reasonable answers to give. I debated calling them myself but their presence would only complicate matters. I'd ring them after I left the property with the key part in hand. Until then, Greenwood's frantic staff were on their own.

Despite my circuitous route, I was quickly back at the rear of the grand house and pleased to see that the emergency exit was now wide open. Entering the supposedly secure building had suddenly become a piece of cake. I raised my eyebrows at Otis and Hester. 'See?' I said.

'It's too dangerous. This is still a very bad idea,' Otis told me.

Hester pursed her lips. 'I'm coming around to it. This might be our chance.'

There was no might about it.

I glanced first to my left and then to my right. Once I was

sure that the way was clear, I abandoned the dubious safety of the undergrowth for the open door and nipped inside. Now all I had to do was find the final part of the Loch Arkaig treasure key. How hard could that be?

'How many rooms do you think there are in this place?' I asked aloud.

'Too many,' Otis muttered.

I wagged my finger at him. 'No black-hat thinking.'

'Hester's the one who wears black hats.' He was clearly confused. 'Not me.'

I didn't bother to explain; armchair psychology could wait. With a determined stride, I headed down the first corridor. *Come on, magic key. Come out, come out, wherever you are.*

There were a lot of antiques in the first room we came to, but they appeared to have been selected as part of the interior design; there were no glass-fronted cases or anything that suggested Jacobean magic. I swivelled towards the second room. That was more promising; there were plenty of gleaming antiquities lining the walls.

I completed a full circuit of the room but there was nothing that appeared to be what I was looking for. Hmm; this was going to take more time than I'd anticipated. My gaze drifted down to my mangled mess of a hand. Maybe I ought to take another spider's silk pill, just to keep my thoughts clear.

'Daisy!' Otis was waving at me from a room across the hall-way. 'I think it's in here!'

All thoughts of drugs fled my mind as I trotted over and followed him into a third room. When I saw its contents, my mouth dropped open. It was crammed with gleaming treasures and, from the way the metal objects caught the light, not even a single speck of dust.

They had obviously been given far greater care and attention than the creatures in the pavilion, I thought bitterly. I was tempted to forego the treasure hunt in favour of confronting Lord Alisdair fucking Greenwood in person. It would probably be worth it.

There was the murmur of voices from somewhere deeper in the house, followed by footsteps heading my way. I smirked: this might be my chance. I waved to Hester and Otis to keep out of sight and ducked behind a large free-standing cabinet in the far corner of the room.

'It's nothing to worry about,' a clipped English voice stated. 'Merely a garden bonfire that got slightly out of control. It's far back from the house – I can assure you we are in no danger.'

That had to be Greenwood. He was doing a reasonable job of projecting an aura of bravura, but I heard the nervousness behind every word. That could only mean that he didn't want his companion to know about the pavilion. I resisted the urge to peek out and listened some more.

'I say, old chap, you ought to be more careful. I can give you the names of some gardeners who would never allow such a thing to happen. You have to be able to trust your staff. I can assure you that the people I know are good fellows.'

Astonishment rendered me rigid. I looked at Hester, who poked her head out to check, and Otis, who was wide-eyed with shock.

That was Humphrey. That was most definitely Humphrey.

'I appreciate the offer,' Greenwood responded stiffly. 'But there are no problems with my people. There are no problems at all.'

'If you say so,' Humphrey burbled.

I risked a look. They had their backs to me and were standing in front of one of the display cabinets. Humphrey appeared as relaxed as usual; by contrast, Greenwood looked stiff and unyielding, tension in every line of his body. He was not a happy man. Good. I wondered if he already knew that his captive menagerie had escaped.

'Let's get this over with, shall we?' he muttered. 'I'm sure you are busy and have plenty of other things to be doing with your time.'

Humphrey clapped him on the back and the sound of his friendly blow echoed through the room. 'No rush, my friend. No rush.'

Greenwood acted as if he hadn't heard him. As he leaned towards the cabinet, he searched his pocket for something. I caught a flash of metal and realised it was a key. He unlocked the cabinet door and reached inside. I already knew what he was extracting and I sagged with disappointment. I had been so close, so damned close.

'Here,' Greenwood said. 'One Jacobean artefact, as requested.' He handed it to Humphrey.

'Wonderful.' Humphrey smacked his lips with satisfaction. 'Simply wonderful.'

Greenwood didn't respond immediately. I twitched; this would be a good time to rush them both. I could take them by surprise, knock them to the floor and snatch the third and final key part from Humphrey's fingers, then it would be only Hugo and me in the final. I'd truly be a treasure hunter extraordinaire. I could do it. I was sure I could do it.

I pulled back. Humphrey had the key part and it belonged to him, fair and square. I didn't know how he'd managed to locate it or persuade Greenwood to hand it over, but it wasn't mine to take.

I'd lost. I wasn't a treasure hunter and I wouldn't be taking part in the final search for the Loch Arkaig gold. It had been a mistake to think I was ever in the running. I was a failure – and I had to acknowledge that sad truth. My hunt was over.

I heard more shouts from outside; the fire at the pavilion was clearly not abating. It was impressive that Greenwood could stand there and hold a polite conversation with Humphrey as if nothing were going on. That vile excuse for a man was obviously an accomplished liar.

'Why don't I stay a little longer?' Humphrey said. 'We can have a good chat over a cup of tea. I remember those wonderful little cakes your cook made last time I was here. I'd love another one of those.'

There was a long pause before Greenwood replied. 'I can speak to her and see what's available.'

'You are a good fellow,' Humphrey told him. 'A very good fellow.' A moment later, they turned and walked out, still oblivious to my presence.

As soon as they'd gone, I leaned against the cabinet and sighed. So that was that.

'I'm sorry, Daisy,' Otis whispered. 'If we hadn't stopped to rescue everyone in the pavilion, you would have got to the key part.'

I managed a half-smile. 'We did the right thing. If I'd had the choice between finding the Loch Arkaig treasure or rescuing those poor bastards, I'd have chosen the rescue. Always.'

'We can't let that man get away with what he's done,' Hester said.

'We won't,' I promised. 'Alisdair Greenwood will get what's coming to him.'

She brightened. 'You'll use Gladys to stab him in the heart?' There was an answering buzz of delight from the blade.

'No. We will not be killing anyone.'

Hester pouted. 'Trust me,' I told her. 'He won't go unpunished.' I pushed away my disappointment and concentrated on the satisfaction I would feel when I saw Greenwood clapped in handcuffs. The day had not been an entire disaster, not by a long shot.

'Let's steal stuff,' Otis said. 'As much as we can carry.' I looked at him and he shrugged. 'What? I have no problem with it now I know what Greenwood is really like.' His tiny face took on a malevolent gleam. 'We need to fuck him up.'

I gave him a pointed look. 'No stealing. And no touching. We can't leave any fingerprints. And stop swearing!'

Now Otis was pouting. I sighed. 'Come on, you two. Let's get out of here.' There was no longer any reason to stay.

It was far easier to sneak out of Greenwood's property than it had been to sneak in. For one thing, most of the staff were occupied with putting out the fire. For another, when I called the police and the fire brigade and they forced Greenwood to open the iron gates at the end of the driveway, I could simply stroll out.

I'd given the police more than enough information over the phone to arrest Greenwood. Once they saw the evidence within the destroyed pavilion, there was no doubt that he'd be sent down for a long time. I didn't have to worry; his comeuppance was on its way.

I moved left, preparing to retrieve the motorbike from its parking spot around the corner. As I lifted my head, I spotted Eleanor standing beside a gleaming black car, watching the commotion at the gates and fiddling nervously with her bag. When she saw me, her mouth dropped open in shock – and relief.

'Daisy!' she exclaimed. 'I had no idea you were here, too! What's happening? Is everything alright? Is Humphrey okay in there? He told me to wait here for him but then I saw the fire engines and the police and—'

I held up my hands to stop her. 'Humphrey's fine. It's Lord Greenwood who's having a few problems. You shouldn't worry.'

She stared at me wide-eyed. 'What sort of problems? He's an old schoolfriend of Humphrey's. They've known each other for years.'

'These are the sort of problems that Humphrey will do well to stay out of,' I said. I had no doubt that he'd keep his distance from Greenwood once he learned the truth.

Eleanor looked me up and down, her expression still fearful. 'Did you get the key part?' she whispered.

I shook my head. 'No. It's Humphrey's.' I smiled ruefully. 'I'm out of the competition.'

Eleanor breathed out and turned away so I couldn't see her face. 'Oh,' she said. 'Oh. That's good.' She swallowed and turned back to me. 'Not for you, of course. I'm sorry for you. It's just that Humphrey needs this more than he's letting on.' Her gaze dropped as if she felt ashamed for telling me, but then her expression changed from concern to downright horror. 'What the hell happened to your hand?'

I looked down. I shouldn't have been surprised by her reaction; my fingers were swollen and twisted and there were suppurating sores all over my hand. It looked like it had been shoved through a mangle.

'Uh ...' Occupational hazard? Wounds gained in the line of duty? I didn't have an appropriate answer so I avoided the question. 'I'm on my way to the hospital to get it checked out. It looks worse than it is.' That was probably a lie but there was enough spider's silk coursing through my body for it to feel like the truth.

I shifted from foot to foot. There was nothing else to say so I shrugged awkwardly. 'I ought to go.' I nodded at the gates.

'Humphrey might take a while. The police will probably want to speak to him, but he won't be in any trouble. I expect they'll interview him and then let him go.'

'What happened in there, Daisy?'

'Honestly, Eleanor,' I said, 'you don't want to know.'

CHAPTER
TWENTY-SIX

I expected to wait several hours in casualty, but as soon as the receptionist saw my hand she bumped me to the top of the list ahead of a crying teenager, a man repeatedly throwing up into a bucket and a pensioner whose creaky bones could be heard from the other side of the waiting room.

'I'm not in any rush,' I told her. 'I don't mind hanging around for a while until a doctor is free.'

Hester was having none of it. She put her hands on her hips and started yelling. It was astonishing how loud her voice could be, given her mouth was barely the size of a pinhead. 'She's in great pain! She needs to be seen now before infection sets in!'

'It's not that bad.' I sent the receptionist an apologetic look.

'It is *quite* bad,' Otis argued.

'If you head to cubicle three a doctor will see you very soon,' the receptionist said, doing a reasonably good job of neither staring nor squealing at the brownies,

I did as I was told; there were some people it was never sensible to argue with – and medical receptionists were near the top of the list. I plonked myself down on a plastic chair in the cubicle, pulled out my phone and passed it to Hester and Otis so they could watch cat videos to their heart's content.

I reached into my bag again, found the satellite phone and turned it on. As soon as it sprang to life, it buzzed with a message. I read it aloud. *The final key part has been located in Dundee by Humphrey Bridger. Only two teams will proceed to Loch Arkaig. My commiserations to the other teams but my congratulations on a good hunt. My best wishes to you all. Nigel.*

Hester was already jabbing at my phone, but Otis gave me a sorrowful look. 'I'm sorry, Daisy. It's all my fault.'

'Don't be daft. It's not your fault – it's not anyone's fault.' I smiled at him. 'Winning was always a long shot. We tried our best and we should be proud of what we achieved.'

Hester didn't look up. 'I am not proud. I hate losing. In fact, I think blaming Otis for this is an excellent idea.' She sniffed loudly, then sprang back half a foot and tumbled through the air with a startled expression as the phone started to ring.

I gazed at the unknown number on the screen. Eventually curiosity got the better of me and I picked it up to answer it, half-expecting to hear an automated voice telling me I'd won a scammy competition – but it wasn't.

'I'm assuming,' Hugo drawled, without bothering to say hello, 'that the reason you're not here in Wales is because you're in Dundee.'

'How did you get this number?' I asked irritably.

He ignored my question. 'And that means that you worked out where the key part was and still let Humphrey get the better of you. *Humphrey!*'

So said the man who was in the wrong country. 'Is there a reason why you're calling?'

'I wanted to pass on my heartfelt commiserations. It was Sir Nigel who gave me your number – I didn't get hold of it through nefarious means.'

I snorted. 'Given that I didn't give Sir Nigel permission to pass my number to you, then it *was* nefarious. We both know that you're only calling to gloat. Heartfelt commiserations? As if. You're probably throwing a party as we speak.'

'I thought we had a truce. We're supposed to be friends now, Daisy.'

'Friendly rivals,' I corrected. 'There's a difference.'

He was silent for a moment. 'If you say so.'

'I just did.' I bit my tongue and grimaced. I was in danger of becoming a very sore loser. 'Sorry.'

'You're as competitive as I am.' Hugo sounded as if he approved. 'You know, if you weren't so caught up in spider's silk, you'd have done a whole lot better. It messes with your brain.'

Tell that to six brownies, two goblins, a leprechaun, a troll and a damned unicorn. I counted to ten in my head before replying as pleasantly as I could, 'Whatever the reason, you can rest easy knowing that I'm out of your hair for good now.'

'Sure. Because I'm going to be standing opposite Humphrey Bridger at noon tomorrow when the location of the gold is revealed. Going up against him is like taking candy from a baby. At least you provided some decent competition.' He actually sounded like he meant it.

I softened a little. 'Humphrey and Eleanor might surprise you. They got this far.'

'As if.' Hugo paused. 'Listen, Daisy, I wanted to ask you if—'

The cubicle curtain was pulled back and a white-coated woman with a friendly face smiled in at me. 'I'm Doctor Flanagan.'

'Gotta go,' I interrupted. 'It's been nice knowing you and all that.'

'Wait. Daisy, I—'

I ended the call. That would probably be the last time I'd

speak to Hugo Pemberville, although no doubt I'd see his irritatingly handsome face on *The One Show* again before too long.

I ignored the odd tug in my chest and sheepishly held out my left hand for Dr Flanagan. I needed to get fixed up; I didn't like the odds of finding a new job in the real world with only one hand.

~

WHEN I WALKED out of the hospital with my hand dressed in pristine white bandages and a bucketload of painkillers that I didn't need yet, the sky was darkening and the first threads of night were making their way across the country.

The prospect of riding the motorbike with only one hand didn't fill me with joy. I'd managed on the way here, but now that I was covered in bandages it wouldn't be easy. I could hardly leave the bike here, though; I had to get it back to Jamila in Derby at some point soon.

I nibbled my bottom lip and considered. Perhaps if I pitched my tent somewhere for the night, I'd be able to remove some of the bandages tomorrow morning. That would make things easier.

As soon as I said as much to the brownies, they started bickering again. 'This is all your fault,' Hester complained to her brother yet again. 'If it weren't for you, Daisy would be on her way to becoming rich. She could afford a hotel.'

'We both decided to cross the salt and attack the pavilion, Hester,' Otis snapped. 'I didn't make the decision alone.'

'You're a nincompoop.'

'Am not!'

'You are! If you hadn't been so afraid to steal a teeny-weeny little key, we wouldn't have been delayed. You're a pathetic excuse for a brownie.'

I glared at her. 'Stop bullying your brother, Hester. We've been through all this before.'

Her eyes widened. 'Bullying? I'm not bullying him! I'm merely stating facts!'

I glanced at Otis, who was flitting from side to side by my shoulder. To be fair, he didn't look intimidated by Hester, merely exasperated. I frowned at him. Then an odd thought tugged at me and I took a step back. Hmm.

'Am I bullying you, Otis?' Hester demanded, in a tone of voice that was aggressive enough to answer the question.

'You're certainly annoying me, Hester,' he replied.

Hester turned to me. 'See? I'm not bullying him, I'm only annoying him. And I'm allowed to do that because I'm his sister – it's my *job* to annoy him. He annoys *me* often enough!'

When I didn't say anything, Hester jabbed my nose. 'Daisy? Did you hear me?'

'Leave her alone,' Otis said. 'She's busy working out how she'll ride a motorbike all the way back to Edinburgh when she's only got one hand.'

My tongue darted out and wet my lips. 'We're not going to Edinburgh,' I said slowly. 'Not yet.'

'I don't want to camp in Dundee,' Hester whined.

I shook my head. 'We're not doing that either.'

The brownies stared at me. 'A hotel then?' Hester asked hopefully. 'Five star? With butler service?'

I smiled. 'Afraid not. We'll still be camping, but we won't be doing it here. We're going to Loch Arkaig.'

'Yessss!' Hester pumped the air with her fists. 'You're going after the treasure anyway, aren't you? We're going to get that gold!'

By contrast, Otis looked horrified. 'But ... but ... but ... that's not the rules. We're not part of the treasure hunt anymore. The gold isn't ours. Only Humphrey and Eleanor and Hugo and his Primes can look for it.'

'Says who?' Hester sneered. 'Nigel Hannigan? The gold doesn't belong to him. Daisy is allowed to find it, no matter what he says. He's not her boss.' She nodded at me. 'This is a sneaky, desperate move, Daisy Carter, and I like it. I like it a lot. This will show Hugo Pemberville who's in charge.' She shrugged. 'He'll probably go back to hating Daisy's guts and she'll never get into his bone zone, but there are other men. It'll be fine.'

'Daisy,' Otis said, 'you can't do this. Hugo will hate you and every high elf in the country will believe you've got no honour. They'll be right – plus, *they'll* all hate you. Sir Nigel will never invite you to take part in another treasure hunt. And what about Humphrey and Eleanor? They're nice people. They're our friends. They—'

I held up my hands. 'I'm not planning to steal the Loch Arkaig gold. Not yet, anyway. I only want to watch what goes on.'

This time both Hester and Otis squinted. 'Eh? Why?'

I tapped the side of my nose. 'I'll tell you later.' I glanced at the motorbike. Riding one-handed was daunting but not impossible. All I had to do was take my time.

I winked at the brownies. 'Buckle up, darlings. This ain't over yet.'

CHAPTER
TWENTY-SEVEN

The excess of spider's silk coursing through my system started to wear off soon after midnight. Between my fear of running out completely and the concern over overdosing until my body ceased to function, I hadn't dared take any more. Instead, I'd been swallowing the painkillers that Dr Flanagan had given to me as if they were sweets.

At least I'd made it to Loch Arkaig before the worst of the pain began, and I had coped with riding the bike one-handed. In fact, it was easier than I'd expected. Unfortunately, after hiding the bike in some scrub, traipsing up a hill until I found a spot to hunker down and spy on proceedings and spending several hours lying flat in damp undergrowth, I was no longer particularly enamoured of my decision to come to the loch.

'Be a treasure hunter, they said,' I muttered aloud. I gazed at the stunning vista with its multi-coloured hills, pretty loch and gleaming blue sky dotted with fluffy clouds. Bah. I was wet and uncomfortable and the pain in my hand was almost unbearable. 'It'll be fun, they said.' I pouted.

'You're not a treasure hunter any longer,' Otis said mournfully in my ear. 'Now you're just a cheat.'

'There's nothing wrong with cheating,' Hester declared in my other ear. 'As long as you win.'

'Shh,' I said. 'You need to be quiet.'

'We're in the middle of nowhere,' Hester said. 'Who will hear us? A sheep?'

I pointed down the slope. The brownies might not have spotted them, but there was a group of people about a mile away. They were walking around the edge of Loch Arkaig, making a beeline for the northern edge that was directly in my eyeline.

I narrowed my eyes. Hugo was at the front of the pack with Sir Nigel next to him. The rest of the Primes were trailing behind, followed by Humphrey and Eleanor, who was waving her hands first towards the glittering blue waters of the Loch and then to the undulating hills on the other side. *Yes, Eleanor. It's pretty here*, I thought. *Stop dilly-dallying*.

My right leg was starting to cramp up and I shifted slightly though I didn't dare move much. Although I was a reasonable distance from the group, I could still be spotted. I knew it wouldn't go well for me if I was.

I kept my head down but I stayed focused. There wasn't long to go.

'I wonder what they're talking about,' Hester whispered. 'It'd be good to know. Shall I fly down and eavesdrop?'

'No, Hester!' Otis gasped.

'They might see you,' I said mildly. 'You should stay here.' But she was right: it *would* be good to hear what they were talking about.

I tilted my head to one side then, with as much care and attention as I could muster, I gently used air magic to create a breeze heading in my direction. I had to be cautious; I couldn't permit any of the people below to sense my magic or to grow suspicious. But when their voices drifted upwards, carried to my ears by the magicked wind, I knew the risk had been worth it.

'I'm glad you've changed your mind about Daisy,' Sir Nigel said.

My stomach dropped. They were talking about me? I strained to hear Hugo's reply. 'I've not changed my mind. She's still untrustworthy and she's still dangerous. Spider's silk shouldn't be messed with – and I'm convinced there's a great deal more to Daisy Carter than meets the eye. There's a lot she's not telling us.'

I wrinkled my nose. I was an open book; I wasn't dangerous or untrustworthy in the slightest.

'Wait until he finds out what you're doing now,' Otis murmured. 'What will he think then?'

My grimace deepened.

'Has she told you why she takes spider's silk?' Sir Nigel asked.

'Does it matter?'

Sir Nigel didn't answer. Hugo sighed. 'She did better in the hunt than I expected. It's only bad luck that she didn't get two of the three key parts. She's resourceful and intelligent. And...' He sighed and didn't finish his sentence.

'You really like her, don't you?' Sir Nigel asked quietly.

I realised suddenly that I didn't want to hear Hugo's answer; maybe it was better not to know. I squeezed my eyes shut and re-directed the breeze towards Humphrey and Eleanor.

'I guess you're right. All you can do is try.' Eleanor was in the middle of a conversation and she seemed hesitant, which immediately put me on edge. Try what?

Humphrey responded cheerfully, 'Absolutely, my dear! It would be the fairest thing to do, and I know that Hugs would appreciate equality.' He paused. 'But maybe it would be better if he heard it from you rather than me. He likes you.'

Eleanor sounded surprised. 'Does he?'

'Everyone likes you.'

Humphrey was probably right. I listened to them for several moments, hoping to learn more, but their chatter drifted to the vitally important topic of what to have for lunch. Apparently smoked salmon was passé these days and smashed avocado was the way to go. Whatever.

I tuned out and waited until they all reached the tip of the loch. As expected, Sir Nigel took the lead. Finally, he motioned to a small patch of land at the water's edge that looked no different to any other spot.

I redirected my air magic again so I could hear their conversation. As I did, Hugo's head jerked up. I stiffened. Shit – I'd clearly not been delicate enough with my touch. I pressed myself further into the undergrowth and held my breath. I was too nervous even to cross my fingers. I had to stay very, very still.

'Hugo?' I heard Becky ask. 'Is there a problem?'

I counted to six before he answered. 'No,' he said. 'Everything is fine.'

I swallowed hard and relaxed slightly, though I chastised myself. As a high elf, his magical skills were far beyond mine. I couldn't grow complacent.

Sir Nigel took out a pocket watch. 'It is midday,' he declared. 'Bring forth your key parts and let us reveal the location of the gold.'

Becky and another Prime stepped forward and crouched down to place their sections on the patch of the ground. Humphrey passed his to Eleanor and nudged her. She twitched and cleared her throat. 'Uh, before we do this,' she said nervously, 'there's something I'd like to suggest.'

They all turned to her. Even from this distance, I saw her cheeks redden. 'Um, so, this isn't about whether the Arkaig treasure will be found. It will turn up very soon, right?'

'That's the plan,' Sir Nigel said. 'The British Museum is already preparing to receive several chests of gold coins.'

Hugo shrugged and Humphrey smiled encouragingly.

'This is a competition to see who can find it first,' Eleanor continued. 'But shouldn't it be a fair competition?'

I raised my eyebrows.

'Are you suggesting that it's not been fair up to now?' Hugo growled.

'No! It's been fair! I'm not saying that at all!' Eleanor sounded panicked and she glanced at Humphrey for help.

He said reassuringly, 'Of course it's been fair. I think Eleanor means something else.'

She nodded vigorously. 'Going forward, I think it'll only continue to be fair if the numbers are even.' She pointed towards the Primes. 'I mean, there are lots of you and only two of us.'

'You can bring as many people as you wish,' Hugo said. 'Nobody is stopping you.'

Eleanor scratched her arms and seemed to fold into herself but, to give her her due, she didn't give up. 'Everyone knows I'm not the one who's the treasure hunter here, it's Humphrey. Maybe the final part of the treasure hunt should be just Humphrey and Hugo. After all, you're the leaders of both teams who've got this far. This competition isn't about who wins the prize money, it's about who wins the hunt and is the best treasure hunter at the end of the day.'

'*Mano a mano*,' Humphrey declared. 'Splendid. What do you say, Hugs old chap? Then it's not down to who has the better resources or the most people. Whoever gets to the Arkaig treasure first is the greatest hunter, hands down.'

I was too far away to read Hugo's expression accurately, but I hoped he'd tell Humphrey to piss off. It was the sensible option. Instead, he shrugged. 'Sure. You versus me. No tricks. No people. Nothing more. Us two against each other.'

I smacked my forehead, wishing that I could smack Hugo instead. Idiot – he was letting his arrogance get the better of him. At least now I knew I'd made the right decision in coming here – I hadn't been sure before but now I was certain. It was the only thing that made any sense.

I sucked a deep breath into my lungs. Humphrey Bridger was a charlatan and he'd lulled every person down there into such a false sense of security that they couldn't see it. Hugo thought that *I* was the dangerous one but it was Humphrey he should be worrying about. It was Humphrey we should *all* be worrying about.

If it hadn't been for Hester and Otis, my suspicions might never have been raised. Otis genuinely wasn't remotely intimidated by Hester; he displayed not a single flicker of fear despite her harsh tone and often nasty words. But when I'd watched Humphrey and Greenwood together, there had been no denying Greenwood's fear. At first I'd put it down to anxiety that his activities at his summer pavilion prison would come to light, but now I reckoned it was something else entirely.

Greenwood had been frightened of *Humphrey* – in fact, not frightened but terrified. Why would a rich, famous, powerful man who happily trapped magical creatures and held them prisoner, be scared of someone like Humphrey? It didn't make sense – unless there was more to Humphrey than met the eye.

Eleanor had said that Greenwood and Humphrey were old school friends but they couldn't have been; Humphrey had told me himself that he'd gone to Eton, and my research showed that Greenwood was at Gordonstoun. They were both posh educational establishments but they were at opposite ends of the British Isles. It was a strange thing to lie about – unless there was a reason to lie.

Eleanor had said that Humphrey needed to win the treasure hunt, but little of what he did or said suggested that he cared about it. For goodness' sake, he'd wandered off for cocktails instead of participating in the search for the first part of the key. He must have known all along that he'd get a key part from Greenwood, so he'd leaned back and played the role of bumbling buffoon who got on with everyone. None of the other treasure hunters – me included – had given him a second thought.

He'd used Eleanor to persuade the Primes to drop out so now he only had Hugo to beat. Had he brought her along because she was sweet and naïve and helped embellish the fiction that he was like that, too? I should have realised that Humphrey was too fucking good to be true.

I didn't have all the answers yet and I didn't yet know everything that was going on, but I did know that the Loch Arkaig treasure was worth ten million pounds and Humphrey was not the man I'd thought he was. I strongly suspected that those two facts were linked.

'I don't understand,' Hester whispered, looking from my face to the group below us and back again. 'What's happening?'

'I'll explain later,' I hissed. 'For now, we need to pay attention.' She pouted but fell silent.

'Excellent!' Sir Nigel clapped his hands. 'I do so enjoy a good competition. Eleanor, would you be so kind as to add your key part to the others? Then we can see exactly where the Arkaig treasure is and, more importantly, who can be named as the greatest treasure hunter this country has to offer.'

I snorted. That was unnecessarily melodramatic. Eleanor, however, appeared moved and curtsied towards him as if he were some kind of prince. She walked forward, carrying the key part reverently in both her hands, then knelt down and held it up like a sacrifice to the gods. While everyone watched, she slowly lowered it into place before standing up and stepping back.

I'd expected a crack of thunder or an earthquake. Maybe a glowing light. Instead, nothing happened.

I stared at the assembled parts of the key from my hiding spot up in the hills. All the people below me were doing the same. Hester clicked her tongue. 'Disappointing.'

Otis was staring ahead rather than at the people below or at the reassembled key. His gaze was fixed on the centre of Loch Arkaig. 'It's a mirage,' he whispered. 'It has to be.'

I looked up. When I saw what he was talking about, I started to gape too. In the centre of the loch, hovering above the water, was a small island. That definitely hadn't been there before.

Hester jumped up and down. 'The treasure must be there! Let's go! Let's go now, before the others get there!'

I grabbed hold of her with one hand before she took off. 'Otis is right. That island's not real, it's an image of where we need to go to find the treasure. A sort of magical hologram'

'A holo ... what?'

'A mirage, right?' Otis beamed. 'I knew it!'

'How do you know it's not real?' Hester demanded. 'Until you reach it and check for yourself, you won't know whether it's there or not.'

'*I* know.' I grinned. 'I'd recognise that island anywhere. I know exactly where it is and it's not in the middle of Loch Arkaig.'

I glanced at the group below us again. They'd finally noticed the hovering 'island' too, and their backs were turned to me as they stared at it. Taking advantage of their distraction, I stood up and jogged to the summit of the hill before scrambling down the other side.

'Come on!' I called to the brownies. 'We're going now! We're heading straight to Edinburgh as fast as we can!'

I grinned. I wasn't done treasure hunting yet.

CHAPTER

TWENTY-EIGHT

T he tidal isle of Cramond is less than a mile from Edinburgh in the grey waters of the Firth of Forth. At low tide it's perfectly accessible on foot, a ten-minute stroll across a stone walkway that stretches from the mainland to the uninhabited island. At high tide it's an entirely different story; as soon as the sea comes in the walkway is submerged and, in theory, the only way to leave the island is to swim or wait until the water recedes.

That would be a very bad idea. The vicious selkies that inhabit the Firth of Forth return to the area at high tide – and woe betide anyone who comes face to face with them. Even the hardiest of fishermen stay well away. Selkies are mesmerisingly beautiful, with huge, liquid, doe eyes and sleek grey fur; they're also highly territorial and very efficient killers. Every year there are grim tales of hapless wanderers who get caught by the tide and try to remain on Cramond until it's safe to walk back. The selkies believe the island belongs to them as much as the waters around it do. Often there are little more than gnawed bones left for grieving families to bury.

I'd never been close to a selkie and I'd never wanted to be.

'It's far too dangerous to cross now,' Otis said as he flitted along the shoreline. 'We have to wait.'

I looked up from the text message on my phone. 'We can't wait. At best we're probably only an hour in front of Hugo and Humphrey. We have to get to the island before they do.'

'The tide is coming in! They won't be able to reach Cramond for hours either.'

'But we can't let them see us,' I reasoned. 'So we have to go now to get there before they do and before they know we're here.'

'Then we'll be trapped on Cramond!' Otis shrieked. 'With the selkies!'

'I don't often agree with my brother,' Hester said, 'but on this occasion I think he's right. We can't risk it.'

I wasn't worried. 'I've been to Cramond at low tide before and I know the layout. There's an old World War II lookout that we can hide in. The selkies won't get to us there. As long as they don't scent us, we'll be fine.'

'Otis and I will be fine – we can fly away,' she muttered. 'You'll be selkie food. And how will you transport the gold away without being seen?' She frowned doubtfully at my arms. 'You can't carry it. You're not that strong.'

I flexed my muscles. 'I'm stronger than I look. Come on! The longer we wait, the harder this will be.' I marched towards the walkway. There was already an inch of sea water covering it.

'Daisy—'

I stopped listening. This wasn't the time for qualms. 'Ready,' I whispered under my breath. 'Set.' I steeled myself. 'Go!'

I took off and jogged towards the small island. I couldn't move too fast for fear of slipping on seaweed but neither could I waste time. For the first fifty metres or so it was reasonably easy going, although my feet and the hem of my jeans were soaked within the first few seconds.

I debated summoning a surge of water magic to propel the water away from me, but I knew the approaching selkies would sense it and immediately head towards me. Besides, no magic in the world was powerful enough to completely halt the tide. Even a high elf couldn't hold back the sea – King Canute had taught us that.

I kept going, splashing onwards, while the sea rushed in faster than I'd expected. By the time I reached the midway point of the causeway, it had reached my calves. It was icy cold and the ever-present wind in this part of Scotland had grown stronger. I gritted my teeth and carried on. As long as I got to Cramond before I was completely submerged and forced to swim, I was pretty sure the selkies wouldn't notice me.

Otis buzzed around my head. 'Come on, Daisy! Go faster!'

'If she goes faster, they'll be more likely to notice her when they swim in with the tide,' Hester hissed.

'I don't like this. I don't like this. I don't like this.' Otis zipped from side to side. Then he screamed abruptly. 'There's one!'

I stiffened and my blood ran cold as I saw a black shape rising out of the water. I reached for Gladys, determined to defend myself if nothing else. I'd thought I'd have longer; I'd thought I could to get to the island.

'It's a fucking rock, you nincompoop!' Hester yelled.

My heart thumping painfully against my ribcage, I stared at it for a second before I realised she was right. I exhaled – then I tried to move faster. There is nothing like the threat of mortal danger to encourage a person to speed up. With the sea water now at my knees, however, I couldn't maintain the pace.

I tore my eyes away from the surface of the water – scanning for the sudden appearance of selkies wouldn't help – and focused on the scrap of land ahead. The sea sloshed around my legs and I was shivering, but forward momentum would get me there. I could do this. I knew I could.

In the distance, there was a juddering scream followed by another and then another. The selkies were on their way back, swimming with the tide as it rose and rose. I gritted my teeth and ploughed on, quashing my anxiety as the water reached my thighs, putting one foot after the other and forcing my way onwards.

And then, just when I thought I wouldn't make it, the sea level dropped. I thrust forward, gasping as I finally reached the rocky shore of Cramond Island itself.

It had been a far more strenuous effort than I'd expected but I resisted the urge to collapse and catch my breath. I needed to get to higher ground and duck out of sight before the shoal of selkies swam past and realised that the island wasn't empty.

'There's the path!' Hester said, urgency colouring her voice.

I nodded and scrambled upwards, ignoring the pebbles that lay closest to the shore. Past them, I was on soft sand so I took the time to scuff away my footprints to ensure there was no sign of me. There were several footprints left by others; the trail led up the beach to a narrow path through the undergrowth and back again. Although the owners of those footprints had already departed, I smoothed them over as well. Discretion was the name of the game now.

I left the beach and plunged up the pathway. Stinging nettles and brambles caught at my skin, occasionally tearing at the bandages on my injured hand. I grimaced; the bandages were already damp from the sea spray and the last thing I needed was for infection to set in. I raised my arm high in the air and continued awkwardly, like a school child in a classroom desperate to be chosen to answer their teacher's question. I guessed that so far my career as a treasure hunter had indeed been an education, albeit one fraught with danger and fool-hardy choices.

The ugly cement lookout was on the other side of the island, facing the sea rather than Edinburgh and the mainland shore. That was hardly surprising, but it was annoying because I wouldn't be able to watch Hugo and Humphrey arrive. However my main priority was staying safe from the selkies so I headed straight for it.

As I crested the highest point on the island and glanced to my left, my breath caught in my chest.

'There,' Otis breathed, as awestruck as I was. 'There is the gold.'

Down below, in a small dip surrounded by dandelions, were three wooden chests. The old magic that surrounded them was potent enough to make my eyes water. It must have taken incredible power to conceal them so effectively for centuries. When the key was re-formed at Loch Arkaig, it wasn't only the mirage of Cramond that had appeared: so had the antique chests filled with Jacobean gold.

I licked my lips, a surge of triumphant glee filling my veins, but I didn't go towards them and take a peek. This wasn't the time to have a rummage.

I turned away and looked towards the old lookout post instead. It wasn't perfect but it would have to do. Ignoring my wet jeans flapping around my legs, I jogged down and went in through the entrance at the side.

It wasn't a comfortable place to rest – there was nothing inside except the dirt on the ground, a few random sticks and stones and a pervasive smell of urine – but it would conceal me. I peered out of the small viewing slots set into the walls. I couldn't see any selkies in the open water but I knew they were out there.

I beckoned to Otis and Hester and drew them in close, then

stood in the very centre of the lookout and concentrated on my air magic. It stilled the breeze around the lookout and created an invisible barrier through which my scent wouldn't travel. It wouldn't be enough to fool any selkie that came close, and it certainly wouldn't prevent them from coming inside to find me, but hopefully it would be enough to keep my presence secret.

All we had to do now was hunker down, stay quiet, and wait for low tide to arrive yet again.

I'D ESTIMATED around five hours before the selkies returned to deeper water and the stone walkway on the opposite side of Cramond Island reappeared as the tide turned. I wasn't far wrong; after four-and-a-half hours of shivering while dusk and then nightfall fell, I heard the echoing hoots of the selkies rippling across the water as they swam away. If any of them had come onto the island, they hadn't ventured near me. It was almost an anti-climax. Almost.

I emerged from my hideout and stretched my aching limbs, then cracked my knuckles in anticipation. It wouldn't be long before Hugo and Humphrey arrived from the mainland.

I sent Otis and Hester off to check; they could flit close enough to see if my competitors were on their way without being noticed. After they'd gone, I headed for the treasure chests and finally gave rein to my eagerness to see what they contained.

The chests, with their warped oak and rusted hinges, certainly looked old. Avoiding the dandelions, I circled around them; I didn't want to trample on anything and leave a trace of myself.

After three complete circuits, I inhaled deeply and reached for the nearest chest. It was fastened by an ancient-looking padlock. It appeared to be a simple mechanism. Concentrating hard, I sent a burst of water magic towards it and the jet of water did its work. There was a faint snick as the lock burst open. I grinned and flipped open the chest.

It was full to the brim. Awe-struck, I stared at the shimmering gold coins before reaching in and picking one up. When I held it up, its shiny edge caught in the moonlight. I hefted it in my hands then raised it to my mouth, biting down on a corner in the same way I'd seen people do in films. Satisfied it was what I'd expected, I tossed the coin into the chest where it made a pleasing clink. Excellent.

I reached across, closed the chest and ensured the padlock was once again in place.

There was a rustle of leaves as Hester and Otis reappeared. 'They're on their way!' Hester screeched. 'Hugo is in the lead. He's going to get to the treasure first!'

Otis buzzed his anxiety. 'We can still return to the old lookout and hide there until all this is over. Nobody will ever know we were here.'

'It's too late for that.' I smiled. 'I was here first. I win.'

'You're out of the competition!'

I shrugged then spun on my heel and headed for a clump of bushes on the slope above the chests. I'd hide there for now; between the thick foliage and the dark sky it would be safe enough, though I doubted I'd stay hidden for long.

I made myself comfortable and adjusted my position until I had a clear view. The brownies joined me, their tiny bodies vibrating with anticipation. It was as well they did because seconds later I heard the crash of approaching footsteps.

Even without Hester's warning, I'd expected Hugo to be first. Humphrey had never shown himself to be particularly fast or strong, and Hugo was an experienced treasure hunter who moved quickly and seemed to have a nose for precious metal.

Maybe, I thought sardonically, that was what life was like when you were a high elf. The rest of us smelled flowers and shit. The likes of Hugo Pemberville smelled gold.

I was right. Before too long his familiar figure appeared at the top of the gentle slope opposite my hiding spot. His blue eyes immediately lit on the chests and a dimple formed in his cheek as he grinned to himself. My heart skipped a beat and I scowled. Then Hugo strode down to the chests and laid his hand on top of the nearest one, his expression full of triumph. Yeah, yeah. He'd won. Or at least he thought he had.

He wasn't as far in front as I'd expected because moments later Humphrey appeared. I held my breath, watching carefully as he gazed down at Hugo. What would he do now?

'You won, old chap!' Humphrey called out. 'Congratulations!'

Hmmm. He didn't sound upset. I pursed my lips. Maybe I'd been wrong. Maybe I'd tied together a few pieces of circumstantial evidence and ended up at entirely the wrong conclusion.

'Thank you,' Hugo said.

'In the end you were too good for me.' Humphrey smiled. 'I should have expected it. You're the greatest treasure hunter this country has ever seen.'

Perched on my shoulder, Hester let out a tiny snort. It was barely audible – but it was enough. Hugo's head jerked up, his eyes piercing the foliage with such laser focus that I was certain he could see me.

Humphrey, by contrast, paid no attention to my hiding place. 'Unfortunately for you, Hugs old chap,' he continued, 'I'm the greatest actor.' He reached into his coat and in one swift movement pulled out a gun. He raised it towards Hugo's back.

Oh shit. So I'd been right then.

CHAPTER

TWENTY-NINE

I didn't hesitate. I flung myself out of the bushes and threw my entire weight at Hugo, smacking into him and bringing him down to the ground in a tangle of limbs. A split second later, the gun went off above our heads.

'Fuck!' Humphrey exploded.

I caught a fleeting glimpse of Hugo's eyes, which were wide with shock as he stared at me. Then he shoved me away and bounded up to face Humphrey, blasting him with air magic so that he was thrown backwards.

'Take that, you bastard!' Otis shrieked, shaking his fists at Humphrey who was writhing on the ground, blinking and grimacing with pain.

Humphrey released another shot, sending it wildly into the sky where it startled a passing seagull but did no actual harm. I clambered awkwardly to my feet and rubbed my eyes while Hugo flung out more magic, snapping together enough molecules to form a plume of water that knocked the gun from Humphrey's hand. He walked over, picked it up and frowned at it before ejecting the ammunition clip and tossing it to the side.

'You're welcome,' I said pointedly.

'What the hell is going on?' Hugo muttered under his breath.

I'd thought he was smarter than that. 'Obviously I just saved your life.' I gestured to the treasure chests. 'And I got here first, so I win. I'm the greatest treasure hunter. Not,' I added with satisfaction, 'you.'

'Daisy,' Hugo said, running a hand through his hair, 'you—'

'—are a fucking bitch,' Humphrey interrupted. Hugo and I glanced towards him; he was still on the ground, flat on his back and red-faced.

I raised an eyebrow. 'Language, Humphrey!' I scolded. 'How very shocking.'

Hugo stared at me. His expression was still confused but I could see that he was starting to work it out. 'When did you get here?' he asked.

'Before the last high tide,' I said smugly. 'I had an inkling that something like this would happen.'

'Daisy,' Otis whispered.

'How?' Hugo asked.

I grinned. 'Well,' I began, 'it started when—'

Otis's voice grew more insistent. 'Daisy!'

Hugo and I glanced at him. His face was strikingly pale as he raised a shaking arm to point at Humphrey. I turned around – and when I saw what was happening, my stomach sank to the soles of my feet.

Humphrey was still on the ground. I'd assumed that being knocked down plus losing his gun had neutralised him, but I couldn't have been more wrong. Something was happening to him. Something very, very wrong.

His body was twisting and jerking as strange red shapes danced across his skin. Bizarre lumps were travelling across his forearms and neck, and one was bulging upwards, pulsating beneath his cheekbone. Another appeared at his right hand, threatening to burst through his skin itself. An inky dark cloud was forming in front of him. It wasn't a random puff of smoke; it appeared to be arranging itself into some sort of symbol.

'Daisy, get back,' Hugo said desperately, his voice low in warning.

I continued to stare as snaking tendrils slithered out of the strange cloud towards us. Otis yelped and flapped out of the way but Hester was braver. She flew towards Humphrey to attack him before being thrust back by some sort of invisible force.

'I said get back!' Hugo repeated. 'We have to get out of here!' He grabbed my hand and yanked me away. Seconds later, we were running through the bush where I'd been hiding.

'I don't understand,' I gasped. 'What's happening? What *is* he?' I glanced over my shoulder. The smoky snakes were speeding through the air, following us.

'Just run!' Hugo yelled. 'We have to get out of here!'

There was a scream from behind and I knew instantly that it had come from Hester. I snatched my hand away from Hugo, turned and drew Gladys. The dark cloud was right there and there was no sign of the little brownie – she'd been swallowed up.

I raised the sword and sliced ineptly at the cloud. Gladys hummed and her hilt grew hot in my hand. From somewhere to my left Otis cried out, 'Hester! Hester!'

Hugo muttered something then I felt a blast of magic as he threw a bolt of air at the cloud. It pulled back, ejecting Hester with a guttural gargle as if vomiting her up.

I grabbed her in my bandaged left hand, crying out in pain as I forced my fingers to hold her. The black cloud stretched out, circling me and Hugo, but still I slashed at it with Gladys in my right hand.

Hugo attacked it again with air magic. I combined my magic

with his to do the same but it wasn't enough. Our united efforts could slow the approach of the dark mass but we couldn't stop it.

My movements became more frantic. I desperately waved Gladys, jabbing and slashing, sending out bolt after bolt of magic, but then the cloud enveloped me. I felt Hugo reach for me for a final time, his arm wrapping around me as if to protect me. It was too late; nothing would protect any of us now.

I coughed and spluttered, clawing at my throat and desperately trying to throw more magic at the thing. A moment later, my knees buckled. I heard a dim groan from Hugo, and then my body slammed into the ground and I lost consciousness.

I NOTICED THE PAIN FIRST. Every part of me hurt. My poor hand was the worst, throbbing in agony, and I moaned softly. Fuck. I was still alive. But *fuck*.

'You only have yourself to blame for this, Daisy.'

Humphrey. I opened one eye and squinted at him. It was still dark so I'd not been unconscious for that long.

He looked even more menacing than before. The bulges beneath his skin remained but the strange twisting shapes had merged across every visible part of his body. He blazed scarlet from head to toe. 'What are you?' I whispered.

It was Hugo, slumped next to me, who answered. 'He's human,' he said dully. 'But he's using blood magic.'

Blood magic? I struggled to understand. I'd never heard of such a thing. That was what happened when you were self-taught; there were vast gaps in your knowledge that sometimes seemed impossible to fill.

'Good old Hugs is right,' Humphrey said cheerfully. 'Those spells cost me a lot of money on the black market, and they weren't easy to track down or to master. But I think you'll agree that the effort was worth it.' He pointed and I realised that Hugo and I were still encircled by the ring of black smoke. 'You two are going nowhere.'

I stiffened as alarm flooded through me. Humphrey clapped a hand to his mouth. 'Oh! Pardon me. I meant the four of you.' He pointed to the ground by my feet. Lying there, breathing but otherwise unmoving, were Otis and Hester.

'You cumbubbling bastard,' I breathed.

Humphrey tutted. 'I told you already, you only have yourself to blame. Their deaths will be your fault, Daisy, as will be your own. If you hadn't come here, you would never have been involved.' He glanced at Hugo. 'You were right. You can't trust anyone who's addicted to spider's silk.'

I stared at him. 'I don't think I'm the untrustworthy one around here.'

He barked a surprised laugh. 'Ha! Good point, good point.' He grinned. 'I liked you, Daisy, and I really wish you hadn't come here. Although after Eleanor told me that you were at Greenwood's place, I suppose there are no more loose ends for me to worry about. I can blame Hugo's death on you and everyone will believe me.

'I've already moved the treasure. The two of you will be eaten by the selkies and no-one will be any the wiser. It's handy that those old Jacobites hid the gold here because it makes my life so much easier. I can maintain that the gold was lost with you and, instead of a paltry fifty-grand reward, I'll get the money I deserve for all this hard work. The British Museum doesn't need the gold but I do. Ten million pounds will do me nicely. And nobody will believe that poor old useless Humphrey was involved in your deaths.'

He smiled then his expression became earnest. 'It's not personal, so don't feel hard done by. In fact, it's rather nice that you'll die together – you clearly have a thing for each other.'

I growled, 'We do not.'

Humphrey chuckled. 'Stubborn to the last, Daisy Carter. Well done.' He raised his head and looked away. 'Well, the tide is returning so it is time for me to leave. I hope for your sake that your endings are swift.'

He bent down and reached for Gladys with his fingertips. As soon as he touched her hilt, he hissed in pain and drew back. He glanced at me. 'Good grief. Is that a magic sword? Bound to you? Of all people?'

'Fuck off, Humphrey,' I muttered.

He tapped his mouth thoughtfully. 'You know, I think that's exactly what I will do.' He kicked Gladys further away. 'Toodle-pip. I'll be sure to say some nice words about you at your funerals.'

'You don't really believe you'll get away with this?' Hugo asked.

Humphrey smiled sadly. 'I already have, dear chap. I already have.' And then he turned on his heel and walked away.

I reached for Hester and Otis and scooped them up carefully in my uninjured hand so I could examine them. They were unconscious but I couldn't see any obvious injuries. 'Are they okay?' Hugo asked gruffly.

'I don't know. I think so, but they're both out for the count.'

'The effects from that blood-magic cloud will probably be more severe for them, given their size. They'll come round soon.'

'In time to be eaten by selkies, you mean?'

Hugo scowled. 'You got here before the last high tide and you managed to avoid them.'

'That was before I was shoved into some sort of magical barrier with you for company,' I said with a derisive sniff.

'You're talking as if this is all my fault. If you suspected Humphrey was up to something, why didn't you come to me?'

I rolled my eyes. 'Because you'd have believed me?' Sarcasm dripped from every word. 'I didn't have any proof, only suspicions.' And I'd only expected Humphrey to steal the treasure, not attempt murder. Now I realised that our deaths were the only way he'd get away with his theft. I'd been as naïve as Hugo – well, almost.

I asked aloud, 'What would you have said if I'd grabbed a word in your shell-like ear and suggested Humphrey was planning to double-cross you?'

'I'd have listened.'

'No, you wouldn't.'

Hugo sighed. 'Alright. I'd have been sceptical.'

'Because I'm a pathetic junkie who can't be trusted.'

He didn't reply but I caught the flash of guilt in his expression. I changed the subject. Sniping at Hugo wouldn't help any of us escape. 'You're a high elf. Can't you use your superior magic to get us out of here?'

Hugo flung out a burst of air magic followed by flames and water, but every attempted enchantment thudded uselessly against the ring of black smoke that surrounded us despite the power that rippled from each attempt. 'I've already tried.'

I dropped Hester and Otis gently into my coat pocket, stood up and dusted myself off. 'There's still earth magic,' I said.

Hugo's eyes met mine. 'I wasn't sure if you'd notice that I'd not tried that yet.'

'I'm not a complete idiot.'

'No,' he said quietly. 'You're not.' He held out his hand. 'Here. If we work together, we can probably manage it.'

I gazed at his outstretched hand then reached across and took it. His fingers closed around mine with reassuring warmth. 'There?' I asked, gesturing towards a barren scrap in front of us.

'It's as good as any spot,' Hugo replied. 'On a count of three. One, two...'

We both directed a massive thrust of earth magic downwards. I felt my magic twist with his, plaiting together before slamming into the ground.

There was a loud rumble and I stumbled sideways,. Hugo's arm shot out and he grabbed my waist to help me stay upright. I coughed and waved away the clouds of dust. 'Thanks,' I muttered.

'No problem.' He gave me a long look.

'What?'

'Your magic is strong.'

I snorted. 'For a low elf, you mean.'

His response was instant. 'For any elf.'

Eventually I ripped my eyes away and looked down at the hole we'd created. 'I suppose your magic is quite strong too,' I said, offering a grudging compliment in return.

He grinned suddenly and his dimple reappeared. 'Ladies first?'

I grinned back. 'I thought you'd never ask.' Then I jumped feet first into the hole.

It took five more bursts of controlled earth magic before we managed to finagle our escape by burrowing through the earth beneath Humphrey's blood-magic ring of smoke. When we finally pulled ourselves out at the other side, I was panting with effort and Hugo's brow was slick with sweat.

Unfortunately, we weren't yet free. No sooner had we exchanged glances of exhausted satisfaction than the air was rent with a bone-juddering screech. The tide was high and the selkies were returning – and this time they'd sensed us.

There was no need for words. I grabbed Gladys and gestured to the left-hand path. Hugo nodded and we plunged towards it, running for the supposed safety of the old lookout.

It was too late to make it to the mainland; we had to stay here until the tide turned yet again and this time that meant fending off the selkies.

We barrelled through the undergrowth, our feet pounding along the narrow dirt path, first up a small hill then down again. Dawn was approaching and the sky was already beginning to lighten, but daylight wouldn't provide a defence: we had to create one for ourselves.

As soon as the lookout came into view, I threw myself towards it with Hugo hot on my heels. We skidded inside and wasted no time. He half-closed his eyes and summoned up another magic circle, made of fire this time. I repeated my air magic spell, hoping it would make it harder for the selkies to find us as well as adding enough oxygen to keep the flames high. Then we backed into the centre of the lookout and waited.

We didn't have to wait for long.

The first selkie that appeared was massive. I'd been expecting something large, but nothing like as big as the creature that was coming towards us. It sniffed the air, keeping its distance from Hugo's fire, but it knew we were just beyond the flames. It knew that we had no way to escape.

It drew its lips back over its mouth, revealing a vast row of sharp yellow teeth. I hissed and pulled back.

'It's okay,' Hugo said. 'The fire will hold.'

From the focused look in the selkie's eyes, I wasn't so sure. I was even less sure when several others came into view. One by one they took up position around the flames until we were completely surrounded. I was absolutely certain they would remain there until Hugo's magic faltered; this was going to be a battle of attrition.

At my side, Gladys started to hum, a discordant sound that did nothing to ease my anxiety. 'Stop that,' I hissed.

'She wants blood,' Hugo said. 'She wants to fight.'

'We can't fight all of them,' I answered. 'Not if we want to win.' He didn't disagree.

One of the selkies screamed and the rest joined in until their chilling chorus echoed around us. I swallowed hard, reached for a spider's silk pill and tossed it into my mouth with shaky haste. One single lapse in concentration and we were done for. I was shivering with fear. I didn't want to be ripped apart. Suddenly I wasn't ready to die.

Hugo cleared his throat. 'My best friend was addicted to spider's silk.'

I jerked. 'Excuse me?'

'Philip Farcastle. We grew up together and for a time we were inseparable. Then he met a girl, a low elf like you.' His voice wasn't judgmental or scathing, he just sounded sad. He sighed heavily and continued. 'Phil knew his parents wouldn't be happy about the relationship but he didn't care. He was smitten. She gave him his first dose of spider's silk. And his second.'

Hugo linked his hands together and stared out at the selkies while they stared in at us. 'By the time I realised what was happening to him, it was already too late. He became strung out and he wouldn't talk to any of us. All he cared about was getting his next hit. He even stopped caring about the girl.

'When he ran out of money, she left him and he spiralled. I tried to help him, lots of people tried, but we could never do enough. Everywhere Philip went, he left devastation in his wake. He brutally attacked his own sister when she tried to persuade him to go to rehab. He stole a small fortune from his parents to fund his habit. It wasn't his fault, not really, but he wouldn't accept any help. He overdosed three years ago and now he's buried in the family plot in Fife.'

He ran a hand through his tawny hair. 'I've still never met anyone as skilled at water magic as he was. If he'd been here, he could probably have held back the tide so we could escape. His powers were that extraordinary. If he'd not become addicted, there's no telling what he might have achieved or gone on to become. The more spider's silk he took, the less power he had – it sapped his magic.'

His voice grew darker. 'And it sapped who he was at his core. Spider's silk caused him to lose his family, his money, his magic and his life.'

'I'm not like that,' I whispered.

Hugo didn't hesitate before answering. 'Not yet.'

I licked my lips. Apparently it was the time for sharing. 'My parents aren't elves. I was adopted as a baby. They don't have magic and they don't understand it. They try, though. They've been good to me and I love them more than anyone else in the world.'

I felt Hugo's eyes on me. I didn't look at him but I did continue. 'I started to have bad dreams when I was a teenager.' I gave a cold laugh. 'Nightmares. I don't remember many of the details but I often woke up screaming. It didn't matter what I tried, they got worse and worse.'

I gazed unseeing into the flames. 'It felt as if something was after me, some monster that was stalking me through my sleep, and I grew too scared to go to bed. When I did fall asleep and the nightmares came, I used magic in my sleep. I had no control and I didn't know what I was doing. There was no-one I knew to ask for help.'

I lifted my head and my eyes met the dark gaze of the first selkie. It was drooling.

'One night it was particularly bad and whatever was after me started closing in. It was almost upon me and I couldn't escape.' I shook my head, remembering. 'I managed to wake myself up somehow, and it was just as well because my bedroom was filled with smoke.'

Hugo clearly understood. 'You threw out fire magic in your sleep.'

I nodded. 'The house burned down and my parents almost died. I almost killed my own mum and dad because I couldn't control the magic inside me.'

'That's not an uncommon phenomenon, Daisy. There were lots of places you could have gotten help. High elves are trained from a young age to deal with that sort of thing.'

'Well, I wasn't trained,' I said flatly. 'And I didn't know where to go to, or who to speak to for help. But I had heard of spider's silk. While my mum and dad were recovering from smoke inhalation in hospital and our home lay smouldering, I went out and found some.'

I finally turned and looked at him. 'I've not had a nightmare since. The drugs dampen my magic so there's less of a danger to me and to others. I'm sorry about your friend, I truly am, but I wouldn't have survived without spider's silk. And now it's too late for me to be anything other than an addict. You told me about your friend to distract me from the selkies. I appreciate that. But you have to understand that spider's silk once distracted me from my nightmares. It will kill me eventually.' I smiled crookedly. 'If the selkies don't get me first, of course. But nobody else will die because of me and that makes every pill worth it.'

Hugo watched me, a grim, speculative expression on his face that I didn't quite understand. 'The fire wasn't your fault.'

'And your friend's death wasn't yours,' I said softly. I touched his hand. 'But we both feel guilty.'

He took a step towards me, raised one hand and cupped my cheek. For a long moment we stared into each other's eyes. But the selkies were still there and they were still watching us. 'We can't lose our concentration,' I whispered.

Hugo's jaw tightened and he dropped his hand. 'You're

right.' He checked his watch. 'Another four hours until the tide will be low enough to return to the mainland. Then we'll be safe.'

I nodded before turning to face the selkies again. Safety, however, is always a relative concept.

THIRTY

'I feel like I've been hit by a train.' Otis rubbed his head over and over again.

'Not a train,' Hester said. 'A ten-tonne weight that fell from the sky and squashed us.'

'Getting hit by a train is more lethal than getting squashed by a weight falling from the sky,' he retorted.

'No.' She shook her head vigorously. 'A ten-tonne weight would be worse.'

'How would it be worse than a train? And how would it happen?' He threw his hands upwards. 'Where would it come from?'

'We're in the middle of the sea! Where would a train come from?'

I smiled at them fondly. The fact that they were bickering again meant that they were recovering. We were going to be okay. All of us.

I'd worried that the selkies would remain when the tide receded, waiting us out. There'd been a few occasions over the last hours when Hugo's defensive fire had faltered, but together we'd managed to keep it burning just enough to keep us safe.

And when enough time had passed and the sea was doing its thing by retreating away as it always did, the selkies snorted in disgust and slipped off, one after the other.

I'd reached for Hugo's hand without thinking and together we stood there, waiting until there was no more sign of the slippery, sharp-toothed creatures. He'd squeezed my fingers in a brief show of reassurance that had warmed me far more than the blistering heat from the fiery circle. I supposed that, bizarrely, we genuinely were friends now. All it had taken was yet another near-death experience. They were becoming a nasty habit.

Hugo allowed the flames to die back, testing to see if the selkies had really gone and weren't skulking around the corner for their final chance at a tasty breakfast. Meanwhile, Hester flew slowly out to the east and Otis headed west. It didn't take them long to return.

'The way is clear,' Hester announced. 'They've gone out with the tide.'

I exhaled and cradled my injured hand. The last hit of spider's silk had kept the worst of the pain at bay, but soon I'd have to resort to weak-ass painkillers again. The once-pristine white bandages were grubby and I'd have to get the dressing changed soon. The last thing I needed was for sepsis to set in.

'You saved my life,' Hugo said. He quirked an eyebrow. 'And you know what that means.'

'Your undying gratitude for the rest of eternity?'

He smirked. 'That part goes without saying. According to the Chinese, you're also now responsible for my life forever.'

I stared at him. 'What? How is that fair?'

Hugo's grin grew. 'We're bonded for life. You have to look out for me until the day you die.'

I folded my arms. 'Technically, you saved me first by giving me spider's silk when I was in withdrawal. You saved my life then, even though you hate the stuff.'

'So I'm responsible for you for the rest of my life? That's what you're saying?'

I shook my head vigorously. 'Our actions cancel each other's out. We can happily go our separate ways with no obligations.'

He gave me a long look. 'Mmm.' What did that mean?

'Before we part company,' he continued, 'you'll need to come with me. We'll have to tell Sir Nigel what happened, and the police will probably want statements from both of us.'

True. I wasn't going to be able to avoid the police, not now. I nodded as Otis reappeared. 'No sign of the selkies,' he said. 'And no sign of the chests, either. Humphrey took them all with him.'

That wouldn't have been an easy feat. I felt a flicker of dark amusement at the effort he'd have had to make to heave them to the mainland.

Hugo sighed. 'It won't be easy to get all that gold back. If he has any sense, he'll already have spirited it away.'

'Humphrey will get his comeuppance.'

'You seem very sure.'

I shrugged. 'You're like a dog with a bone. You have an inflated desire for justice that won't let him get away.'

'As if *you* would forget what he's done,' Hugo snorted. 'You'd be as likely to commandeer a troupe of vampires to do your bidding and send them after him for bloody vengeance as you would be to let him go.'

'Vampires are not a bad idea.' I grinned. 'Between you and me, Humphrey is toast.'

Hugo smiled at me.

'I'm sorry that I sent Duchess to your posh castle,' I said quietly.

'I'm sorry I judged you and got you fired.'

I nodded, acknowledging his sincerity. 'I'm *not* sorry that I found the necklace before you.'

Hugo was suddenly no longer smiling. He dipped his head towards me and murmured in my ear, 'Neither am I, Daisy.'

'If this continues,' Hester muttered from the side, 'it'll be high tide again and we'll be stuck here again because you two couldn't stop making googly eyes at each other.'

I licked my lips. She was right: we had to get off Cramond and find Sir Nigel. Besides, this wasn't over yet. In fact, the best part was about to begin.

ALTHOUGH I BELIEVED we were now genuine friends, I couldn't prevent the delicious thrill of satisfaction that my ability to weave between traffic on Jamila's motorbike meant I arrived in front of the Royal Elvish Institute before Hugo. I was handicapped by the injury to my hand but I was still faster than him. It was a childish, petty joy – and I relished it.

As I heaved myself off the bike and strode up the steps, I immediately recognised the two doormen. Bonus. When they caught sight of me and their expressions hardened into identical glares, my smile broadened. 'Fellas! How fabulous to see you both again!'

From their perch on my shoulder, Hester and Otis waved. Neither doorman reacted.

'You're not carrying anything,' the first doorman said. 'So you're not making a delivery.'

'And your name,' the second doorman added without missing a beat, 'is not down on today's list of guests.' The pair of them stepped closer to each other to ensure that my way was barred. 'You are not welcome here.'

Otis gasped in melodramatic horror but Hester took a more

pragmatic approach. 'Kick them where it hurts, Daisy! You can take them!'

There was a pointed cough from behind us and both doormen looked over my shoulder. Their demeanour altered drastically. 'Lord Pemberville.'

I raised an eyebrow. Lord? Hugo was even posher than I'd realised.

'Don't you know who this is?' he asked in such a civilised tone that I almost laughed. 'This is Daisy Carter. She's an esteemed elf who is one of the greatest treasure hunters our country has to offer.'

There was a moment's silence then the doormen shuffled to the side, one heading right while the other stepped to the left. 'I apologise,' the first one said stiffly.

'We didn't know,' replied the second.

I was reasonably certain they both hated me more than ever now. I turned away, partly so they wouldn't see the smile on my face and partly so I could tease Hugo. 'Beat you,' I grinned.

'You had an unfair advantage.'

I held up my bandaged hand. 'I disagree.'

'Next time I'll tie one hand behind my back and get a motor-bike of my own,' he growled. 'Then we'll see who's fastest.'

Next time?

Hugo looked at the doormen. 'Is Sir Nigel in attendance?'

'Yes, sir.'

'How about Humphrey Bridger?'

'He arrived about twenty minutes ago, just after we opened up.'

Hugo and I exchanged glances. 'Yahtzee,' I whispered. He held out his arm and I took it, placing my hand on it as if I were a proper lady. Together we waltzed past the goggle-eyed door-men. Hester blew them a raspberry as we passed.

Hugo steered us not towards the large dining room but into

a smaller, albeit equally grand, drawing room. The walls were panelled with oak on which were hung old paintings of hunting scenes, and a vast fireplace with decorative crossed swords above it occupied the far side.

In front of the fireplace there was a large group of people. I instantly recognised Hugo's Primes, together with Eleanor and Sir Nigel. Becky was crying, Eleanor was dabbing at her eyes with a handkerchief, and even Sir Nigel looked on the brink of tears.

Humphrey was facing them with his back turned to us. 'You all know that he was a better treasure hunter than me. He got to Cramond before I did. The tide was high and I was too late to cross, but I saw him standing on the shore. He was looking at something.' His voice cracked. Damn, he was a good actor. 'Then I realised what – or rather *who* – he was looking at.'

'Who?'

Humphrey knew how to play his audience. He paused several seconds for effect, building up the tension and appearing too overcome to speak. 'It – it – it was Daisy. She was quite some distance away from me, but I'm sure it was her on the island. I recognised her clothes.'

There was a swift intake of breath from around the room.

'I don't understand,' Eleanor said. 'Why would Daisy have been there?'

Humphrey exhaled a long, strangled breath. 'I've been over and over it in my head. She must have been at Loch Arkaig and spied on us when we re-formed the key. She went to Cramond to steal the treasure before Hugo or I could get there.'

He hung his head. 'I didn't think she was like that – I thought she was a good fellow. But I saw her – I saw her holding something. I think it was a wooden chest. Hugo tried to take it from her.' His voice dropped to a pained whisper. 'That was when the selkies appeared.'

Several of the Primes cried out.

Humphrey remained hunched over himself. 'I waited until low tide and ventured across but I couldn't see either of them. I checked the whole island but there was no sign of them or of the gold. I think the selkies killed Hugo and Daisy and hauled the chests into the sea. Nothing else makes any sense.'

'Hugo could have fought off selkies!' Becky burst out. 'He has more than enough magic to defend himself!'

'Not if he was distracted by that junkie,' another Prime snarled.

I stiffened. Hugo straightened his shoulders and stepped forward. 'It's strange, Humphrey,' he drawled, 'that you saw all that happen from the mainland yet you didn't think to call anyone for help. Didn't you have your phone with you?'

The whole group whirled to face us, each face blank with astonishment. Then every single one of the Primes flung themselves towards Hugo. 'You're alive!'

While they hugged him and cried, I kept my focus on Humphrey. 'My good fellow,' I said. 'You're looking pale.'

Humphrey stared at me and swallowed hard. Here we go. I tensed my body. A heartbeat later, he rushed towards me. I thought he was going to attack despite the large audience; instead he enveloped me in a tight hug.

'You're alright! You're safe!' His mouth twisted to my ear. 'Half the gold is yours if you help me get out of here,' he murmured so that only I could hear him.

I didn't react.

'Five million pounds and you'll be set for life, Daisy.'

Indeed I would. Five million pounds in the bank and I could do whatever the fuck I wanted. I thought of all the spider's silk I could buy with that money. And I smiled.

THIRTY-ONE

I yanked myself away from Humphrey. He looked into my eyes, registered what I was thinking and his expression twisted. 'You fucking idiot, Daisy,' he muttered.

I shrugged. Yeah, maybe. 'I guess it's not the money I want,' I told him. 'It must be the thrill of the hunt that I enjoy. And now I've hunted you down.'

Humphrey snarled. Before I could stop him, he leapt backwards and grabbed Eleanor while the strange, intricate, red shapes swirled across his skin again.

Hester and Otis shrieked with terror and abandoned their position on my shoulder in favour of flying at high speed out of the room before they had to face Humphrey's disturbing blood-magic powers for a second time.

'Hugo!' I yelled.

Hugo wasted no time in extricating himself from his over-joyed team, and I felt the rush of power as he flung a burst of magic straight at Humphrey. I followed it up with one of my own. Three of the Primes did the same, not understanding what was happening but determined to follow Hugo's lead, whatever it was.

Each one of the bolts of brutal magic slammed uselessly into some sort of invisible wall around Humphrey. The strange powers he was tapping into had grown since the previous night on Cramond.

I sucked in a breath and drew Gladys. Humphrey roared in anger and held Eleanor in front of him as a shield. 'You bastard!' she yelled, writhing against him and kicking back with her heels in a vain bid to free herself. 'You're using blood magic!'

Was I the only person in the world who'd never heard of fucking blood magic? How did Eleanor, of all people, know of it?

Sir Nigel strode forward. 'Let her go, Bridger,' he commanded, his tone brooking no argument.

Humphrey, however, wasn't playing ball. 'I don't think I'll do that. Not yet.'

The two doormen from outside skidded to a halt beside me and their jaws dropped. I guessed this sort of thing didn't often happen in the Royal Elvish Institute.

I held Gladys tightly with my good hand and brandished her at Humphrey in what I hoped was a threatening manner. He barely blinked; instead, he gazed around the room, his eyes narrowing as he assessed the situation. Eventually he nodded as he apparently came to a decision. 'I have the Loch Arkaig gold,' he declared. 'I will return half of it to you, Sir Nigel, in exchange for my safe passage out of this building.'

'You don't have the gold,' Becky burst out. 'You're a shit treasure hunter! How would you have it?'

Humphrey looked at Hugo and raised a questioning eyebrow. Hugo nodded grimly. 'He's got it. But I reckon he's also the only person here who believes that gold is worth more than a life,' he drawled. 'No deal, Humphrey. You're not getting out of here.'

Humphrey laughed. 'Oh, I think I am.'

I decided that the trouble with posh people was that there

was far too much talking and far too little action. I sidled to the left, skirting behind the shocked group and aiming to position myself behind Humphrey. As I did so, the same choking black cloud of dangerous magic he'd conjured up on Cramond started to swirl at his feet. Eleanor yelped and tried to jerk away but he was still holding her fast.

'Instead of only killing poor Eleanor,' Humphrey cackled, 'I suppose I'll have to kill all of you.' With that single, ominous statement, a tendril of the smoke snapped out in Sir Nigel's direction and wrapped his neck in a stranglehold.

Hugo snarled then leapt towards the gigantic fireplace and reached above the mantelpiece for the hanging swords. With one tug he grabbed them, one in each hand. Then he turned to face Humphrey yet again.

Sir Nigel was already on his knees, his face turning purple. Several of the Primes were trying to help him, using both magic and brute force in an attempt to pry away the tightening smoke ring from around his neck. They didn't appear to be succeeding.

Hugo advanced. 'You won't escape, Humphrey.'

'I've already beaten you once. Are you so keen to try again, Hugs old chap?'

Hugo replied by swinging one sword expertly towards Humphrey, followed in quick succession by the other one. 'Dear fellow, be careful!' Humphrey protested. 'You almost took off Eleanor's ear!'

On cue, Eleanor began shrieking. 'Let me go! Let me go, you bastard!'

A second snaky black section of the cloud spat out in Hugo's direction. He dodged it once, twice, but it was obvious he couldn't stay out of its path for long. Humphrey laughed coldly and started dragging Eleanor towards the door. 'Come along, my dear. I think it's time we made our exit.'

She continued struggling. 'Stop it! Humphrey! Stop it!'

I took another step until I was finally in the right position behind Humphrey's back. Gladys was already humming, eager to draw blood. I looked to my right and caught Hugo's eye as he fended off the black smoke. I gave him a meaningful look and raised Gladys. We couldn't delay if we were going to help Sir Nigel.

Thankfully, Hugo understood. He jerked his head to the side and I nodded once in agreement. I mouthed a silent count-down. Three. Two. *One.*

Hugo sprang upwards, jumping over the smoke tendril with both his swords raised. Eleanor squeaked in terror as Humphrey thrust her in Hugo's path, more than prepared to let the blades kill her if that was what it took to ensure his escape. But he hadn't been paying enough attention and he hadn't realised I was behind him. It was easy to underestimate a low-elf junkie – but it wasn't smart.

I pulled Gladys backwards then, with as much force as I could, I rammed her forward, tip first. She slid into the space between Humphrey's shoulder blades with a sound that I could only describe as a squeal of joy.

For one long, strange moment Humphrey froze, seemingly suspended in time. Then he uttered a single, surprised word. 'Oh.'

He pitched forward, face first onto the gleaming wooden floor. I grabbed Eleanor and yanked her out of the way before reaching for Gladys and pulling her towards me. She slid out of Humphrey's body with a wet smack while the dangerous black smoke dissipated as if it had never existed in the first place.

The doormen jumped towards Humphrey and turned him over. He was gasping for air, still alive. Becky reached for her phone to call for an ambulance and the police.

I crouched down next to Humphrey and Hugo joined me. 'I

don't think I hit any major organs,' I told Humphrey cheerfully. 'You'll be fine in no time to face trial.'

'It was an inelegant move, Daisy,' Hugo said. 'You could do with some sword lessons.'

I eyeballed him. 'I did considerably better than you. It's thanks to me that he's down and nobody's dead.'

'Beginner's luck.'

I pulled an irritated face but then Humphrey wheezed and we both returned our attention to him. 'You ... won't ... get ... the gold,' he managed in a strained whisper. 'You'll ... never ... find ... it.'

'Don't be so sure,' Hugo growled. 'You forget who I am.'

'Even ... you ... won't ... be able ... to locate ... it.'

Yeah, yeah.

Humphrey smiled to himself then his eyes rolled back into his head as he finally passed out. I checked his vitals until I was satisfied that he was unconscious and not dead. I could already hear the sirens in the distance.

I turned my head to check on Sir Nigel, who was still surrounded by Primes. 'I'm alright,' he managed. 'I'm going to be alright.' He blinked blearily in our direction. 'Humphrey really did steal the Loch Arkaig treasure?'

'Yes,' Hugo said.

I grinned. 'No.'

Everyone looked at me. I curtsied in return as Hester and Otis peered nervously towards us from the doorway. 'Is it safe?' Otis called in. 'Because there's a delivery guy at the front door.'

Bang on time. My smile grew. 'Let him through.'

The two doormen glared at me. 'Hey!' snarled the taller of the two. 'That's not for you to decide!'

'Do it,' Sir Nigel ordered, watching me carefully.

Hugo nodded. 'Let him in.'

It didn't take Billy long to trundle in with three heavy boxes on a squeaky trolley. He grinned and waved. 'Hey, Daisy! How's things?' His gaze dropped to Humphrey's unmoving body and he whitened. 'Uh...'

'Don't worry about him. Paramedics are on their way.'

Hugo had folded his arms. 'Who is he?'

I beamed. 'This is Billy. He's from SDS. They deliver,' I chanted in a sing-song voice, 'when it counts.'

Billy looked up from Humphrey. 'We don't only deliver,' he said faintly. 'We do pick-ups as well.'

Hugo glowered at him suspiciously then strode forward and reached for the first box. He ripped away the cardboard; within seconds, the ancient, warped wood of an old chest was revealed.

'Uh,' Billy swallowed and shot me a nervous glance. 'I'm supposed to deliver these to Sir Nigel Hannigan,' he said. 'Not you.'

Sir Nigel raised a weak hand from where he lay on the floor. 'That's me. It's alright. Hugo can open them.'

'I'll need a signature,' Billy said.

Hugo didn't look up. Instead, he fiddled with the chest lid and flipped it open. He gazed at the contents then glanced at me. 'What is the meaning of this, Daisy?'

I shrugged. 'I knew it would take me a while to get to Cramond from Loch Arkaig, and I couldn't be sure if I was right about Humphrey or what he was planning. So I took out a little insurance.'

Billy nodded. 'I picked up the chests from Cramond last night with instructions to deliver them here at 10am precisely.'

'He'd have brought them earlier, but deliveries are only permitted between the hours of ten and four.' I winked at the doormen. 'See? I do pay attention.' They stared at me.

'What about the gold that Humphrey took?' Hugo asked.

'Fake. Billy delivered fake pirate chests bought from a fancy-dress supply shop. They were pre-filled with gold coins fashioned out of aluminium. He delivered them to Cramond at low tide and took the real treasure away with him.' I spread my arms wide. 'Daisy Carter saves the day.'

Billy frowned. 'With Billy's help,' I added hastily.

'Oi!'

I looked towards a pouting Hester. 'And with the invaluable aid of the two bravest brownies in the kingdom.' I turned to Hugo. 'Admit it. I'm magnificent.'

There was the loud sound of running feet and a moment later a posse of police officers barrelled into the room. 'Everyone down!'

I was starting to lower myself as instructed when an older officer appeared in front of me. His face twisted as he yelled, 'Drop the weapon! Now!'

Oops. I was still holding Gladys. I straightened, released my grip on her hilt and she clattered to the floor. Humphrey's blood still clung to her blade. That probably didn't look good for me.

'Hands behind your back!' the policeman screamed. I did exactly as he ordered. 'No magic!' he added.

'I'm not using any,' I told him. 'I admit I stabbed that man, but it was in self-defence. I promise.'

A paramedic was already by Humphrey's side. 'He's been stabbed in the back,' she said.

Shit. That didn't look very good for me, either. As the policeman hauled me away, all I could hear was Billy mumbling, 'I only need a signature. Then I'll get out of everyone's way. Daisy promised me this would be an easy job.'

My shoulder banged painfully into the door frame on the way out. Hmm. Maybe my magnificence could do with some work.

'You're lucky that so many people were willing to vouch for you,' the desk officer told me. 'Especially when those people include Sir Nigel Hannigan and Lord Hugo Pemberville.'

I opened my mouth to tell her that they were lucky I'd been around to save their sorry arses. Then I thought better of it, signed the piece of paper and grabbed my belongings. I needed a hot shower, new dressings for my hand and some spider's silk. Not in that order.

Shielding my eyes from the bright sunlight as I tripped down the steps of the police station, I looked around for anyone I knew. It didn't take long to spot Hester and Otis hovering anxiously by the exit. Beside them stood a familiar figure. I pretended that I wasn't disappointed that it was Eleanor who was waiting for me. There was no reason why Hugo would have come. He probably had far better things to do.

'I'm so glad they released you without charge.' She held out her arms and I stepped forward, enjoying the hug. Hester and Otis joined in, squashing themselves between us.

'Are you okay, Daisy?' Otis asked anxiously.

'Peachy.' I grinned and stepped back.

'Are you sure?' Hester sniffed. 'Because I can go in there and beat up those nasty police officers if you like.' She held her fists up. 'I've got your back.'

'Not a good idea,' I told her with a small smile. 'Everything's fine.' I looked up. 'But what about you? Are *you* alright, Eleanor?'

She sniffed and nodded. 'I feel so stupid. I should have seen what Humphrey was like. I knew he was desperate to get his hands on that gold even though he didn't act that way in public. I should have realised what sort of man he really was.'

'He fooled all of us. It's not your fault.' I gazed at her. 'Is he...?'

'Humphrey's alright. It wasn't a serious wound. You didn't

hit any major organs. He's lost some blood but he'll be released into police custody later today.'

Good. I smacked my lips in satisfaction. All was well that ended well, then.

Eleanor bit her lip. 'He's going to get into a lot of trouble. All that stuff he did...' She shivered. 'And the blood magic too.'

I gave her a curious look. 'How did you know it was blood magic?'

She wetted her lips. 'Because that's how I met Humphrey in the first place,' she whispered. 'After the vampire incident when you saved me, I went to a little sorcerer's shop I'd heard about to get something to defend myself with in case it happened again. Humphrey was there talking to someone. He told me that the only way I could defend myself against a vampire and be sure that I was safe was to use blood magic, but it was extremely rare, highly illegal and very dangerous and I shouldn't go near it. We got chatting and went for a drink and then...' She shrugged helplessly. 'In the end it turns out I'd have been safer with the vampires.'

I knew she was trying to make light of the situation. 'He fooled all of us, Eleanor. In the end, everything worked out.'

I would, however, be very happy if I never crossed paths with blood magic ever again. I crossed my fingers and muttered a brief wish to whoever might be listening. Then I smiled at her. 'I need to go home and freshen up, but would you like to meet up later for a drink or two? I owe Billy a pint and you'd be very welcome to join us.' I had a strong suspicion that Eleanor was in dire need of some real friends.

A genuine smile grew across her face. 'I'd love that. I'd *really* love that.'

THE DOORBELL RANG when I was towelling off my hair. 'Hester,' I called. 'Can you go and see who that is?'

'Why do I have to do it? Why can't Otis do it?'

'I'm watching cat videos!' he yelled.

I rolled my eyes. It was easier to answer the door myself. I padded down the narrow corridor and opened the door. When I saw who was standing on my doorstep, I blinked in genuine surprise.

'Hi Daisy.' Mr McIlvanney twisted his hands together and gave me a nervous look. 'How are you?'

'Fine.'

He looked down at his feet. Silence stretched out.

'Can I help with you something?' I asked eventually.

He sighed and twitched. 'I want to apologise to you for what happened before. I shouldn't have sacked you like that. You deserve support, not censure, and you've been an excellent SDS employee.'

Uh-huh. I *had* been an excellent SDS employee – but that didn't explain what my ex-boss was doing here now. I waited, using my own sudden silence as a weapon against him.

McIlvanney cleared his throat. 'I'd like it if you came to work for us again. I'll give you a raise. You can work whichever shifts you like. I want to make amends.'

'I'm still a drug addict. That's not changed.'

'We can work around that,' he said. 'It's not a problem. Maybe in time we can find a rehab programme that suits, but it doesn't matter. We want you as you are.'

I watched him for a long moment. 'I'm not coming back,' I said quietly.

He gnawed on his bottom lip. 'Okay.' He didn't seem surprised. 'I'll give you an excellent reference.'

'I don't need a reference. I'll work for myself from now on.'

He raised his head. 'As a freelance delivery driver?'

'As a freelance treasure hunter.' I hadn't thought about it until now but as soon as I said the words they made sense. I was good at it. Sometimes. I also enjoyed it. Sometimes. Mostly, it felt right; it was what I *wanted* to do.

McIlvanney looked thoroughly confused but he seemed to know better than to question me. 'If you change your mind, you can always come back to SDS. In the meantime...' He thrust an envelope in my direction.

'What's that?'

'Severance pay.'

I looked at the envelope, then I took it. I'm not completely stupid. 'Thanks.'

'You're welcome.' He shuffled his feet. 'I should go.'

He twisted around and walked away. Hester flapped up to my ear. 'Stab him in the back! You did it to Humphrey. You can do it to him!'

'Hush.' I leaned out and peered around the corner. 'You can come out now.'

Hugo didn't hesitate, neither did he look particularly sheepish at getting caught. He simply gave me a long curious look. 'A freelance treasure hunter?'

'Are you saying that I won't be good enough?'

'No. I'm saying that it won't be easy.'

I snorted. 'If I've learned anything over the last few weeks, it's that.'

He smiled slightly. 'If I've learned anything over the last few weeks, it's that I shouldn't judge people before I get to know them.' He shoved his hands into his pockets. 'And that I kind of like you.'

I stared at him.

'Instead of friendly rivals,' he said, 'how about simply friends?'

'What's the catch?'

Amusement glinted in his eyes. 'You have to accept that I'm superior in all things.'

'In *all* things?'

'Yup.'

'I'm about to wax my bikini line.'

'Alright,' he conceded. 'You might be better at that than I am.'

'I'm better at riding a motorbike one-handed.'

He shook his head. 'Unproven.'

'I'm better at lassoing giant snakes.'

'Also unproven.'

I pursed my lips. 'I'm better at stabbing people in the back.' I met his eyes. 'Only literally, though.'

Hugo met my gaze. 'That goes without saying.' He hesitated. 'Friends, then?'

'Alright. Friends.'

His smile grew. He leaned forward and gave me a brief kiss on my cheek. The touch of his lips was so light that I barely felt it. 'Sealed with a kiss, Daisy. You can't change your mind now.'

'I'll change my mind whenever I want to,' I retorted.

He laughed. 'Fair enough.' He raised his hand in a mock salute. 'Give me a call when you need help with your treasure hunting.' He turned and started to walk away.

'I won't need help!' I called back. Cumbubbling bastard. I wanted the last word.

'We'll see about that.' He disappeared around the corner.

'Yes, we will!' I shouted. I ground my teeth. What a glittering rejoinder that had been. *Not.*

Then, I heard a soft noise drifting towards me. It was unmistakably the sound of Hugo laughing. I harrumphed loudly and closed my door. But I smiled to myself, too.

· · ·

***

THANK you so very much for reading Tattered Huntress! I truly hope you've enjoyed it. Any and all reviews are always massively appreciated. They make a huge difference to indie authors like me.

If you want to make sure you never miss a release, you can sign up to my newsletter at https://shorturl.at/blvBC

There are details of more of my books over the next few pages - and the second book in Thrill of the Hunt will be released in March 2024 - https://mybook.to/Thrill2

HELEN X

Author's Notes

Although Pemberville Castle, the Royal Elvish Institute and Alisdair Greenwood's Dundee-based mansion are invented, the majority of the places in in *Tattered Huntress* do indeed exist.

Devil's Beef Tub is a deep hollow located north of the Scottish town of Moffat. It was once famed for its sulphur baths and possibly derived its name from being a hiding place for stolen cattle, or because Beef Tub is a derivation of Bath Tub.

Hurley Cave is an artificial tunnel, which was created in 1742, reached via a small bridge on the Penicuik estate in Midlothian, Scotland. It is currently closed to the public (not because of trolls) but is being restored to its former glory.

Neidpath Castle is close to Peebles and started its life in 1190 although it has undergone various re-modellings since then. It is available for hire as a wedding venue.

Doctor's Gate is an old Roman road named after Dr John Talbot, who is believed to have improved a section of it in the fifteenth century. Snake Pass, which runs close by, forms part of the A57 between the cities of Manchester and Sheffield. There are, unsurprisingly, no giant snakes but the road is winding and has several sharp bends.

Smoo Cave is both a freshwater and seawater cave near Durness in Scotland. Dye tests have suggested that there is indeed a secondary section of caves via an underwater passage that is currently inaccessible.

Cramond is a tidal island in the Firth of Forth, just off Edinburgh. It is only accessible when the tide is low and people are often accidentally stranded on it when the sea comes in. The World War II lookout shelter that Daisy hides in is located in the far corner of the small island.

The Loch Arkaig Treasure did exist and was brought to Scotland to aid the Jacobite cause, as described by Sir Nigel. It went missing after the Jacobite rebellion in 1745, and its disappearance caused considerable controversy and rancour. Some people believe that it is still buried somewhere around Loch Arkaig, although evidence was recently uncovered that suggests most of the gold was smuggled to France and into the hands of Bonnie Prince Charlie.

Acknowledgments

Thank you so much to everyone who helped bring Daisy's first book to life. Clarissa Yeo and JoY Cover Designs created the wonderful cover, which depicts her character perfectly. Karen Holmes, as always, did an excellent job with editing my mess and Ruth Urquhart has produced a wonderful audiobook and aided with any errant typos along the way.

There are many ARC readers who have made an impact - in fact there are too many to name although each and every one of them has been wonderful. I'd also like to drop in a special mention to Marvellous Maps and their Great British Folklore and Superstition Map which provided a great deal of inspiration for the many places which Daisy visits.

Finally, thank to you, dear reader. I've loved writing Daisy's story and it means more than you can know to have you along for the ride too.

Helen x

Also by Helen Harper

The *FireBrand* series

A werewolf killer. A paranormal murder. How many times can Emma Bellamy cheat death?

I'm one placement away from becoming a fully fledged London detective. It's bad enough that my last assignment before I qualify is with Supernatural Squad. But that's nothing compared to what happens next.

Brutally murdered by an unknown assailant, I wake up twelve hours later in the morgue – and I'm very much alive. I don't know how or why it happened. I don't know who killed me. All I know is that they might try again.

Werewolves are disappearing right, left and centre.

A mysterious vampire seems intent on following me everywhere I go.

And I have to solve my own vicious killing. Preferably before death comes for me again.

The *WolfBrand* series

Devereau Webb is in uncharted territory. He thought he knew what he was doing when he chose to enter London's supernatural society but he's quickly discovering that his new status isn't welcome to everyone.

He's lived through hard times before and he's no stranger to the murky underworld of city life. But when he comes across a young werewolf girl who's not only been illegally turned but who has also committed two brutal murders, he will discover just how difficult life can be for supernaturals - and also how far his own predatory powers extend.

Book One – The Noose Of A New Moon

Book Two – Licence To Howl

The complete *Blood Destiny* series

"A spectacular and addictive series."

Mackenzie Smith has always known that she was different. Growing up as the only human in a pack of rural shapeshifters will do that to you, but then couple it with some mean fighting skills and a fiery temper and you end up with a woman that few will dare to cross. However, when the only father figure in her life is brutally murdered, and the dangerous Brethren with their predatory Lord Alpha come to investigate, Mack has to not only ensure the physical safety of her adopted family by hiding her apparent humanity, she also has to seek the blood-soaked vengeance that she craves.

Book One - Bloodfire

Book Two - Bloodmagic

Book Three - Bloodrage

Book Four - Blood Politics

Book Five - Bloodlust

Also

Corrigan Fire

Corrigan Magic

Corrigan Rage

Corrigan Politics

Corrigan Lust

The complete *Bo Blackman* series

A half-dead daemon, a massacre at her London based PI firm and evidence that suggests she's the main suspect for both ... Bo Blackman is having a very bad week.

She might be naive and inexperienced but she's determined to get to the bottom of the crimes, even if it means involving herself with one of London's most powerful vampire Families and their enigmatic leader.

It's pretty much going to be impossible for Bo to ever escape unscathed.

Book One - Dire Straits

Book Two - New Order

Book Three - High Stakes

Book Four - Red Angel

Book Five - Vigilante Vampire

Book Six - Dark Tomorrow

The complete *Highland Magic* series

Integrity Taylor walked away from the Sidhe when she was a child. Orphaned and bullied, she simply had no reason to stay, especially not when the sins of her father were going to remain on her shoulders. She found a new family - a group of thieves who proved that blood was less important than loyalty and love.

But the Sidhe aren't going to let Integrity stay away forever. They need her more than anyone realises - besides, there are prophecies to be fulfilled, people to be saved and hearts to be won over. If anyone can do it, Integrity can.

Book One - Gifted Thief

Book Two - Honour Bound

Book Three - Veiled Threat

Book Four - Last Wish

The complete *Dreamweaver* series

"I have special coping mechanisms for the times I need to open the front door. They're even often successful..."

Zoe Lydon knows there's often nothing logical or rational about fear. It doesn't change the fact that she's too terrified to step outside her own house, however.

What Zoe doesn't realise is that she's also a dreamweaver - able to access other people's subconscious minds. When she finds herself in the Dreamlands and up against its sinister Mayor, she'll need to use all of her wits - and overcome all of her fears - if she's ever going to come out alive.

Book One - Night Shade

Book Two - Night Terrors

Book Three - Night Lights

Stand alone novels

Eros

William Shakespeare once wrote that, "Cupid is a knavish lad, thus to make poor females mad." The trouble is that Cupid himself would probably agree...

As probably the last person in the world who'd appreciate hearts, flowers and romance, Coop is convinced that true love doesn't exist – which is rather unfortunate considering he's also known as Cupid, the God of Love. He'd rather spend his days drinking, womanising and generally having as much fun as he possible can. As far as he's concerned, shooting people with bolts of pure love is a waste of his time...but then his path crosses with that of shy and retiring Skye Sawyer and nothing will ever be quite the same again.

Wraith

Magic. Shadows. Adventure. Romance.

Saiya Buchanan is a wraith, able to detach her shadow from her body and send it off to do her bidding. But, unlike most of her kin, Saiya doesn't deal in death. Instead, she trades secrets - and in the goblin besieged city of Stirling in Scotland, they're a highly prized commodity. It might just be, however, that the goblins have been hiding the greatest secret of them all. When Gabriel de Florinville, a Dark Elf, is sent as royal envoy into Stirling and takes her prisoner, Saiya is not only going to uncover the sinister truth. She's also going to realise that sometimes the deepest secrets are the ones locked within your own heart.

The complete *Lazy Girl's Guide To Magic* series

Hard Work Will Pay Off Later. Laziness Pays Off Now.

Let's get one thing straight - Ivy Wilde is not a heroine. In fact, she's probably the last witch in the world who you'd call if you needed a magical helping hand. If it were down to Ivy, she'd spend all day every day on her sofa where she could watch TV, munch junk food and talk to her feline familiar to her heart's content.

However, when a bureaucratic disaster ends up with Ivy as the victim of a case of mistaken identity, she's yanked very unwillingly into Arcane Branch, the investigative department of the Hallowed Order of Magical Enlightenment. Her problems are quadrupled when a valuable object is stolen right from under the Order's noses.

It doesn't exactly help that she's been magically bound to Adeptus Exemptus Raphael Winter. He might have piercing sapphire eyes and a body which a cover model would be proud of but, as far as Ivy's concerned, he's a walking advertisement for the joyless perils of too much witch-work.

And if he makes her go to the gym again, she's definitely going to turn him into a frog.

Book One - Slouch Witch

Book Two - Star Witch

Book Three - Spirit Witch

Sparkle Witch (Christmas short story)

The complete *Fractured Faery* series

One corpse. Several bizarre looking attackers. Some very strange magical powers. And a severe bout of amnesia.

It's one thing to wake up outside in the middle of the night with a decapitated man for company. It's another to have no memory of how you got there - or who you are.

She might not know her own name but she knows that several people are out to get her. It could be because she has strange magical powers seemingly at her fingertips and is some kind of fabulous hero. But then why does she appear to inspire fear in so many? And who on earth is the sexy, green-eyed barman who apparently despises her? So many questions ... and so few answers.

At least one thing is for sure - the streets of Manchester have never met someone quite as mad as Madrona...

Book One - Box of Frogs

SHORTLISTED FOR THE KINDLE STORYTELLER AWARD 2018

Book Two - Quiver of Cobras

Book Three - Skulk of Foxes

The complete *City Of Magic* series

Charley is a cleaner by day and a professional gambler by night. She might be haunted by her tragic past but she's never thought of herself as anything or anyone special. Until, that is, things start to go terribly wrong all across the city of Manchester. Between plagues of rats, firestorms and the gleaming blue eyes of a sexy Scottish werewolf, she might just have landed herself in the middle of a magical apocalypse. She might also be the only person who has the ability to bring order to an utterly chaotic new world.

Book One - Shrill Dusk

Book Two - Brittle Midnight

Book Three - Furtive Dawn

Made in the USA
Las Vegas, NV
13 March 2024

87171687R00173